Ellen Glasgow

Phases of an inferior planet

Ellen Glasgow

Phases of an inferior planet

ISBN/EAN: 9783743330399

Manufactured in Europe, USA, Canada, Australia, Japa

Cover: Foto ©ninafisch / pixelio.de

Manufactured and distributed by brebook publishing software (www.brebook.com)

Ellen Glasgow

Phases of an inferior planet

Phases of an Inferior Planet

By ELLEN GLASGOW
Author of "*The Descendant*"

HARPER & BROTHERS PUBLISHERS
NEW YORK AND LONDON
1898

Phase First

"Some turned to folly and the sweet works of the flesh."
—Hymn to Zeus.

PHASES OF AN INFERIOR PLANET

CHAPTER I

ALONG Broadway at six o'clock a throng of pedestrians was stepping northward. A grayish day was settling into a gray evening, and a negative lack of color and elasticity had matured into a positive condition of atmospheric flatness. The air exhaled a limp and insipid moisture, like that given forth by a sponge newly steeped in an anæsthetic. Upon the sombre fretwork of leafless trees, bare against red-brick buildings, drops of water hung trembling, though as yet there had been no rainfall, and the straggling tufts of grass in the city parks drooped earthward like the damp and uncurled fringe of a woman's hair.

Spanning the remote west as a rainbow stretched an unfulfilled pledge of better things, for beyond the smoke-begrimed battalion of tenement chimney-pots a faint streak of mauve defined the line of the horizon —an ineffectual and transparent sheet of rose - tinted vapor, through which the indomitable neutrality of background was revealed. The city swam in a sea of mist, and the electric lights, coming slowly into being, must have seemed to a far - off observer a galaxy of wandering stars that had burst the woof of heaven and fallen from their allotted spheres to be caught like blossoms in the white obscurity of fog. Above them their deserted habitation frowned blackly down with closed doors and impenetrable walls.

The effect of the immortal transformation of day into night was singularly elusive. It had come so stealthily that the fleet-footed hours seemed to have tripped one another in the fever of the race, the monotonous grayness of their garments shrouding, as they fluttered past, the form of each sprightly elf.

Along Broadway the throng moved hurriedly. At a distance indescribably homogeneous, as it passed the lighted windows of shops it was seen to be composed of individual atoms, and their outlines were relieved against the garish interiors like a panorama of automatic silhouettes. Then, as they neared a crossing, a flood of radiant electricity, revealing minute details of face and figure, the atoms were revivified from automatic into animal existence.

With an inhuman disregard of caste and custom, the aberrant shadows of the passers-by met and mingled one into another. A phantasmagoric procession took place upon the sidewalk. The ethereal accompaniment of the physical substance of a Wall Street plutocrat glided sedately after that of a bedizened daughter of the people, whose way, beginning in the glare of the workhouse, was ending in the dusk of the river; a lady of quality, whose very shadow seemed pregnant with the odor of spice and sables, melted before the encroaching presence of a boot-black fresh from the Bowery; a gentleman of fashion gave place to the dull phantom of a woman with burning brows and fingers purple with the stain of many stitches. It was as if each material substance, warm with the lust of the flesh and reeking with a burnt-offering of vanity, was pursued by the inevitable presence of a tragic destiny.

At the corner of Seventeenth Street, a girl in a last season's coat left the crowd and paused before a photographer's window. As she passed from shadow into light the play of her limbs was suggested by the close folds of her shabby skirt. She had the light and steadfast gait of one to whom exercise is as essential as food, and more easily attained.

A man coming from Union Square turned to look at her as she passed.

"That girl is a *danseuse*," he said to his companion, "or she ought to be. She walks to music."

"Your induction is false," retorted the other. "She happens to be—"

And they passed on.

As the girl paused before the lighted window the outlines of head and shoulders were accentuated, while the rest of her body remained in obscurity. Her head was shapely and well poised. Beneath the small toque of black velvet, an aureole of dry brown hair framed her sensitive profile like a setting of old mahogany. Even in the half-light silhouette it could be noticed that eyes, hair, and complexion differed in tone rather than in color. Her sallow skin blended in peculiar harmony with the gray-green of her eyes and the brown of her hair. Her face was long, with irregular features and straight brows. The bones of cheek and chin were rendered sharper by extreme thinness.

A new photograph of Alvary was displayed, and a small group had assembled about the window.

The girl looked at it for a moment; then, as some one in the crowd jostled against her, she turned with an exclamation of annoyance and entered the shop. Hesitating an instant, she drew a worn purse from her pocket, looked into it, gave a decisive little shrug, and approached the counter.

The shop-girl came up, and, recognizing her, nodded.

"Music?" she inquired, glancing at the leather roll which the other carried.

The girl shook her head slowly.

"No," she replied, "I want a photograph of Alvary —as Lohengrin. Oh, the Swan Song—"

A man who was sorting a pile of music in the rear of the shop came forward smiling. He was small and dark and foreign.

"Ah, mademoiselle," he said, "it ees a plaisir for w'ich I live, ees ze Elsa of your."

The girl smiled in return. In the clear light the glint of green in her eyes deepened.

"No," she replied, "this is Elsa." She pointed to a photograph in the case. "This is the only Elsa. I should not dare."

He bowed deprecatingly.

"Zat ees ontil you come," he said. "I live for ze day w'en we sing togezzer, you an' I. I live to sing wiss you in ze grand opera."

"Ah, monsieur," lamented the girl, regretfully, "one cannot live forever. The Lord has allotted a term."

She took her change, nodded gayly, and departed.

In the street she passed unheeded. She was as ignored by the crowd around her as the colorless shadow at her side. Upon a massive woman in a feather boa a dozen men gazed with evident desire, and after the sables enveloping the lady of quality the eyes of the boot-black yearned. But the girl moved among them unnoticed — she was insignificant and easily overlooked.

A violet falling upon the pavement from the breast of a woman in front of her, the girl lifted her skirt, and, to avoid crushing it, made a slight divergence from her path. Then impulsively she turned to rescue it from the cold sidewalk, but in so doing she stumbled against a man whose heel had been its Juggernaut. A tiny blot of purple marked the scene of its destruction.

Over the girl's face a shadow fell; she glanced up and caught the courteous smile of an acquaintance, and the shadow was lifted. But before her upward glance tended earthward it rested upon an overdriven horse standing in the gutter, and the shadow that returned had gathered to itself the force of a rain-cloud.

An impressionable and emotional temperament cast its light and darkness upon her features, as the shifting clouds cast their varying shades upon an evening landscape. With such a face, her moods must be as evanescent as the colors of a kaleidoscope.

As she neared an electric light she slipped the photograph she carried from its envelope, and surveyed it with warming eyes. She spoke in a soft whisper—

"I shall never sing Elsa—never—never! Lehmann is Elsa. But what does it matter? By the time I reach grand opera I shall have dinners—real dinners—with napkins the size of a sheet and vegetables of curious kinds. Then I'll grow fat and become famous. I may even sing Isolde."

She broke into a regretful little sigh. "And Alvary will be too old to be my Tristan."

At the corner of Twenty-third Street she took a crosstown car. It was crowded, and, with half-suppressed disgust, she rested the tips of her fingers upon a leather strap. The gloves covering the fingers were worn and badly mended, but the touch was delicate.

Something graceful and feminine and fragile in her unsteady figure caused half a dozen men to rise hastily, and she accepted a proffered seat with the merest inclination of her head.

With an involuntary coquetry she perceived that, as the newest feminine arrival, she was being stealthily regarded from behind the wall of newspapers skirting the opposite seat. She raised her hand to her loosened hair, half frowned, and glanced at the floor with demure indifference.

Beside her sat an Irishwoman with a heavy basket and a black bruise upon her temple. The girl looked at the woman and the bruise with an expression of repugnance. The repugnance was succeeded by a tidal wave of self-commiseration. She pitied herself that she was forced to make use of public means of conveyance. The onions in the Irishwoman's basket offended her nostrils.

Her gaze returned to her lap. As daintily as she had withdrawn her person from contact with the woman beside her, she withdrew her finely strung senses from contact with the odor of onions and the closeness of the humanity hemming her in.

She sat in disdainful self-absorption. Her sensitive features became impassive, her head drooped, the green in her eyes faded into gray, and the lashes obscured them. The shadow of her heavy hair rested like a veil upon her face.

When the car reached Ninth Avenue she got out, walked to Thirtieth Street, and crossed westward. Facing her stood the immense and unpicturesque apartment-house known as "The Gotham"—a monument of human Philistinism and brownstone-finished effrontery. She entered and passed through the unventilated hall to the restaurant at the rear.

As she crossed the threshold, a man seated at one of the larger tables looked up.

"My dear girl," he said, reproachfully, "lateness for dinner at The Gotham entails serious consequences. We were just planning a search-party."

His right-hand neighbor spoke warningly. "Don't believe him, Miss Musin; he refused to get uneasy until he had finished his dinner."

"When one is empty," retorted the first, "one can't

get even uneasy. Anxiety can't be produced from a void."

The girl nodded good-evening, took her seat, and unfolded her napkin. The first gentleman passed her the butter, the second the water-bottle. The first was named Nevins. He was fair and pallid, with a long face that would have been round had nature supplied gratification as well as instinct. His shoulders were high and narrow, suggesting the perpetual shrug with which he met his fate. He was starving upon an artistic career. The second gentleman—Mr. Sellars—was sleek and middle-aged. Providence had intended him for a poet; life had made of him a philosopher —and a plumber. He was still a man of sentiment.

At the head of the table sat Mr. Paul—an apostle of pessimism, whose general flavor marked the pessimist rather than the apostle. The peculiarity of his face was its construction—the features which should have gone up coming down, and the features which should have come down going up. Perhaps had Mr. Paul himself moralized upon the fact, which is not likely, he would have concluded that it was merely a physical expression of his mental attitude towards the universe. He had long since arrived at the belief that whatever came in life was the thing of all others which should have kept away, and its coming was sufficient proof of its inappropriateness. He had become a pessimist, not from passion, but from principle. He had chosen his view of the eternal condition of things as deliberately as he would have selected the glasses with which to survey a given landscape. Having made his choice, he stood to it. No surreptitious favors at the hands of Providence were able to modify his honest conviction of its general unpleasantness.

The remaining persons at this particular table were of less importance. There was Miss Ramsey, the journalist, who was pretty and faded and harassed, and who ate her cold dinner, to which she usually arrived an hour late, in exhausted silence. Miss Ramsey was one whom, her friends said, adversity had softened; but Miss Ramsey herself knew that the softness of adversity is the softness of decay. There was Mr. Ardly, a handsome young fellow, who did the dramatic column of a large daily, and who regarded life as a gigantic jag, facing failure with facetiousness and gout with inconsequence. There was Mr. Morris, who was thin, and Mr. Mason, who was fat, and Mr. Hogarth, who was neither.

The restaurant consisted of a long and queerly shaped room. It had originally been divided into two apartments, but when the house had passed into the present management the partition had been torn down, and two long and narrow tables marked the line where the division had been. The walls were dingy and unpapered. Where the plaster was of an unusual degree of smokiness, several cheap chromos, in cheaper frames, had been hung, like brilliant patches laid upon a dingy background. Above the chromos lingered small bunches of evergreen—faded and dried remnants of the last holiday season—and from the tarnished and fly-specked chandelier hung a withered spray of mistletoe.

. The room was crowded. There was not so much as a vacant seat at the tables. The hum of voices passed through the doors and into the rumble of the street without. In a far corner a lady in a blouse of geranium pink was engaged in catching reckless flies for the sustenance of the chameleon upon her breast; nearer at hand a gentleman was polishing his plate and knife with his napkin. It was warm and oppressive, and the voices sounded shrilly through the glare. The girl whom they had called "Miss Musin" looked up with absent-minded abruptness.

"I had as soon wear wooden shoes as eat with a pewter fork!" she remarked, irritably.

PHASES OF AN INFERIOR PLANET

Mr. Nevins shook his flaxen head and laid down his spoon.

"So long as it remains a question of forks," he observed, "let us give thanks. Who knows when it may become one of food?" Then he sighed. "If it is only a sacrifice of decency, I'm equal to it, but I refuse to live without food."

"The audacity of youth!" commented Mr. Sellars, the philosopher. "I said the same at your age. But for taking the conceit out of one, commend me to experience."

"From a profound study of the subject," broke in Mr. Paul, grimly, "I have been able to calculate to a nicety that each one of these potatoes, taken internally, lessens an hour of one's existence. As a method of self-destruction"—and he proceeded to help himself—"there is none more efficacious than an exclusive diet of Gotham potatoes. Allow me to pass them." He looked at Miss Musin, but Mr. Nevins rose to the occasion.

"After such an analysis, my gallantry forbids," and he intercepted the dish.

The girl glanced up at him.

"Extinction long drawn out is boring," she said. "And is food the only factor of human life? It may be the most important, I admit, but important things should not always be talked of."

"I declare it quite staggers me," interrupted a cheerful individual, who was Mr. Morris, "to think of the number of things that should not be talked of—some amazingly interesting things, too! Do you know, sometimes I wonder if social intercourse will not finally be reduced to a number of persons assembling to sit in silent meditation upon the subjects which are not to be spoken of? One so soon exhausts the absolutely correct topics."

"We are a nation of prudes," declared Mr. Paul, with

emphasis, "and there is no vice that rots a people to the core so rapidly as the vice of prudery. All our good red blood has passed into a limbo of social ostracism along with ladies' legs."

"I was just thinking," commented Mr. Hogarth, who aspired to the rakish and achieved the asinine, "that the last-named subject had been particularly in evidence of late. What with the ballet and the bicycle—" He blushed and glanced at Miss Musin.

She was smiling. "Oh, I don't object," she said, "so long as they are well shaped."

Mr. Nevins upheld her from an artistic stand-point.

"I hold," he said, authoritatively, "that indecency can only exist where beauty is wanting. All beauty is moral. I have noticed in regard to my models—"

"On the contrary," interrupted Mr. Paul, "there is no such thing as beauty. It is merely the creation of a diseased imagination pursuing novelty. We call nature beautiful, but it is only a term we employ to express a chimera of the senses. Nature is not beautiful. Its colors are glaringly defective. It is ugly. The universe is ugly. Civilization is ugly. We are ugly—"

"Oh, Mr. Paul!" said Miss Musin, reproachfully.

"Our one consolation," continued Mr. Paul, in an unmoved voice, "is the knowledge that if we could possibly have been uglier we should have been so created. Providence would have seen to it."

"When Providence provided ugliness," put in Mr. Morris, good-naturedly, "it provided ignorance along with it."

Mr. Ardly, who was eating his dinner with a copy of the *Evening Post* spread out upon his knees, looked up languidly.

"We are becoming unpleasantly personal," he remarked. "Personalities in conversation should be avoided as sedulously as onions in soup. They are stimulating, but vulgar."

PHASES OF AN INFERIOR PLANET

Mr. Paul seized the bait of the unconscious thrower with avidity.

"Vulgarity," he announced, with ringing emphasis, "is the most prominent factor in the universe. It is as essential to our existence as the original slime from which we and it emanated. If there is one thing more vulgar than nature, it is civilization. Whatever remnant of innocence nature left in the mind of man civilization has wiped out. It has debased the human intellect—"

"And deformed the human figure," interpolated Mr. Nevins, with a sigh. "Oh, for the days of Praxiteles!"

The emotionless tones of Mr. Paul flowed smoothly on.

"And if there is one thing more vulgar than civilization, it is art."

Mr. Nevins retorted in a voice of storm.

"Sir," he cried, "art is my divinity!"

"A vulgar superstition," commented Mr. Paul, calmly; and he pointed to a poster beside Mr. Nevins's plate. "You call that art, I suppose?"

Mr. Nevins colored, but met him valiantly. "No," he returned; "I call that bread and meat."

As the girl next him rose from her chair she bestowed upon him an approving smile, which he returned with sentimental interest.

"You haven't finished," he remonstrated, in an aside. "My posters aren't only bread and meat; they are pie—principally pie."

The girl laughed and shook her head.

"And principally pumpkin," she returned. "No, thank you!"

She left the dining-room and mounted the stairs to the fourth landing. Her room was in the front of the house, and the way to it lay through a long and dimly lighted corridor, the floor of which was covered with figured oil-cloth.

As she slipped the key into the lock the door swung back, and a blast of damp air from the open window blew into her face. She crossed the room and stood for a moment with her hand upon the sash, looking down into the street. A train upon the elevated road was passing, and she saw the profiles of the passengers dark against the lighted interior. Clouds of white smoke, blown rearward by the engine's breath, hovered about the track, too light to fall. Then, as the wind chased westward, the clouds were torn asunder, and stray wreaths, deepening into gray, drifted along the cross street leading to the river.

The girl reached out and drew in a can of condensed milk from the fire-escape. Then she lowered the window and turned on the steam-heater in the corner, which set up a hissing monotone.

The room was small and square. There was a half-worn carpet upon the floor, and the walls were covered with cheap paper, the conspicuous feature of which was a sprawling design in green and yellow cornucopias. In one corner stood a small iron bedstead, partially concealed by a Japanese screen, which extended nominal protection to the wash-stand as well. On the wall above the screen an iron hook was visible, from which hung a couple of bath-towels and a scrubbing-brush suspended by a string. Nearer the window there was an upright piano, with a scarf of terra-cotta flung across it and a row of photographs of great singers arranged along the ledge. Here and there on the furniture vivid bits of drapery were pinned over barren places.

But with the proof of a sensuous craving for color a latent untidiness was discernible. Her slippers lay upon the hearth-rug where she had tossed them when dressing for the street; a box of hair-pins had been upset upon the bureau, and a half-open drawer revealed a tangled mass of net veiling.

PHASES OF AN INFERIOR PLANET

Throwing her hat and coat upon the bed, the girl turned up the lights, selected a score of "Lucia" from a portfolio under the piano, and, seating herself at the music-stool, struck the key-board with sudden fervor. The light soprano notes rang out, filling the small room with a frail yet penetrating sweetness. It was a clear and brilliant voice, but it was a voice in miniature, of which the first freshness was marred—and it was not the voice for Lucia.

With quick dismay the girl realized it, and rising impatiently, tossed the score upon the carpet and left the piano.

Standing before the long mirror on the wall, she slipped off her walking-gown, letting it fall in a black heap to her feet. Then stepping over it, she kicked it aside and stood with gleaming arms and breast in the flickering gas-light. She loosened her heavy hair, drawing the pins from it one by one, until it fell in a brown mane upon her shoulders.

Doffing her conventional dress, she doffed conventionality as well. She was transformed into something seductive and subtle—something in woman's flesh as ethereal as sea-foam and as vivid as flame.

She smiled suddenly. Then to a humming accompaniment she twirled upon her toes, her steps growing faster and faster until her figure was obscured in the blur of action and her hair flew about her face like the hair of a painted witch.

The words of the air she hummed came with a dash of bravado from between her lips:

"—Ange ou diable,
Écume de la mer?"

Still smiling, she sank in an exhausted heap upon the floor.

Then she went to bed and fell asleep, lamenting that her head rested upon a cotton pillow-slip.

CHAPTER II

In time long past, when the Huguenots were better known, if less esteemed, an impecunious gentleman of France left his native land for the sake of faith and fortune.

Lured by that blatant boast of liberty which swelled the throats of the Western colonies, even while their hands were employed in meting out the reward of witchcraft and in forging the chains of slavery, he directed his way towards American soil.

His mission failed, and, in search of theological freedom, he only succeeded in weaving matrimonial fetters. Amid an unassorted medley of creeds and customs he came upon the red-cheeked daughter of a Swiss adventurer—an ambitious pioneer who lived upon the theory that the New World having been created for the service of its foreign invaders, the might of the sword was the right of possession.

The gentleman of France, deciding to found a farm and family in the land of his adoption, awoke suddenly to the knowledge that, to insure the success of such an enterprise, feminine intervention is a necessary evil.

Accordingly, he set about his preparations with an economic industry. Casting his eye upon a tract of land upon a Southern river, he acquired it for certain services rendered in an unguarded moment to the Swiss adventurer, who had acquired it in a manner that concerned himself alone.

The next step of the French gentleman was to build

beside the Southern river a family mansion, whose door he promptly closed upon the Swiss adventurer, since virtue consists not so much in refusing to benefit by vice as in refusing to acknowledge the benefit. Not without a sense of nervous perturbation, he then proceeded to cast his gaze upon the most promising feminine pledges of progeny. From among a dozen or so of his fair neighbors he selected, with the experienced eye of a woman-fancier, the blooming specimen of Swiss buxomness, and, the adventurer coming to terms, the marriage had been celebrated without the retarding curtain-raiser of a romantic prelude.

The gentleman's name was Marcel Musin de Biencourt; the lady's has no place in the following history.

For a period matters progressed in natural sequence. The land was tilled, the cotton picked, and the lady installed in the best bedroom of the newly erected mansion. Had she played the part for which nature and her lord intended her, there is reason to suppose that she would have become a serviceable instrument in the preservation of the species.

But the gentleman had reckoned without Providence. With the ending of the year of her bridehood the roses in the lady's cheeks grew waxen, and she turned with a sigh of relief from the labor of travail to the rest of the little church-yard upon the hill.

The aspens shivered above her, the river purled between level fields far down below, and from the uprooted furrows around the dutiful corn put forth tender sprouts; but the lady had shirked her mission in its first fulfilment, and with the birth-time of the year she neither rose nor stirred.

In the best bedroom the dust thickened upon the chintz curtains, and a weak and sickly hostage to fortune yelled his new throat hoarse with premonition of the inhospitality of the planet upon which he had been precipitated.

PHASES OF AN INFERIOR PLANET

Disappointed in his estimate of woman's nature, the gentleman of France decided to economize in material, and to rear a race from the unpromising specimen in his possession. Faithfully he strove to fulfil his part, and when the boy reached manhood, he laid himself down beside his wife upon the hill.

From this time on the family record is biblically concise. Marcel begot Marcel, and again Marcel begot Marcel, and yet again.

While the root Musin languished, De Biencourt, the lofty family tree, withered and died, to be forgotten. Neither in history nor in tradition, nor in the paths of private virtue, was a Musin known to have distinguished himself. If he took up arms in the American Revolution, he took them up in a manner unworthy of record; if he favored the Declaration of Independence, he did not commit his preference to paper; if he excelled in any way, it was in the way of mediocrity —which is perhaps the safest way of all.

But extinction was not to be the end of the venturesome blood of the French gentleman. His spirit animated one of his name to confide to the care of his ex-slaves the mansion crumbling above his head, and to become a wanderer in the States which had been so nearly disunited. Like the minstrels of old, he strung his harp from his shoulder, and journeyed from South to North and from East to West. His Norman blood still ran blue in his veins, and his faith was the faith of his fathers.

In his travels he played his passage into the vivacious affections of an Irish maiden, who wore a rosary about her neck and a cross upon her sleeve. But these conspicuous badges of Popery failed to chill the passion of Marcel. And, in truth, if the maiden's heart was as black as the arch-fiend, her eyes (which is more to the point) were not less blue than heaven. With an improvidence sufficient to bleach the ghost of his

PHASES OF AN INFERIOR PLANET

colonial progenitor, he tossed forebodings into the capacious lap of the future, and stormed the yielding heart of young Ireland.

Love was lord, and their marriage-bonds were double-locked and barred by Protestant and Catholic clergy. But there is a power which laughs at religious locksmiths. Within six months the illusions with which each had draped the other melted before the fire and brimstone of ecclesiastical dispute. Between the kisses of their lips each offered petitions to a patient Omnipotence for the salvation of the other's soul. As the kisses grew colder the prayers grew warmer. There is a tendency in man, when he has fallen out with the human brother whom he has seen, to wax more zealous in his attentions to the Divine Father whom he has not. To be courteous to one's neighbor is so much more difficult than to be cringing to one's God.

And then a child was given. In the large family Bible upon the father's desk the event is recorded in two different hands, and the child was christened with two different names.

The first reads:

"MARIE MUSIN, *born April* 24, 1868."

And the second:

"MARY ANN MUSIN, *born April* 24, 1868."

After fifteen years the matter was settled, as were most family matters, by the child herself.

"I will be both," she said, decisively. "I will be Mariana."

And Mariana she became.

In the same high-handed fashion the theological disputes of the parents were reduced to trifles as light as air.

"I will be a Presbyterian one Sunday and a Catholic

the next," she concluded, with amiable acquiescence; "only on fast-days and lecture-nights I'll be a heathen."

For a time these regulations were observed with uncompromising impartiality, but, upon moving to a smaller town, she foresaw a diplomatic stroke.

"I think it better," she announced, sweetly, "for one of us to become an Episcopalian. I have noticed that most of the society people here are Episcopalians—and in that way the family will be so evenly distributed. I see that it will be easier for me to make the sacrifice than for either of you. Of course, I should love to go with you, mamma, but incense makes me sneeze; and you know, papa, I can't stand congregational singing. It grates upon my nerves. And I must be something, for I have so much religious feeling. I will be an Episcopalian."

She cast herself into the arms of the Church with all the zeal of a convert. From an artistic stand-point she repudiated insincerity, and, though cultivated, her professions were as fertile as the most natural product. Even to herself she scorned to admit that her alliance with a particular creed was the result of aught but a moral tendency in that direction. And the burden of the truth was with her. She was as changeable as wind and as impressionable as wax, and the swelling tide of sentiment had taken an ecclesiastical turn.

She dressed in sober grays, and attended service with the regularity of the sexton; she decorated her walls with Madonnas; and she undertook, by way of the Sunday-school room, to lead a class of eight small boys into the path of righteousness. She read Christina Rossetti and George Herbert, and she placed tiny silver crosses, suspended from purple ribbons, in her school-books.

At the age of sixteen she attached herself to a society whose mission it was to cultivate, by frequent calls, the religious poor, and she neglected social observances to retard by her presence the domestic duties of the indigent members of the community. She descended in a special detachment upon a series of beer saloons, enforcing the pledge upon a number of helpless gentlemen, and thereby multiplying the sin of intemperance by that of perjury. While her mother mended the rents in her garments, Mariana promoted a circle of stocking-darners for the inhabitants of the almshouse.

At that period her expression was in perfect harmony with the tenor of her mind. The dramatic effect was always good.

In the daily school, which she attended when the fancy seized her, she ruled as a popular fetish. Between the younger children, whom she terrorized, and the elder, whom she mesmerized, there was an intermediate class with whom she was in high favor. As a tiny child she had caught the street songs quicker than any other, and had sung them better; and to the accompaniment of a hand-organ she could render a marvellous ballet.

During her tenth year she fell into a passionate friendship for one of the scholars—a stately girl with phlegmatic eyes of gray. For six months she paid her lover-like attentions in surreptitious ways, and expended her pocket-money in nosegays, with which to adorn the desk of her divinity. She wore a photograph of the gray-eyed girl above her heart, and lingered for an hour to walk home with her upon Fridays.

The friendship was sundered at last by visits exchanged between them, and Mariana's emotions became theological.

But this passed also. Vague amatory impulses of old racial meaning were born. At sixteen she was precipitated into a sentiment for the photograph, printed by the daily press, of a young fellow who was at that time in the custody of the State, preparatory to responding to a charge of highway-robbery. The photograph was romantic, the crime was also. It was a nineteenth-century attempt at a revival of the part of Claude Duval.

Mariana attended missions less and meditated more. She divided her time between her journal and the piano, showing a preference for songs of riotous sentiment. Without apparent trouble to herself, she grew wan and mysteriously poetic. She wore picturesque gowns with romantic draperies. Her hair possessed a charming disorder, the expression of her face passed from the placid into the intense. The dramatic effect was as good as ever. Her journal of that year contains a declaration of undying constancy. The object of this avowal is nominally the young highwayman—in reality the creation of an over-fertile brain craving the intoxicant of a great passion. The highwayman was but a picturesque nucleus round which her dreams clustered and from which they gathered color. She existed in a maze of the imagination, feasting upon the unsubstantial food of idealism. Her longings for fame and for love were so closely interwoven that even in her own mind it was impossible to disassociate them. If she bedewed her pillow with tears of anguish for the sake of a man whom she had never seen, and whom, seeing, she would have passed with averted eyes, the tears were often dried by ecstatic visions of artistic aspirations. And yet this romance of straw was not the less intense because it was the creation of overwrought susceptibilities; perhaps the more so. If real troubles were the only troubles, how many tortured hearts would be uplifted to the hills. And Mariana's mystical romance was a *daemon* that lured her in a dozen different disguises towards the quicksands of life.

But this passed also and was done with.

PHASES OF AN INFERIOR PLANET

Her mother died, and her father married an early love. Mariana, who had been first, declined to become last. Dissensions followed swiftly, and the domestic atmosphere only cleared when Mariana departed from the paternal dwelling-place.

From the small Southern village, under the protection of an elderly female relation, she had flown to New York in search of theatrical employment. Failing in her object, she turned desperately to the culture of her voice, living meanwhile upon a meagre allowance donated by her father. The elderly female relation had remained with her for a time, but finding Mariana intractable in minor ways, and foreseeing a future in which she would serve as cat's-paw for the girl's vagaries, she had blessed her young relative and departed.

"One must either worship or detest you, my dear," she remarked as a parting shaft. "And to worship you means to wait upon you, which is wearing. Your personality is as absorbent as cotton. It absorbs the individual comfort of those around you. It is very pleasant to be absorbed, and you do it charmingly; but there is so much to see in the world, and I'm getting old fast enough."

So she went, leaving Mariana alone in a fourth-story front room of The Gotham apartment-house.

CHAPTER III

Mr. Nevins once said to Mariana: "You are as elusive as thistle-down whipped up with snow."

Mariana smiled that radiating, indescribable smile which dawned gradually from within, deepening until it burst into pervasive wealth of charm.

"Why snow?" was her query.

Mr. Paul, who apparently had been engrossed in his dinner, glanced up grimly. "The only possible reason for a metaphor," he observed, "is lack of reason."

Mr. Nevins dismissed him with a shrug and looked in sentimental perplexity at Mariana.

"Merely because it is impossible to whip up ice with anything," he replied.

"I should have supposed," interrupted Mr. Paul, in unabashed disapproval, "that the same objection would apply to thistle-down. It would certainly apply to a woman."

Miss Ramsey, who sat opposite, turned her tired eyes upon him.

"Life is not of your opinion, Mr. Paul," she said. "It whips us up with all kinds of ingredients, and it never seems to realize when we have been reduced to the proper consistency."

She looked worn and harassed, and had come in to dinner later than usual. It was the first remark she had made, and, after making it, she relapsed into silence. Her small red hands trembled as she lifted her fork, the rebellious lines between her brows grew deeper, and she ate her dinner with that complete ex-

PHASES OF AN INFERIOR PLANET

haustion which so often passes for resignation in the eyes of our neighbors. Nervous prostration has produced more saints than all the sermons since Moses.

Mariana watched her sympathetically. She wondered why the gravy upon Miss Ramsey's plate congealed sooner than it did upon any one else's, while the sobbiest potatoes invariably fell to her share.

"A false metaphor!" commented Mr. Paul. "Most metaphors are false. I don't trust Shakespeare himself when he gets to metaphor. I always skip them."

"Oh, they have their uses," broke in the cheery tones of the optimist. "I'm not much on Shakespeare, but I've no doubt he has his uses also. As for metaphor, it is a convenient way of saying more than you mean."

"So is lying," retorted Mr. Paul, crossly, and the conversation languished. Mariana ate her dinner and looked at the table-cloth. Mr. Nevins ate his dinner and looked at Mariana. He regarded her as an artistic possibility. Her appearance was a source of constant interest to him, and he felt, were he in the position of nature, with the palette and brush of an omnipotent colorist, he might blend the harmonious lines of Mariana's person to better advantage. He resented the fact that her nose was irregular and her chin too long. He wondered how such a subject could have been wilfully neglected.

As for himself, he honestly felt that he had wasted no opportunities. Upon their first acquaintance he had made a poster of Mariana which undeniably surpassed the original. It represented her in a limp and scantily made gown of green, with strange reptiles sprawling over it, relieved against the ardor of a purple sunset. The hair was a marvel of the imagination.

Mariana had liked it, with the single exception of the reptilian figures.

"They have such an unpleasant suggestion," was her critical comment. "I feel quite like Medusa. Couldn't you change them into nice little butterflies and things?"

Mr. Nevins was afraid he could not. The poster satisfied him as it was. Miss Musin could not deny, he protested, that he had remodelled her nose and chin in an eminently successful job, and if the hair and eyes and complexion in the poster bore close resemblance in color, so did the hair and eyes and complexion in the original. He had done his best.

Mariana accepted his explanation and went complacently on her way, as enigmatical as a Chinese puzzle. She was full of swift surprises and tremulous changes, varying color with her environment; gay one moment, and sad before the gayety had left her lips—cruel and calm, passionate and tender—always and ever herself.

Twice a week she went to Signor Morani's for a vocal lesson. Signor Morani was small and romantic and severe. In his youth he had travelled as Jenny Lind's barytone, and he had fallen a slave to her voice. He had worshipped a voice as other men worship a woman. Unlike other men, he had been faithful for a lifetime—to a voice.

When Mariana had gone to him, an emotional and aspiring soprano of nineteen, he had listened to her quietly and advised patience.

"You must wait," he said. "All art is waiting."

"I will not wait," said Mariana. "Waiting is starvation."

He looked at her critically.

"More of us starve than the world suspects," he answered. "It is the privilege of genius. This is a planet, my dear child, where mediocrity is exalted and genius brought low. It is a living fulfilment of the scriptural prophecy, 'The first shall be last and the last shall be first.'" Then he added: "Sing again."

Mariana stood up and sang. His words had depressed her, and her voice trembled. She looked at him wistfully, her hands hanging at her sides, her head thrown back. It was an aria from "Faust." He shook his head slowly.

"You will never be great," he said. "I can give you technique, but not volume. Your voice will never be great."

With a half-defiant gesture Mariana broke forth again. This time it was a popular song, with a quick refrain running through it. As she sang she acted the accompaniment half unconsciously.

Signor Morani frowned as she commenced, and then watched her attentively. In the fragile little girl, with the changeable eyes of green and the aureole of shadowless hair, he scented possibilities.

"Your voice will never be great," he repeated; "but you may make men believe so."

"And you will take me?" pleaded Mariana. She stretched out her beautiful hands. Her eyes prayed. Her flexible tones drooped.

Signor Morani took her hands in his with kindly reassurance.

"Yes," he said—"yes; it will keep you out of mischief, at least."

And it had kept her out of mischief. It had opened a channel for her emotions. Like a tide, the romanticism of her nature veered towards art. She became the most fanatical of devotees. She breathed it and lived it. In her heart it transplanted all other religions, and the æstheticism of its expression gained a marvellous hold upon her faith. Above the little mosaic altar at her bedside she enshrined a bust of Wagner, and she worshipped it as some more orthodox believer had once worshipped an enshrined Madonna. At midnight she held devotional services all alone, sitting before the piano, bending to the uses of a litany the intellectual rhapsodies of Beethoven or the sensuous repinings of Chopin, while the little red flame sent up praise and incense from dried rose leaves and cinnamon to the memories of dead musicians. She introduced a rare, sensuous beauty into this new worship, as she had introduced it into the old. She typified the Church when, in its fresh young passion, and suffused with the dying splendors of paganism, it turned from the primitive exercises of its founders and revived the worship of the gracious Madonna of Old Egypt in the worship of the Madonna of Nazareth, and the flower-scented feasts of Venus in the Purification of the Virgin. There existed in the girl an unsatisfied restlessness of self, resulting in the desire for complete submergence of soul in idea. Her nature veered constantly from extreme to extreme; there was no semblance of a saner medium, and as a system must have exponents, the high priests and priestesses of art became her lesser divinities.

She began to haunt the Metropolitan Opera-house. From the fifth gallery she looked down every evening upon an Italian or German landscape. She herself trembled like a harp swept by invisible fingers; she grew pale with Marguerite, wept over the dead Juliet, and went mad with the madness of Lucia.

When the voice of that fair Bride of Lammermoor who sang for us that season was borne to her on the notes of a flute which flagged beneath the exceeding sweetness of the human notes they carried, Mariana grasped the railing with her quivering hands and bowed her head in an ecstasy of appreciation. It was the ecstasy with which a monk in mediæval days must have thrilled when he faced in a dim cathedral some beautiful and earthly Virgin of the great Raphael. It was the purest form of sensuous self-abnegation.

Then, as the curtain fell, she would rise and step gropingly towards the door, cast into sudden darkness. Wrapped in that mental state as in a mantle, she would descend the stairs and pass out into the street. At such times she was as far removed from the existence to which she was returning as was the poor mad Lucia herself. And then in the night she would awake and sing softly to herself in the stillness, lying with seraphic eyes and hands clasped upon her breast, until the morning sun flashed into her face and the day began.

There was also a tragic side to her emotions. Her past inheritance of ages of image-worshippers laid hold upon her. From being merely symbols of art the singers became divinities in their own right. She haunted their hotels for fleeting glimpses of them. She bought their photographs with the money which should have gone for a winter hat. She would gladly have kissed the dust upon which they trod. After her first hearing of "Tristan and Isolde," she placed the prima donna's photograph beneath the bust of Wagner, and worshipped her for weeks as a bright particular star.

In the evening she attended the opera alone. Returning when it was over, she crossed Broadway, boarded a car, and, reaching The Gotham, toiled up to the fourth landing. She was innocent of prudery, and she went unharmed. Perhaps her complete absorption in something beyond herself was her safeguard. At all events, she brushed men by, glanced at them with unseeing eyes, and passed placidly on her way.

Mariana was famished for romance, but not for the romance of the street. She had an instinctive aversion to things common and of vulgar intent. Her unsatisfied desire was but the craving of a young and impressionable heart for untried emotion. It was the poetry of living she thirsted for—poetry in æsthetic proportions, with a careful adjustment of light and shade. She desired harmonious effects and exquisite schemes of color, all as appropriate settings to a romance which she could arrange and blend in treatment as an artist arranges models of still life. So, for a time, she expended herself upon great singers. A new tenor appeared as Edgardo. Upon the stage he was dark and fierce and impassioned. He made an adorable lover. He sang to Lucia, not to the audience, and he threw half his arias into his eyes. Mariana was enraptured. She fell desperately in love. During the day she went about in meditative abstraction; during the night she turned upon her little cotton pillow-slip, and wept to think how far below him she must ever remain. She even wished herself a chorus girl, that she might intercept his glances. She grew frantically jealous of the prima donna, whom, also, she adored. She imagined innumerable romances in which he enacted upon the stage of life the part of Edgardo. Then, through the kindness of Signor Morani, she was introduced to the object of her regard, and the awakening was abrupt. He was fat and commonplace. He proved to be the faithful husband of a red-faced little German wife, and the devoted father of a number of red-faced German children. He possessed no qualities for romantic development, and Mariana recovered.

For a period her susceptibilities abated. The wave of activity spent its violence. Life flowed for her like a meadow stream, sensitive to faint impressions from a passing breeze, but calm when the breeze was afar.

Upon a night of "Carmen" she saw from the fifth gallery a velvet rose fall from the prima donna's bosom to the stage. When the curtain fell she rushed madly down and begged it of an usher. She carried it home, and hung it upon the wall above her bed. At night, before falling asleep, she would draw the curtains aside, and, in the electric light that flooded the room, cast her eyes upon the vivid bit of color. In the early morning she would awake, and, raising herself upon her elbow, touch it reverently with her hand. It was homage rendered to her own ambition.

At The Gotham, her bare little chamber, with its garish wall-paper, was a source of acute discomfort to her. Once, after a long spell of pneumonia, she had fallen into a fit of desperation, and had attacked the paper with a breakfast-knife. The result was a square of whitewashed wall above the bureau. An atmosphere of harmony was so necessary to her growth that she seemed to droop and pine in uncongenial environment. In the apartment-house, with its close, unventilated halls, its creaking elevator, its wretchedly served dinners, she had always felt strangely ill at ease. Her last prayer at night was that the morrow might see her transplanted to richer soil, her first thought upon awakening was that the coming day was pregnant with possibilities. Life in its entirety, life with passionate color and emotional fulfilment, was the food she craved.

Of Mariana, Mr. Ardly had made a laborious and profound analysis.

"That young person is a self-igniting taper," he had concluded. "If some one doesn't apply the match, she will go off of her own accord—and she will burn herself out before time has cast a wet blanket upon her."

He himself was a self-contained young fellow, who, like a greater before him, followed with wisdom both wine and women. His life was regulated by a theory which he had propounded in youth and attempted to practice in maturer years. The theory asserted that experience was the one reliable test of existing conditions. "I refused to believe that alcohol was an intoxicant," he had once said, "until I tested it."

PHASES OF AN INFERIOR PLANET

When Mariana first arrived, he surprised in his heart an embryonic sentiment concerning her, and proceeded to crush it as coolly as he would have crushed a fly that encroached upon the private domain of his person.

"I have no dissipations," he explained, when discussing the affair with Mariana. "I neither drink nor love."

"Which is unwise," retorted Mariana. "I do both in moderation. And a man who has never been in love is always a great school-boy. I should be continually expecting him to tread upon my gown or to break my fan. Sentiment is the greatest civilizer of the race. If I were you I would begin immediately."

"I dislike all effort," returned Ardly, gravely, "and love is cloying. Over-loving produces mental indigestion, as over-eating produces physical. I have suffered from it, and experience has made me abstemious. I shall abstain from falling in love with you."

"What a pity!" sighed Mariana, lifting her lashes.

"Well, I can't agree with you," argued Ardly, "and I don't regret it. I am very comfortable as I am."

"I am not," retorted Mariana. "I detest the dinners. Who could be comfortable on overdone mutton and cold potatoes?"

"Even in the matter of food I am without prejudices," declared the other. "I had as soon want a good dinner and have a poor one as have a good one and want none. These are the only conditions with which I am acquainted. There may be estates where things are more equally adjusted, but I know nothing of them; I have not experienced them."

Mariana sighed. "You are as depressing as Mr. Paul," she complained.

"I only speak of what I know," explained Ardly, complacently. "Upon other matters I have no opinions, and I calmly repeat that I have found appetite

PHASES OF AN INFERIOR PLANET

and gratification to be situated upon opposite sides of a revolving globe. When one's up the other's down."

"I shall cut a passage through," said Mariana. "If life doesn't equalize things, I will."

"And I will watch the process," remarked Ardly, indolently.

It was shortly after this that Mariana went to Long Island for a holiday, spending a couple of weeks in the cottage of an acquaintance, who, by dint of successive matrimonial ventures, had succeeded in reaching the equilibrium to which Mariana aspired.

Upon returning to New York the girl found her distaste for The Gotham to have trebled. When she had toiled up the dingy stairway and installed herself in her old place, she sat upon her trunk and looked about her. Never had the room appeared so dull, so desperately plain. The close odor caused by lack of ventilation offended her nostrils, and yet she hesitated to fling back the shutters and reveal the rusty balcony with its spindling fire-escape, beyond which stretched the sombre outlook, the elevated road looming like a skeleton in the foreground. The door into the hall was ajar, and she could see a dull expanse of corridor, lighted day and night by a solitary and ineffectual electric jet.

A sob stuck in her throat, and, crossing to the window, she raised it and threw back the shutters, letting in a thin stream of dust and sunshine. Her geranium stood where she had left it, and its withered and yellow leaves smote her with accusing neglect.

"Oh, you poor thing!" she cried, in an impulsive burst of pity.

Then she saw that it had been freshly watered, and that its famished leaves were unfolding. Turning her eyes, they encountered a row of small pots containing seedlings which lined her neighbor's window, encroaching slightly upon her own possession. Before them a man was standing, a watering-can in one hand, a small trowel in the other. As Mariana stepped upon the fire-escape he turned in evident resentment, glanced at her indifferently, and resumed his task of invigoration.

The afternoon sun shone full upon him, and Mariana saw him plainly. He was young, with stooping shoulders, and he wore a cheap and shabby suit of clothes, with apparent disregard of their quality. His face was thin and cleanly shaven, there was a nervous tension about the mouth, and the hair, falling dark and heavy upon the temples, lent a haggardness to his colorless and burned-out profile. It was a face in which the poetic principle was obscured by an ascetic veneering. In his whole appearance was borne out the suggestion flashing from the eyes—a suggestion of mental sustentation upon physical force.

Mariana regarded him mutely. Her gaze was almost tragic in its intensity. For a moment her lips quivered and her fingers interlaced. Then she retreated into her room, slamming the shutters after her. Throwing herself into a chair, she buried her face in her hands.

"I—I can't have even that to myself!" she said, and burst into tears.

CHAPTER IV

MARIANA's neighbor sat in his room. He sat motionless, his head resting upon his hands, his arms resting upon an office desk, which was plainly finished and of cheap walnut. At his left elbow a lamp cast an illumination upon his relaxed and exhausted figure, upon the straight, dark hair, upon the bulging brow, and upon the sinewy and squarely shaped hands, with their thin and nervous fingers.

The desk upon which he leaned was covered with a litter of closely written letter-sheets, and at the back a row of pigeon-holes contained an unassorted profusion of manuscripts.

The walls of the room were lined with roughly constructed shelves of painted wood, which were filled to overflowing with well-worn volumes in English, French, and German, Oken's *Die Zeugung* upon the north side confronting Darwin's *The Variation of Animals and Plants Under Domestication* upon the south. A cabinet in one corner contained a number of alcoholic specimens of embryonic development, and a small table near by supported a microscope and several instruments for physiological experiments. Above the mantel, perhaps arranged in freakish disregard of superstition, hung a skull and a pair of cross-bones, and beneath them a series of photographs illustrating the evolution of rudimentary nervous systems.

Upon the hearth, within convenient reach of the desk, stood a small spirit-stove, and on it a coffee-pot, which emitted a strong and stimulating aroma. Beside it a table was spread, with the remains of a cold supper and an unused cup and saucer.

The man lifted his head from his hands, turned up the wick of the lamp, and took up his pen.

From without came the rumble of the elevated road and the shrill cries of a newsboy proclaiming the redundant virtues of the *Evening Post*. A warm August breeze, entering at the open window, which was raised from the floor, caused the flame of the lamp to flicker slightly. Outside upon the fire-escape the young plants were arranged in rows of systematic precision, their tender leaves revealed in the narrow path of lamplight leading from the heated room to the iron railing overlooking the street. With absent-minded elaboration the man drew an irregular line upon the paper before him. The line bore no relation whatever to the heading of the paper, which was written in a remarkably firm and heavy hand, and read:

"*Transmission of Acquired Characteristics.*"

Suddenly he laid the pen aside, and rose, wiping the moisture from his brow with his handkerchief. Then he threw off his coat and drew up his shirt-sleeves. It was oppressively warm, and the lamp seemed to possess the heating qualities of a Latrobe stove. For a couple of minutes he walked slowly up and down the uncarpeted floor. From the adjoining room came the sound of a piano and a woman singing. He shook his head impatiently, but the sound continued, and he yawned and stretched his arms with resentful resignation. After which he lifted the coffee-pot from the little stove and filled the cup upon the table.

Returning to his seat, he drank his coffee slowly, allowing his abstracted gaze to wander through the window and into the city night without. Upon the drawn shades of the opposite tenement-house he could trace the shadows of men and women passing to and fro like the unsubstantial outlines of figures remembered

PHASES OF AN INFERIOR PLANET

in a dream. His thoughts fluttered restlessly. He was tired. Yes, but the coffee would get him into shape again, and he must work. It was barely ten o'clock. The day had been trying. The experiments made in the college labarotory had been unsuccessful. He had gone about them wrongly. Professor Myers had been mistaken in his calculations. It was unfortunate. The opportunity for work had been excellent, and in September, when the session began, his lectures at that infernal Woman's College would take a good two hours daily, to say nothing of the preparations. What a bore it would be! If he had only money enough to follow out his work independently he might make a splendid success of it. True, he had spent enough on those travels and excavations in Egypt and Assyria to have supported an ordinary Philistine in comfort for an ordinary lifetime. But he did not regret them. They had given balance to his judgment, and he had acquired an immense amount of information. And those studies in Ancient India. Why, they had even more direct bearing upon his theories. Involuntarily his glance strayed round the book-lined walls and to the manuscripts in his desk. He devoured the closely written, almost illegible pages with insatiable eyes—eyes stricken with the mania for knowledge. The bronzed and sallow face he turned towards the light was suffused with the glow of a consuming purpose. In its deep-eyed, thin-lipped severity of drawing, every sensuous curve had been erased by lines of toil.

He set the cup aside and returned to his work. From a drawer of his desk he drew a thick volume, consisting of a number of legal-cap sheets, bound with a systematic regard for subject. Upon the cover was written in printed letters: "Notes," and beneath: "A History of Man, with Special Application of the Science of Ontogeny."

After consulting this briefly he laid it away and fell to writing. From the adjoining room still came the sound of a woman singing. The voice was light and flippant.

"Damn it!" said the man, suddenly, with angry impatience. He said it vehemently, looking up from his work with nervous irritability. At the same moment there came a slight tap at his door.

He laid aside his pen, rose, and opened it. Mr. Paul stood upon the outside.

"Well, Mr. Algarcife," he began, grimly, "you see I have broken a life-long principle and taken a man at his word. I came for the book you spoke of."

Algarcife welcomed him impatiently. "So I suppose I must prove your principle relative, if not erroneous," he answered. His voice was singularly full and clear. "It was *Milligan on the Vocabulary of Aboriginal Tasmanians*, was it not? Yes, I think it will aid you."

Mr. Paul came in and they sat down. Algarcife offered him coffee and cigars, but he declined. He sat stiffly in his chair and looked at the other with cynical interest.

"You write all night on this lye, I suppose?" he said, abruptly. "A combined production of brains and coffee."

Algarcife lighted his pipe and leaned back in his chair, blowing gray circles of smoke upon the atmosphere.

"You are right," he responded; "I find I do my best work after midnight, when I am drunk on caffeine or coffee. I suppose it will do for me in the end."

Mr. Paul returned his indifferent gaze with one of severity. "You are all nerves as it is," he said. "You haven't an ounce of good barbarian blood in your body—merely a colorless machine for ratiocination. I tell you, there is no bigger fool than the man who,

PHASES OF AN INFERIOR PLANET

because he possesses a few brains, forgets that he is an animal."

The other laughed abstractedly.

"What wholesome truths you deliver," he said. "I think Luther must have had your manner. Well, if I were in your place, I should probably say the same, though less forcibly. But they are theories. You see, I argue this way: with one man's mind and one man's power of work, I could never accomplish what I have before me—any more than poor Buckle, with the brain of a giant, could accomplish what he undertook. It is too big for a single man in this stage of development. So, with one man's mind, I intend to do six men's amount of labor. If I hold out, I will have my reward; if I go to pieces, I shall at least have the satisfaction of a good fight."

His voice was distinct and forcible, with a widely varied range of expression.

There was a second tap at the door, and Mr. Nevins entered, looking depressed and ill-humored.

"Hello, Anthony!" he called. "What! is Mr. Paul squandering your midnight oil? You should have sent him to bed long ago."

"It is not my hour for retiring," responded Mr. Paul.

Anthony interrupted pacifically.

"Mr. Paul is exhorting me," he said, "and I have no doubt that, with slight modifications, his sermon may be adapted to your case. He predicts brain-softening and general senility."

"An inspired prophecy," returned Mr. Nevins, crossly, "and savoring of Jeremiah. As for myself, it is but common justice that a man who has conscientiously refused the cultivation of the mind should not be called upon to lose what he doesn't possess." Then he grew suddenly cheerful. "Confound it! What's the use of being a philosopher on paper when you can be one in practice. What's the use of dying when you can eat, drink, and be merry?"

"Eating," remarked Mr. Paul, with depressing effect, "produces dyspepsia, drinking produces gout."

"And thought, paresis," added Anthony, lightly. "They are all merely different forms of dissipation. I have chosen mine; Nevins has chosen his. Only, as a matter of taste, I'd rather die by work than wine. Personally, I perfer consumption to apoplexy."

"There is such a thing as the means justifying the end," responded Mr. Nevins, in reckless ill-humor. "And it is a great principle. If I wasn't a fool, I'd make a bonfire of my brush and palette, and start afresh on a level with my appetite. I would become the apostle of good-living, which means fast living. I tell you, an hour of downright devilment is worth all the art since Adam. Aristippus is greater than Raphael."

"What has gone wrong?" demanded Algarcife, soothingly. "Too much purple in the 'Andromeda'? I always said that purple was the imperial color of his satanic majesty. If you had followed the orthodox art of your college days, and hadn't gone wandering after strange gods, you might have escaped a dash of that purple melancholia."

"You're a proper fellow," returned Mr. Nevins, with disgust. "Who was it that won that last debate in '82 by a glowing defence of Christianity against agnosticism, and, when the Reverend Miles lit out about the new orator in his flock, floored him with: 'Was that good? Then what a magnificent thing I could have made of the other side!'"

Mr. Paul had opened his book, and glanced up with candid lack of interest. Anthony laughed languidly.

"I saw Miles some weeks ago," he said, "and he is still talking about my 'defection,' as he calls it. I couldn't convince him that I was merely the counsel for a weak case, and that I was always an agnostic at heart."

Mr. Nevins lighted a cigar in silence. Then he nodded abruptly towards the wall. "What's that noise?" he demanded, irritably.

"That," replied Algarcife, "is a fiend in woman's form, who makes night hideous. I can't begin to work until she sings herself hoarse, and she doesn't do that until midnight. Verily, she is possessed of seven devils, and singing devils at that."

Mr. Nevins was listening attentively. His irritability had vanished.

"Why, it's Mariana!" he exclaimed. "Bless her pretty throat! An hour of Mariana is worth all the spoken or unspoken thoughts of—of Marcus Aurelius, to say nothing of Solomon."

Mr. Paul closed his book and looked up gravely. "A worthy young woman," he observed, "though a trifle fast. As for Solomon, his wisdom has been greatly exaggerated."

"Fast!" protested Mr. Nevins. "She's as fast as—as Mr. Paul—"

"Your insinuation is absurd," returned Mr. Paul, stiffly. But Mr. Nevins was not to be suppressed.

"Then don't display your ignorance of such matters. As for this St. Anthony, he thinks every woman who walks the New York streets a bleached pattern of virtue. I don't believe he'd know a painted Jezebel unless she wore a scarlet letter."

Anthony turned upon him resentfully. "Confound it, Nevins," he said, "I am not a born fool!"

"Only an innocent," retorted Mr. Nevins, complacently.

A resounding rap upon the panels of the door interrupted them. Mr. Nevins rose.

"That's Ardly," he said. "He and I are doing New York to-night."

PHASES OF AN INFERIOR PLANET

Ardly came inside, and stood with his hand upon the door-knob.

"Come on, Nevins," he said. "I've got to do a column on that new *danseuse*. She dances like a midge, but, by Jove! she has a figure to swear by—"

"And escape perjury," added Mr. Nevins. "Mariana says it is false."

"Mariana," replied Ardly, "is a sworn enemy to polite illusions. She surveys the stage through a microscope situated upon the end of a lorgnette. It is a mistake. One should never look at a woman through glasses unless they be rose-colored ones. A man preserves this principle, and his faith in plumpness and curves along with it; a woman penetrates to the padding and powder. Come on, Nevins."

Mr. Nevins followed him into the hall, and then turned to look in again. "Algarcife, won't you join us on a jolly little drunk? Won't you, Mr. Paul?"

When they had gone, and Mr. Paul had gone likewise, though upon a different way, Anthony heated the coffee, drank two cups, and resumed his work.

"Taken collectively," he remarked, "the human race is a consummate nuisance. What a deuced opportunity for work the last man will have—only, most likely, he'll be an ass."

The next day he passed Mariana on the stairs without seeing her. He was returning from the college laboratory, and his mind was full of his experiments. Later in the afternoon, when he watered his plants, he turned his can, in absent-minded custom, upon the geranium, and saw that there was a scarlet bloom among the leaves. The sight pleased him. It was as if he had given sustenance to a famished life.

But Mariana, engrossed in lesser things, had seen him upon the stairs and upon the balcony. She still cherished an unreasonable resentment at what she considered his trespass upon her individual rights; and yet, despite herself, the trenchant quality in the dark, massive-browed face had not been without effect upon her. The ascetic self-repression that chastened his lips, and the utter absence of emotion in the mental heat of his glance tantalized her in its very unlikeness to her own nature. She, who thrilled into responsive joy or gloom at reflected light or shade, found her quick senses awake to each passing impression, and had learned to recognize her neighbor's step upon the stair; while he, wrapped in an intellectual trance, created his environment at will, and was as oblivious of the girl at the other end of the fire-escape as he was to the articles of furniture in his room.

It was as if semi-barbarism, in all its exuberance of undisciplined emotion, had converged with the highest type of modern civilization—the civilization in which the flesh is degraded from its pedestal and forced to serve as a jangled vehicle for the progress of the mind.

The next night, as Algarcife stood at his window looking idly down upon the street below, he heard the sound of a woman sobbing in the adjoining room. His first impulse was to hasten in the direction from whence the sound came. He curbed the impulse with a shake.

"Hang it," he said, "it is no business of mine!"

But the suppressed sobbing from the darkness beyond invited him with its enlistment of his quick sympathies.

The electric light, falling upon the fire-escape, cast inky shadows from end to end. They formed themselves into dense outlines, which shivered as if stirred by a phantom breeze.

He turned and went back to his desk. Upon the table he had spread the supper of which he intended partaking at eleven o'clock. For an unknown reason he had conceived an aversion to the restaurant in the basement, and seldom entered it. He slept late in the day and worked at night, and his meals were apt to be at irregular hours.

He wrote a line, and rose and went back to the window. For an instant he stood and listened, then stepped out upon the fire-escape and walked across the shivering shadows towards the open window beyond.

Upon the little door beneath the window a girl was leaning, her head bowed upon her outstretched arm. The light in the room beyond was low, but he could see distinctly the slight outlines of her figure and the confusion of her heavy hair. She was sobbing softly.

"I beg your pardon," he said, the sympathetic quality in his voice dominating, "but I am sure that I can help you."

His forcible self-confidence exercised a compelling effect. The girl lifted her head and looked at him. Tears stood in her eyes, and as the electric light caught the clear drops they cast out scintillant flashes. Against the dim interior her head, with its nimbus of hair, had the droop and poise of the head of a mediæval saint.

"Oh, but you don't know how unhappy I am!" she said.

He spoke as he would have spoken to Mr. Paul in the same circumstances. "You have no one to whom you can go?"

"No."

"Then tell me about it."

His tone was that in which a physician might inquire the condition of a patient's digestion. It was absolutely devoid of the recognition of sex.

"Oh, I have worked so hard!" said Mariana.

"Yes?"

"And I hoped to sing in opera, and—Morani tells me that—it will be impossible."

"Ah!" In the peculiar power of his voice the exclamation had the warmth of a handshake.

PHASES OF AN INFERIOR PLANET

Mariana rested her chin upon her clasped hands and looked at him. "He says it must be a music-hall—or—or nothing," she added.

He was silent for a moment. He felt that it was a case in which his sympathy could be exceeded only by his ignorance. "And this is why you are unhappy?" he asked. "Is there nothing else?"

She gave a little sob. "I am tired," she said. "My allowance hasn't come—and I missed my dinner, and I am—hungry."

Algarcife responded with relieved cheerfulness.

"Why, we are prepared for that," he said. "I was just sitting down to my supper, and you will join me."

In his complete estrangement from the artificial restraints of society, it seemed to him the simplest of possible adjustments of the difficulty. He felt that his intervention had not been wholly without beneficial results.

Mariana glanced swiftly up into his face.

"Come!" he said; and she rose and followed him.

CHAPTER V

As Mariana crossed the threshold the light dazzled her, and she raised her hand to her eyes. Then she lowered it and looked at him between half-closed lids. It was a trick of mannerism which heightened the subtlety of her smile. In the deep shadows cast by her lashes her eyes were untranslatable.

"You are very hospitable," she said.

"A virtue which covers a multitude of sins," he answered, pleasantly. "If you will make yourself at home, I'll fix things up a bit."

He opened the doors of the cupboard and took out a plate and a cup and saucer, which he placed before her. "I am sorry I can't offer you a napkin," he said, apologetically, "but they allow me only one a day, and I had that at luncheon."

Mariana laughed merrily. The effects of recent tears were visible only in the added lustre of her glance and the pallor of her face. She had grown suddenly mirthful.

"Don't let's be civilized!" she pleaded. "I abhor civilization. It invented so many unnecessary evils. Barbarians didn't want napkins; they wanted only food. I am a barbarian."

Algarcife cut the cold chicken and passed her the bread and butter.

"Why, none of us are really civilized, you know," he returned, dogmatically. "True, we have a thin layer of hypocrisy, which we call civilization. It prompts us to sugar-coat the sins which our forefathers swal-

PHASES OF AN INFERIOR PLANET

lowed in the rough; that is all. It is purely artificial. In a hundred thousand years it may get soaked in, and then the artificial refinement will become real and civilization will set in."

Mariana leaned forward with a pretty show of interest. She did not quite understand what he meant, but she adapted herself instinctively to whatever he might mean.

"And then?" she questioned.

"And then we will realize that to be civilized is to shrink as instinctively from inflicting as from enduring pain. Sympathy is merely a quickening of the imagination, in which state we are able to propel ourselves mentally into conditions other than our own." His manner was aggressive in its self-assertiveness. Then he smiled, regarded her with critical keenness, and lifted the coffee-pot.

"I sha'n't give you coffee," he said, "because it is not good for you. You need rest. Why, your hands are trembling! You shall have milk instead."

"I don't like milk," returned Mariana, fretfully. "I'd rather have coffee, please. I want to be stimulated."

"But not artificially," he responded. His gaze softened. "This is my party, you know," he said, "and it isn't polite to ask for what is not offered you. Come here."

He had risen and was standing beside his desk. Mariana went up to him. The power of his will had enthralled her, and she felt strangely submissive. Her coquetry she recognized as an unworthy weapon, and it was discarded. She grew suddenly shy and nervous, and stood before him in the flushed timidity of a young feminine thing.

He had taken a bottle from a shelf and was measuring some dark liquid into a wine-glass. As Mariana reached him he took her hand with frank kindliness.

PHASES OF AN INFERIOR PLANET

In his cool and composed touch there was not so much as a suggestion of sexual difference. The possibility that, as a woman, she possessed an attraction for him, as a man, was ignored in its entirety.

"You have cried half the evening?"

"Yes."

"Drink this." His tone was peremptory.

He gave her the glass, watching her as she looked into it, with the gleam of a smile in his intent regard. Mariana hesitated an instant. Then she drank it with a slight grimace.

"Your hospitality has taken an unpleasant turn," she remarked. "You might at least give me something to destroy the taste."

He laughed and pointed to a plate of grapes, and they sat down to supper.

The girl glanced about the room critically. Then she looked at her companion.

"I don't quite like your room," she observed. "It is grewsome."

"It is a work-shop," he answered. "But your dislike is pure nonsense. Skulls and cross-bones are as natural in their way as flesh and blood. Nothing in nature is repellent to the mind that follows her."

Mariana repressed a shudder. "I have no doubt that toads are natural enough in their way," she returned, "but I don't like the way of toads."

Anthony met her serious protest lightly.

"You are a beautiful subject for morbid psychology," he said. "Why, toads are eminently respectable creatures, and if we regard them without prejudice, we will discover that, as a point of justice, they have an equal right with ourselves to the possession of this planet. Only, right is not might, you know."

"But I love beautiful things," protested Mariana. She looked at him wistfully, like a child desiring approbation. There was an amber light in her eyes.

He smiled upon her.

"So do I," he made answer; "but to me each one of those nice little specimens is a special revelation of beauty."

The girl broke her bread daintily. "You misunderstand me," she said, with flattering earnestness and a deprecatory inflection in her voice. Her head drooped sideways on its slender throat. There was a virginal illusiveness about her that tinged with seriousness the lightness of her words. "Surely you love art," she said.

"Oh, I like painting, if that is what you mean," he answered, carelessly, though her image in his eyes was relieved against a sudden warmth. "That is, I like Raphael and Murillo and a few of the modern French fellows. As for music, I don't know one note from another. The only air I ever caught was 'In the Fragrant Summer-time,' and that was an accident. I thought it was 'Maryland.'"

Mariana did not smile. She shrank from him, and he felt as if he had struck her.

"It isn't worth your thinking of," he said, "nor am I."

Mariana protested with her restless hands.

"Oh, but I can't help thinking of it," she answered. "It is dreadful. Why, such things are a part of my religion!"

He returned her startled gaze with one of amusement.

"I might supply you with an alphabetical dictionary of my peculiar vices. An unabridged edition would serve for a criminal catalogue as well. A—Acrimony, Adhesiveness, Atheism, Aggressiveness, Aggravation, Ambition, Artfulness—"

"Oh, stop!" cried Mariana. "You bewilder me."

He leaned back in his chair and fixed his intent gaze upon her. His eyes were so deeply set as to be almost indistinguishable, but in the spell of lamplight she saw that the pupils differed in color, one having a hazel cast, while the other was of a decided gray.

"Why, I thought you displayed an interest in the subject!" he rejoined. "You lack the genius of patience."

"Patience," returned Mariana, with a swift change of manner, "is only lack of vitality. I haven't an atom of it."

A shade of the nervous irritability, which appeared from apparently no provocation, was in his voice as he answered:

"There is nothing fate likes better than to drill it into us. And it is not without its usefulness. If patience is the bugbear of youth, it is the panacea of middle age. We learn to sit and wait as we learn to accept passivity for passion and indifference for belief. The worst of it is that it is a lesson which none of us may skip and most of us are forced to learn by heart." He spoke slowly, his voice softened. Beneath the veneering of philosophic asceticism, the scarlet veins of primeval nature were still palpitant. The chill lines of self-restraint in his face might, in the whirlwind of strong passions, become ingulfed in chaos.

With an effort Mariana threw off the spell of his personality. She straightened herself with an energetic movement. From the childlike her manner passed to the imperious. Her head poised itself proudly, her eyes darkened, her lips lost their pliant curve and grew audacious.

"That is as grewsome as your room," she said. "Let's talk of pleasant things."

The changes in her mystified Algarcife. He regarded her gravely. "Of yourself, or of myself?" he demanded.

"The first would only display your ignorance. I

should prefer the latter. Begin, please." She had grown vivid.

He spoke jestingly. "Here goes. Name, Algarcife. Christened Anthony. Age, twenty-seven years, three weeks, ten days. Height, five feet eleven inches. Complexion, anæmic. Physique, bad. Disposition, worse. Manners, still worse. Does the exactness of my information satisfy you?"

"No;" she enveloped him in her smile. "You haven't told me anything I want to know. I could have guessed your height, and your manners I have tested. What were you doing before I came in?"

"Cursing my luck."

"And before that?" She leaned forward eagerly.

"Dogging at a theory of heredity which will reconcile Darwin's gemmules, Weismann's germ-plasm, and Galton's stirp."

She wrinkled her brows in perplexity. Her show of interest had not fled. A woman who cannot talk of the things she knows nothing about might as well be a man.

"And you will do it?" she asked. He had a sudden consciousness that no one had ever been quite so in sympathy with him as this elusive little woman with the changeable eyes.

"Well, I hardly think so," he said. "At any rate, I expect to discover what Spencer would call the germ of truth in each one of them, and then I suppose I'll formulate a theory of my own which will contain the best in all of them."

Her manner did not betray her ignorance of his meaning.

"And you will explain it all to me when it is finished?" she asked.

His smile cast a light upon her.

"If you wish it," he answered, "but I had no idea that you cared for such things."

"You did not know me," she responded, reproachfully. "I am very, very ignorant, but I want so much to learn." Then her voice regained its brightness. "And you have read all these books?" she questioned.

He followed with his eyes her swift gestures.

"Those," he answered, pointing to the north shelves, "I have skimmed. Those behind you, I have read; and those," he nodded towards his right, "I know word for word."

"And what do you do?" The delicacy of her manner imbued the question with unconscious flattery.

"I—oh, I eke out an existence with the assistance of the Bodley College."

"What have you to do with it? Oh, I beg your pardon! I had forgotten we were almost strangers."

He answered, naturally.

"It is my unhappy fate to endeavor to instil a few brains and a good deal of information into the heads of sixty-one young females."

"And don't you like them?" queried Mariana, eagerly.

"I do not."

"Why?"

"What an inquisitor you are, to be sure!"

"But tell me," she pleaded.

"Why?" he demanded, in his turn.

She lowered her lashes, looking at her quiet hands.

"Because I want so much to know."

His smiling eyes were probing her. "Tell me why."

She raised her lashes suddenly and returned his gaze. There was a wistful sincerity in her eyes.

"I wish to know," she said, slowly, "so that I may not be like them."

For a moment he regarded her silently. Then he spoke. "My reasons are valid. They giggle; they flirt; and they put candy in my pockets."

"And you don't like women at all?"

"I like nice, sensible women, who wear square-toed shoes, and who don't distort themselves with corsets."

The girl put out her pretty foot in its pointed and high-heeled slipper. Then she shook her head with mock seriousness.

"I don't suppose you think that very sensible?" she remarked.

He looked at it critically.

"Well, hardly. No, it isn't in the least sensible, but it—it is very small, isn't it?"

"Oh yes," responded Mariana, eagerly. She felt a sudden desire to flaunt her graces in his face. He was watching the play of her hands, but she became conscious, with an aggrieved surprise, that he was not thinking of them.

"But you don't like just mere—mere women?" she asked, gravely.

"Are you a mere—mere woman?"

"Yes."

"Then I like them."

The radiance that overflowed her eyes startled him.

"But you aren't just a mere—mere man," she volunteered.

"But I am—a good deal merer, in fact, than many others. I am a shape of clay."

"Then I like shapes of clay," said Mariana.

For an instant they looked at each other in silence. In Mariana's self-conscious eyes there was a soft suffusion of shyness; in his subjective ones there was the quickening of an involuntary interest.

"Then we agree most amicably," he remarked, quietly. As she rose he stood facing her. "It is time for your sleep and my work," he added, and held out his hand.

As Mariana placed her own within it she flashed whitely with a sudden resentment of his cool dismissal.

"Good-night!" she said.

He looked down at her as she lingered before him. "I want to be of use to you," he said, frankly, "but things have an unfortunate way of slipping my memory. If at any time I can serve you, just come to the fire-escape and call me."

"No," answered the girl, pettishly, "certainly not."

His brow wrinkled. "That was rude, I know," he rejoined, "but I meant it honestly."

"I have no doubt of it."

As she turned to go he detained her with a compelling touch.

"You aren't angry?"

"No."

"And you forgive me?"

"I have nothing to forgive. Indeed, I am grateful for your charity."

He surveyed her in puzzled scrutiny. "Well, I am sure I sha'n't forget you," he said. "Yes, I am quite sure of it."

"What a marvellous memory!" exclaimed Mariana, crossly, and she stepped out upon the fire-escape.

"Good-night!" he called.

"Good-night!" she responded, and entered her room.

"He is very rude," she whispered as she closed the shutters. In the half-light she undressed and sat in her night-gown, brushing the heavy tangles of her hair. Then she lighted the flame before the little altar and said her prayers; kneeling with bowed head. As she turned off the light she spoke again. "I am not sure that I don't like rudeness," she added.

Meanwhile Algarcife had watched her vanish into the shadows, a smile lightening the gravity of his face. When she had disappeared he turned to his desk. With his singular powers of concentration, he had not taken up his pen before all impressions save those relating to the subject in hand had been banished from his mind. His expression was buoyant and alert. Turning over his papers, he passed with a sense of reinvigoration to the matter before him.

"Yes; I think, after all, that a strongly modified theory of pangenesis may survive," he said.

CHAPTER VI

AT the extreme end of the corridor upon which Mariana's door opened there was a small apartment occupied by three young women from the South, who were bent upon aims of art.

They had moved in a month before, and had celebrated a room-warming by asking Mariana and several of the other lodgers to a feast of beer and pretzels. Since then the girl had seen them occasionally. She knew that they lived in a semi-poverty-stricken Bohemia, and that the pretty one with pink cheeks and a ragged and uncurled fringe of hair, whose name was Freighley, worked in Mr. Nevins's studio and did chrysanthemums in oils. She had once heard Mr. Nevins remark that she was a pupil worth having, and upon asking, "Has she talent?" had met with, "Not a bit, but she's pretty."

"Then it is a pity she isn't a model," said Mariana.

"An example of the eternal contrariness of things," responded Mr. Nevins. "All the good-looking ones want to paint and all the ugly ones want to be painted." Then he rumpled his flaxen head. "In this confounded century everything is in the wrong place, from a woman to her waist-line."

After this Mariana accompanied Miss Freighley on students' day to the Metropolitan Museum, and watched her make a laborious copy of "The Christian Martyr." Upon returning she was introduced to Miss Hill and Miss Oliver, who shared the apartment, and was told to make herself at home.

Then, one rainy Saturday afternoon there was a knock at her door, and, opening it, she found Miss Freighley upon the outside.

"It is our mending afternoon," she said, "and we want you to come and sit with us. If you have any sewing to do, just bring it."

Mariana picked up her work-basket, and, finding that her thimble was missing, began rummaging in a bureau-drawer.

"I never mend anything until I go to put it on," she said. "It saves so much trouble."

Then she found her thimble and followed Miss Freighley into the hall.

Miss Freighley laughed in a pretty, inconsequential way. She had a soft, monotonous voice, and spoke with a marked elimination of vowel sounds.

"We take the last Saturday of the month," she said. "Only Juliet and I do Gerty's things, because she can't sew, and she cleans our palettes and brushes in return."

She swung open the door of the apartment, and they entered a room which served as studio and general lounging-room in one.

A tall girl, sitting upon the hearth-rug beside a heap of freshly laundered garments, stood up and held out a limp, thin hand.

"I told Carrie she would find you," she said, speaking with a slight drawl and an affected listlessness.

She was angular, with a consumptive chest and narrow shoulders. She wore her hair—which was vivid, like flame, with golden ripples in the undulations—coiled confusedly upon the crown of her head. Her name was Juliet Hill. A mistaken but well-known colorist had once traced in her a likeness to Rossetti's "Beata Beatrix." The tracing had resulted in the spoiling of a woman without the making of an artist.

Mariana threw herself upon a divan near the hearth-rug and looked down upon the pile of clothes.

"What a lot of them!" she observed, sympathetically.

Miss Hill drew a stocking from the heap and ran her darning-egg into the heel to locate a hole.

"It is, rather," she responded, "but we never mend until everything we have is in rags. I couldn't find a single pair of stockings this morning, so I knew it was time."

"If you had looked into Gerty's bureau-drawer you might have found them," said Miss Freighley, seating herself upon the end of the divan. "Gerty never marks her things, and somehow she gets all of ours. Regularly once a month I institute a search through her belongings, and discover more of my clothes than I knew I possessed. Here, give me that night-gown, Juliet. The laundress tore every bit of lace off the sleeve. What a shame!"

Mariana removed a guitar from the couch and leaned back among the pillows, glancing about the room. The walls were covered with coarse hangings, decorated in vague outlines of flying cranes and vaguer rushes. Here and there were tacked groups of unframed water-colors and drawings in charcoal—all crude and fanciful and feminine. Upon a small shelf above the door stood a plaster bust, and upon it a dejected and moth-eaten raven—the relic of a past passion for taxidermy. In the centre of the room were several easels, a desk, with Webster's Unabridged for a foot-stool, and a collection of palettes, half-used tubes of paint, and unassorted legs and arms in plaster.

"How do you ever find anything?" asked Mariana, leaning upon her arm.

"We don't," responded a small, dark girl, coming from the tiny kitchen with a dish of cooling caramels in her hand; "we don't find, we just lose." She placed the dish upon the table and drew up a chair. "I would mortgage a share of my life if I could turn my old mammy loose in here for an hour."

"Gerty used to be particular," explained Miss Freighley; "but it is a vicious habit, and we broke her of it. Even now it attacks her at intervals, and she gets out a duster and goes to work."

"I can't write in a mess," interrupted Miss Oliver, a shade ruefully. "I haven't written a line since I came to New York." Then she sighed. "I only wish I hadn't written a word before coming. At home I thought I was a genius; now I know I am a fool."

"I have felt the same way," said Mariana, sympathetically, "but it doesn't last. The first stage-manager I went to I almost fell at his feet; the next almost fell at mine. Neither of them gave me a place, but they taught me the value of men."

"I don't think it's worth learning," returned Miss Oliver, passing her caramels. "Try one, and see if they are hard."

"Poor Gerty!" drawled Miss Hill, watching Mariana bite the caramel. "She faces editors and all kinds of bad characters. Her views of life are depressing."

"They are not views," remonstrated Miss Oliver, "they are facts. Facts are always depressing, except when they are maddening."

"I have begged her to leave off writing and take to water-color or china painting," said Miss Freighley, cheerfully, "but she won't."

"How can she?" asked Mariana.

"Of course I can't," retorted Miss Oliver, shortly. "I never had a paint-brush in my hand in my life, except when I was cleaning it."

Miss Freighley laid her sewing aside and stretched her arms.

"It only requires a little determination," she said, "and I have it. I got tired of Alabama. I couldn't come to New York without an object, so I invented one. It was as good as any other, and I stuck to it."

Miss Hill shook her head, and her glorious hair shone like amber.

"Art is serious," she said, slowly. She was just entering the life-class at the Art League.

"But the artist is not," returned Miss Freighley, "and one can be an artist without having any art. I am. They think at home I am learning to paint pictures to go on the parlor wall in place of the portraits that were burned in the war. But I am not. I am here because I love New York, and—"

"Claude Nevins," concluded Miss Oliver.

Mariana looked up with interest. "How nice!" she said. "He told me you were awfully pretty."

Miss Freighley blushed and laughed.

"Nonsense!" she rejoined; "but Gerty is so faithful to her young fellow down South that it has gone to her brain."

"I am faithful because I have no opportunity for faithlessness," sang Gerty to an accompaniment she was picking upon the guitar. "I have been in love one—two—six times since I came to New York. Once it was with an editor, who accepted my first story. He was short and thick and gray-haired, but I loved him. Once it was with that dark, ill-fed man who rooms next to Mariana. He almost knocked me down upon the stairway and forgot to apologize. I have forgotten the honorable others, as the Japanese say, but I know it is six times, because whenever it happened I made a little cross-mark on my desk, and there are six of them."

"It must have been Mr. Ardly," said Mariana. "I never look at him without thinking what an adorable lover he would make."

"He has such nice hands," said Miss Oliver. "I do like a man with nice hands."

"And he is clean-shaven," added Miss Freighley. "I detest a man with a beard."

PHASES OF AN INFERIOR PLANET

Miss Hill crossed her thin ankles upon the hearth.

"Love should be taken seriously," she said, with a wistful look in her dark eyes.

Miss Freighley's pretty, inconsequent laugh broke in.

"That is one of Juliet's platitudes," she said. "But, my dear, it shouldn't be taken seriously. Indeed, it shouldn't be taken at all—except in cases of extreme *ennui*, and then in broken doses. The women who take men seriously—and taking love means taking men, of course—sit down at home and grow shapeless and have babies galore. To grow shapeless is the fate of the woman who takes sentiment seriously. It is a more convincing argument against it than all the statistics of the divorce court—"

"For the Lord's sake, Carrie, beware of woman's rights," protested Miss Oliver. "That is exactly what Mrs. Simpson said in her lecture on 'Our Tyrant, Man.' Why, those dear old aunts of yours in Alabama have inserted an additional clause in their Litany: 'From intemperance, evil desires, and woman's suffrage, good Lord deliver us!' They are grounded in the belief that the new woman is an *édition de luxe* of the devil."

Mariana rose and shook out her skirts. "I must go," she said, "and you haven't done a bit of work."

"So we haven't," replied Miss Hill, picking up her needle. "But take some caramels—do."

Mariana took a caramel and went out into the hall. Algarcife's door was open, and he was standing upon the threshold talking to Claude Nevins.

As Mariana passed, Nevins smiled and called to her:

"I say, Miss Musin, here is a vandal who complains that you make night hideous."

Algarcife scowled.

"Nevins is a fool," he retorted, "and if he doesn't know it, he ought to be told so."

PHASES OF AN INFERIOR PLANET

"Thanks," returned Nevins, amiably, "but I have long since learned not to believe anything I hear."

Anthony's irritation increased. 'I should have thought the presumptive evidence sufficient to overcome any personal bias," he replied.

Nevins spread out his hands with an imperturbable shrug.

"My dear fellow, I never found my conclusions upon presumptive evidence. Had I done so, I should hold life to be a hollow mockery—whereas I am convinced that it is a deuced solid one."

"You are so bad-tempered—both of you," said Mariana; "but, Mr. Algarcife, do you really object to my singing? I can't keep silent, you know."

Algarcife smiled.

"I never supposed that you could," he answered. "And as for music, I had as soon listen to you as to—to Patti."

"Not that he values your accomplishments more, but Patti's less," observed Nevins, placidly.

"On the other hand, I should say that Miss Musin would make decidedly the less noise," said Anthony.

"He's a brute, isn't he, Mariana?" asked Nevins—and added, "Now I never said you made anything hideous, did I?"

Mariana laughed, looking a little vexed. "If you wouldn't always repeat everything you hear other people say, it would be wiser," she responded, tartly.

"Such is the reward of virtue," sighed Nevins. "All my life I have been held as responsible for other people's speeches as for my own. And all from a conscientious endeavor to let my neighbors see themselves as others see them—"

Algarcife smiled good-humoredly. "Whatever bad qualities Nevins may possess," he said, "he has at least the courage of his convictions—"

Nevins shrugged his shoulders.

"I don't know about the convictions," he rejoined, "but I've got the courage all right." Then he looked at Mariana. "Is that an implement of housewifery that I see?" he demanded.

"I have been to a darning-party," she answered, "but we didn't darn anything—not even circumstances."

"Lucky circumstances!" ejaculated Nevins. Then he lowered his voice. "I should not have believed it of you," he protested; "to attend a darning-party, and to leave not only me, but my socks, outside."

Mariana flushed angrily.

"You are insufferable," she said, "and you haven't a particle of tact—not a particle. Only yesterday I heard you tell Mr. Morris that his head looked like an advertisement for sapolio, and the day before you told Miss Freighley that I said she didn't know how to dress her hair."

"It was true," said Nevins. "You can't make a liar of me, Mariana."

"I wish you wouldn't call me Mariana," she retorted; and he went upon his way with a lament.

As Mariana laid her hand upon her door-knob she looked at Anthony.

"Mr. Algarcife," she said, "do you really mind my singing so very much?"

From the end of the corridor Nevins's voice was heard chanting:

"How fickle women are,
Fickle as falling star."

"I wish that Nevins would attend to his own affairs," Algarcife responded. "As for me, you may dance a break-down every night of your life, and, if it amuses you, I'll grin and bear it."

CHAPTER VII

During Algarcife's first term at college, a fellow fraternity man remarked of him that he resembled the eternal void, in that he might have been anything and was nothing. Algarcife accepted the criticism with a shrug.

"Wait and see," he responded, shortly, and the fraternity man had waited and had seen.

In that first year Anthony succeeded in sowing a supply of wild oats sufficient for the domestication of the species. He was improvident from principle and reckless from an inborn distrust of accepted dogmas. "I shall live as I please," he replied, in answer to the warnings of a classmate, "and I shall think as I damn please."

For a year he went about his dissipations in a kind of inquiring ardor. He called it "seeing life," and he pursued his observations with entire obliviousness to public regard, but with philosophic concern as to the accuracy of the information obtained. He was known to have got drunk upon whiskey and light wine in order to test the differences in effect, and it was rumored that he made love to the homeliest and most virtuous daughter of the saloon-keeper that he might convince himself whether her virtue was the logical resultant of her homeliness. Into all experiments he carried an entire absence of prejudice, and a half-defiant acceptance of consequences.

"It is a sheer waste of time," said John Driscoll, of the Senior class. "You haven't learned the first prin-

PHASES OF AN INFERIOR PLANET

ciple of scientific dissipation. Instead of plunging into excesses, you stroll into them. By Jove! if you broke every command in the Decalogue, you would appear to sin in moderation."

Algarcife laughed. "I am going to reform," he said. "I am not enough of an artist to see the æsthetic values of vice. Let's become decent. It is more economical."

It was at this time that he reduced his living expenses one-half, and appropriated the surplus funds to the support of a young mechanic, whose health had collapsed in the struggle to work his way to a university degree. "He not only gave it," declared the young mechanic, in a burst of gratitude, "but he gave it without knowing that he did a generous thing."

When Algarcife left college that summer he followed Driscoll to his cabin in the Adirondacks and spent several months botanizing. The chance application to science decided the tenor of his mind, and, upon his return to study, he refused to bow beneath the weight of authority hurled upon him. He denounced the classics and a classical training. Several courses he declared superficial, and he mastered various systems of moral philosophy that he might refute the fallacies of the professor. The brilliancy which he had frittered during the preceding year was turned into newer channels, and the closeness of his reliance upon inductive reasoning caused him to become at once a source of amusement to his classmates and of annoyance to his instructor. To see him rise in class, his face charged with the nervous vigor which seized him in moments of excitement, his keen glance riveted upon the professor as he mercilessly dissected his utterances, was an event which, to his fellow-students, rendered even old Monckton's lectures of interest.

Then he took a prominent part in a debating society. With a readiness which his friends declared to spring from love of logic, his enemies from lack of principle, he accepted either side of a given argument, and had been known to undertake at once the negative and the affirmative, detecting his own weaknesses as ruthlessly as he had detected those of old Monckton.

Before leaving college, and at the urgency of his guardian, he had carried through with dogged distaste a course in dogmatic theology. It was then that he fell into the way of writing theses from opposite sides of a subject, and when handing in a treatise upon "Historical Evidences of Christianity," or "The Pelagian Heresy," it was invariably accompanied by the remark: "I wish you'd look over that 'Lack of Historical Evidences,' or 'Defence of Pelagianism,' at the same time. You know, I always do the other side."

And it was "the other side" which finally drove him out of theology and his guardian into despair. Whether it was an argument in moral philosophy, a mooted question in Egyptology, or a stand in current politics, Algarcife was ready with what his classmates called "the damned eternal opposition." It was even said that a facetious professor, in remarking to his class that it was "a fine day," had turned in absent-minded custom and called upon Mr. Algarcife for "the other side," an appeal which drew a howl of approbation from hilarious students.

Anthony was not popular at college, though his friends were steadfast. It was not until later years, when life had tempered the incisive irony of his speech and endowed him with the diplomacy of indifference, that men fell beneath the attraction of his personality. At that time he was looked upon in an ominous light, and the scintillant scepticism which he carried fearlessly into every department of knowledge caused him to be regarded as one who might prove himself to be an enemy to society. Even his voice, which long afterwards exerted so potent an influence, had not then gained its varied range and richness of expression.

So, when, years later, the public lauded the qualities they had formerly condemned, there was no inconsistence—since life is more colored by points of view than by principles. At the end of his theological course he had delivered an address, at the request of his class, upon the "Christian Revelation." When it was over he went into his guardian's room, the flame of a long determination in his eyes. The paper which he had read was still in his hands, and he laid it upon the table as he spoke.

"It can't be," he said. "I give it up."

The man whom he addressed rose slowly and faced him, standing, a tall, gaunt figure in his clerical coat. His hair was white, and at a first glance he presented the impression of a statue modelled in plaster, so much did the value of form outweigh that of color in his appearance. In meeting his eyes an observer would, perhaps, have gained a conception of expression rather than shade. One would have said that the eyes were benevolent, not that they were gray or blue. His forehead was high and somewhat narrow, three heavy furrows running diagonally between the eyebrows—ruts left by the constant passage of perplexities. He was called Father Speares, and was an impassioned leader of the High Church movement.

"Do you mean it?" he asked, slowly—"that you give up your faith?"

Algarcife's brow wrinkled in sudden irritation. "That I have given up long ago," he answered. "If I ever had any, it was an ingrafted product. What I do mean is that I give up the Church—that I give up theology—that I give up religion."

The other flinched suddenly. He put out one frail, white hand as if in protest.

"I—I cannot believe it," he said.

"And yet I have been honest."

"Honest! Yes, I suppose so. Honest—" he lifted the paper from the table and unfolded it mechanically. "And yet you could write this?"

Anthony shook his head impatiently. "I was but a special pleader with the side assigned, and you knew it."

"But I did not know your power—nor do you. It convinced me—convinced me, though I came with the knowledge that your words were empty—empty and rotten—"

"They were words. The case was given me, and I defended it as a lawyer defends a client. What else could I do?"

Father Speares sighed and passed his hand across his brow.

"It is not the first disappointment of my life," he said, "but it is the greatest."

Algarcife was looking through the open window to the sunlight falling upon the waving grass. A large butterfly, with black and yellow wings, was dancing above a clump of dandelions.

"I am sorry," he said, more gently—"sorry for that —but it can't be helped. I am not a theologian, but a scientist; I am not a believer, but an agnostic; I am not a priest, but a man."

"But you are young. The pendulum may swing back—"

"Never," said Algarcife—"never." He lifted his head, looking into the other's eyes. "Don't you see that when a man has once conceived the magnitude of the universe he can never bow his head to a creed? Don't you see that when he has grasped the essential verity in all religions he no longer allies himself to a single one? Don't you see that when he has realized the dominance of law in religions—the law of their growth and decay, of their evolution and dissolution, when he has once grasped the fact that man creates, and is not created by, his god—don't you see that he can never bind himself to the old beliefs?"

"I see that he can awake to the knowledge of the spiritual life as well as to the physical—that he can grasp the existence of a vital ethical principle in nature. I shall pray for you, and I shall hope—"

Algarcife frowned. "I am sick of it," he said—"sick to death. To please you, I plodded away at theology for three solid years. To please you, I weighed assumptions as light as air. To please you, I read all the rot of all the Fathers—and I am sick of it. I shall live my own life in my own way."

"And may God help you!" said the elder man; and then, "Where will you go?"

"To Egypt—to India—to the old civilizations."

"And then?"

"I do not know. I shall work and I shall succeed—with or without the help of God."

And he had gone. During the next few years he travelled in Africa and Asia, when the sudden loss of his income recalled him to America. Finding it fruitless to rebel, he resigned himself philosophically, secured a position as instructor in a woman's college, made up an annual deficit by writing for the scientific reviews, and continued his studies. His physical nature he believed he had rendered quiescent.

Some days after his encounter with Mariana he came upon her again. He had just entered the park at the Seventy-second Street entrance, on his way from his lecture at the Bodley College. The battered bonnet of a beggar-woman had blown beneath the horses' hoofs in the drive, and he had stopped to rescue it, when he heard his name called, and saw Mariana beside him.

She spoke impulsively.

"I have been watching you," she said.

He looked at her in perplexity.

PHASES OF AN INFERIOR PLANET

"Indeed! And what have you discovered?"

"I discovered that you are a gentleman."

He laughed outright.

"Your powers of intuition are positively miraculous," he replied.

She upbraided him with a glance.

"You are unkind," she said.

"Am I?"

"You are unkind to me." Her manner had grown subtly personal. He felt suddenly as if he had known her from the beginning of time and through various transmigrations.

"You laugh at me," she added. "You were kinder to that woman—"

He broke in upon her, perplexity giving place to amusement.

"Oh!" he said; "so that is what you mean! Why, if you were to lose your hat, I shouldn't laugh, I assure you."

Mariana walked on silently. Her eyes were bent upon the gray sidewalk, there was a faint flush in her face. A line of men seated upon the benches beside the way surveyed her with interest.

"Miss Musin!"

Her face quickened.

"I have a confession to make."

She looked up inquiringly. A finger of sunlight pierced the branches of an elm and pointed to her upraised face.

"I have rather bad manners," he went on. "It is a failing which you must accept as you accept the color of my hair—"

Mariana smiled.

"I say just what I think," he added.

Mariana frowned.

"That is what I complain of," she responded. Then she laughed so brightly that a tiny child, toddling with a toy upon the walk, looked up and clapped its hands.

His eyes warmed.

"But you will take me for better or for worse?" he demanded.

"Could it be better?" she asked, demurely.

"That is a matter of opinion."

They left the park and turned into a cross-town street. The distant blocks sloped down into the blue blur of the river, from which several gaunt, gray masts rose like phantom wrecks evolved from the mist. Beyond them the filmy outline of the opposite shore was revealed.

Suddenly Mariana stopped.

"This is Morani's, and I must go in." She held out her hand.

"How is the voice?" he asked.

"I am nursing it. Some day you shall hear it."

"I have heard it," he responded.

She smiled.

"Oh, I forgot. You are next door. Well, some day you shall hear it in opera."

"Shall I?"

"And I shall sing Elsa with Alvary. My God! I would give ten years of my life for that—to sing with Alvary."

He smiled at the warmth in her words and, as he smiled he became conscious that her artistic passion ignited the fire of a more material passion in himself. A fugitive desire seized him to possess the woman before him, body and brain. From the quivering of his pulses he knew that the physical nature he had drugged had stirred in response to a passing appeal.

"Good-bye," said Mariana. She tripped lightly up the brown-stone steps. As she opened the outer door she turned with a smile and a nod. Then the door closed and he went on his way. But the leaping of his pulses was not appeased.

CHAPTER VIII

ONE morning, several days later, Mariana, looking from her window, saw Anthony standing upon the fire-escape. He had thrown a handful of crumbs to a swarm of noisy sparrows quarrelling about his feet.

As he stood there with the morning sunlight flashing upon his face and gilding the dark abundance of his hair, the singularly mystic beauty of his appearance was brought into bold relief. It was a beauty which contained no suggestion of physical supremacy. He seemed the survival of a lost type—of those purified prophets of old who walked with God and trampled upon the flesh which was His handiwork. It was the striking contrast between the intellectual tenor of his mind and its physical expression which emphasized his personality. To the boldest advance in scientific progress he had the effect of uniting a suggestion of that poetized mysticism which constitutes the charm of a remote past. With the addition of the yellow robe and a beggar's bowl, he might have been transformed into one of the Enlightened of nigh on three thousand years ago, and have followed the Blessed One upon his pilgrimage towards Nirvana. The modernity of his mind was almost tantalizing in its inconsistency with his external aspect.

Mariana, looking through the open window, smiled unconsciously. Anthony glanced up, saw her, and nodded.

"Good-morning," he called. "Won't you come out and help quiet these rogues?"

PHASES OF AN INFERIOR PLANET

Mariana opened the little door beneath the window and stepped outside. She looked shy and girlish, and the flutter with which she greeted him had a quaint suggestion of flattery.

He came towards her, and they stood together beside the railing. Beneath them the noise of trade and traffic went on tumultuously. Overhead the sky was of a still, intense blueness, the horizon flecked by several church-spires, which rose sharply against the burning remoteness. Across the tenement roofs lines of drying garments fluttered like banners.

Mariana, in her cotton gown of dull blue, cast a slender shadow across the fire-escape. In the morning light her eyes showed gray and limpid. The sallow tones of her skin were exaggerated, and the peculiar harmony of hair and brows and complexion was strongly marked. She was looking her plainest, and she knew it.

But Anthony did not. He had seen her, perhaps, half a dozen times, and upon each occasion he had discovered his previous conceptions of her to be erroneous. Her extreme mobility of mood and manner at once perplexed and attracted him. Yesterday he had resolved her character into a compound of surface emotions. Now he told himself that she was cool and calm and sweetly reasonable.

"I am glad you like sparrows," she said, "because nobody else does, and, somehow, it doesn't seem fair. You do like them, don't you?"

"I believe," he answered, "that I have two passions beyond the usual number with which man is supplied —a passion for books and a passion for animals. I can't say I have a special regard for sparrows, but I like them. They are hardy little fellows, though a trifle pugnacious, and they have learned the value of co-operation."

"I had a canary," remarked Mariana, with pathos,

PHASES OF AN INFERIOR PLANET

"but it died. Everything that belongs to me always dies, sooner or later."

He laughed, looking at her with quizzical humor. "Do you expect them to escape the common fate?" he demanded; and then: "If there is anything that could give me an attack of horrors sooner than a dancing dog—and there isn't—it would be a bird in a cage. I left my last lodgings because my neighbor kept a mocking-bird outside of her window. If it had been a canary I might have endured it, but I knew that if I stayed there a week longer I should break in and set that bird free. I used to hear it at night beating itself against the cage."

"Oh, hush!" said Mariana, putting her hands to her ears. She wondered vaguely at his peculiar sensitiveness of sympathy. It was a type of manhood that she had not before encountered—one as unlike the jovial, fox-hunting heroes of her childish days as mind is unlike matter. She remembered that among them such expressions would have been regarded as a mark of effeminacy and ruthlessly laughed to scorn. She even remembered that her own father had denounced a prohibition of prize-fighting as "mawkish rot." This eccentric type of nervous vigor, in which all remnants of semi-barbarism were apparently extinguished, possessed a fascination for her in its very strangeness. In his character all those active virtues around which her youthful romances were woven held no place. Patriotism was modified into a sense of general humanity; chivalry was tempered into commonplace politeness. She did not know that the force which attracted her was but a dominant mentality; that where the mind holds sway the character is modified accordingly. With a great expenditure of nerve force those attributes which result from physical hardihood occupy a less prominent part. In Anthony she beheld, without knowing it, a forced and abnormal result of existing

PHASES OF AN INFERIOR PLANET

conditions. Nature often foreshadows a coming civilization by an advance-guard of individuals. As a supreme test she places a century before his time the victim of her experiments in vivisection. And a character that might have fitted with uncut edges into the circle of existence, had he but been permitted to insert himself at the proper moment, has often been trampled into nothingness by the incessant trend of the inopportune. The priest of the coming generation is the pariah of the present, and the dogma of to-morrow the heresy of to-day.

To Mariana's ignorant eyes Anthony seemed one in whom passion had been annihilated. In reality it was only smothered beneath the weight of a strenuous will. Let the pressure be removed, and it would burst forth the fiercer for its long confinement, ingulfing perhaps the whole organism in its destructive flame.

"Oh, hush!" Mariana had said, and turned from him. "You seem to delight in unpleasant things. I make it a point to believe that suffering and death do not exist. I *know* they do, but I *believe* they do not."

He drew nearer. Across his face she saw a sudden flash—so vivid that it seemed the awakening of a dormant element in his nature. "You are wonderfully vital," he said. "There is as much life in you as there is in a dozen of us poor effete mortals. What is your secret?"

The girl leaned her arm upon the railing and rested her chin in her hand. She looked up at him and her eyes grew darker. "It is the pure animal love of existence," she answered. "I love the world. I love living and breathing, and feeling the blood quicken in my veins. I love dancing and singing and eating and sleeping. The simple sensuousness of life is delicious to me. If I could not be a queen, I had rather be a beggar upon the road-side than to be nothing. If I could not be a human being, I had rather be a butterfly

PHASES OF AN INFERIOR PLANET

in the sunshine than not to be at all. So long as I had the blue sky and the air and the world about me I could not be miserable. It is life—life in its physical fulfilment—that I love. So long as they leave me the open world I can be happy. Only, if I were taken and shut up in an ugly dungeon I should want to die. And even then there would be hope."

She had spoken passionately, the words coming quickly from between her parted lips. She seemed so light and etherealized as to be almost bodiless. The materialistic philosophy to which she gave utterance was spiritualized by her own illusiveness.

For an instant she hesitated, looking across the tenement roofs to the horizon beyond. Then she went on: "I am different from you—oh, so different! Where you think, I feel. You are all mind, I am all senses. I am only fulfilling my place in nature when I am hearing or seeing or feeling beautiful things. My sense of beauty is my soul."

Anthony watched her with steadfast intentness. He had never before seen her in this mood, and it was a new surprise to him. His former generalizations were displaced.

But if he had known it, the present aspect was a result of his own influence upon Mariana. In a moment of contrition for small deceptions, she had been precipitated into an extravagant self-abasement.

"You are disappointed," she added, presently, meeting his gaze. "You expected something different, but I am shallow, and I can't help it." It was like her that in the tendency to self-depreciation she was as sincere as she had been in the former tendency to self-esteem.

And perhaps Anthony was the juster judge of the two. He was certainly the more dispassionate.

"I have told you," concluded Mariana, with an eager catch at the redeeming grace, "because I want to be truthful."

PHASES OF AN INFERIOR PLANET

"My dear girl," responded Anthony, a warm friendliness in his voice, "you might have spared yourself this little piece of analysis. It is as useless as most morbid rot of the kind. It doesn't in the least affect what I think of you, and what I do think of you is of little consequence."

"But what do you think?" demanded Mariana.

"I think that you know yourself just a little less well than you know that old lady wheeling her cart of vegetables in the street below. Had she, by the way, known herself a little better she would not have flown into such a rage because she spilled a few. If we knew ourselves we would see that things are not very much our fault, after all, and that a few slips the more or less on our up-hill road are very little matter."

Mariana glowed suddenly. She looked up at him, a woman's regard for power warming her eyes. To her impressionable temperament there seemed an element of sublimity in his ethical composure.

"Teach me," she said, simply. Anthony smiled. If he seemed a Stoic to Mariana, it was not because he was one, and perhaps he was conscious of it. But our conceptions of others are colored solely by their attitudes towards ourselves, and not in the least by their attitudes towards the universe, which, when all is said, is of far less consequence.

"I should have first to learn the lesson myself," he answered.

"Would you, if you could?" asked Mariana.

For an instant he looked at her thoughtfully. "Teach you what?" he questioned. "Teach you to endure instead of to enjoy? To know instead of to believe? To play with skulls and cross-bones instead of with flowers and sunshine? No, I think not."

Mariana grew radiant. She felt a desire to force from him a reluctant confession of liking. "Why wouldn't you?" she demanded.

"Well, on the whole, I think your present point of view better suited to you. And everything, after all, is in the point of view." He leaned against the railing, looking down into the street. "Look over and tell me what you see. Is it not the color of those purple egg-plants in the grocer's stall? the pretty girl in that big hat, standing upon the corner? the roguish faces of those ragamuffins at play? Well, I see these, but I see also the drooping figure of the woman beside the stall; the consumptive girl with the heavy bundle, going from her work; the panting horses that draw the surface cars."

They both gazed silently from the balcony. Then Mariana turned away. "It is the hour for my music," she said. "I must go."

The sunlight caught the nimbus around her head and brightened it with veins of gold.

"All joy goes with you," he answered, lightly. "And I shall return to work."

"All frivolity, you mean," laughed Mariana, and she left him with a nod.

CHAPTER IX

ACCORDING to the theory that vices are but virtues run to seed, moderation was the dominant characteristic of Anthony Algarcife. At the time of his meeting with Mariana, his natural tendencies, whatever they may have been, were atrophied in the barren soil of long self-repression. It is only when one is freed from the prejudices engendered by the play of the affections that one's horizon is unbroken by a vision of the objects in the foreground, and the forest is no longer lost in consideration of the trees.

And it was under the spell of this moderation that Mariana had fallen. Her own virtues were of that particular quality of which the species is by no means immutable, and of which the crossing often produces an opposite variety, since a union of negative virtues has not infrequently begotten a positive vice. But Mariana's character, of which at that time even the verdict of society had not deprived her, possessed a jewel in its inconsistency. Her very faults were rendered generous by their vivacity, and redeemed her from inflexibility, that most unforgivable trait in womanhood, which, after all, is merely firmness crystallized. And as the lack of formativeness in Mariana left her responsive to the influences beneath which she came, so the anger of yesterday was tempered into the tenderness of to-day, and her nature modified by the changes rung upon her moods.

So far, the influence of Anthony had worked for good. The girl was startled at the wave of gentleness which pervaded her. With a sudden fervor she strained towards an indistinct ideal of goodness, an ideal borrowed in its sanctity from a superficial study of Thomas à Kempis, and in its unreality from the faded recollection of certain Sunday-school literature read in her childhood. She aspired to be good almost as much as she had once aspired to be famous, and set about it with quite as unprincipled an abandon. But her ambition for holiness was ill-timed. An excess of virtue is often as disastrous a form of dissipation as an excess of vice, and the wreck of one's neighbor's peace of mind no less to be deplored than the wreck of one's own physique. For a fool may jog shoulder to shoulder with a comfortable sinner, but it takes a philosopher to support the presence of an unmitigated saint.

So it was as well that Mariana's aspirations were short-lived. She confessed them to Anthony, and they were overruled.

"My dear girl," he said, "stop fasting, and don't wear away your knees at prayer. All the breath in your body isn't going to affect the decision of Omniscience. The only duty you owe to the universe is to scatter as much pleasure in life as you can. Eat good red beef and ward off anæmia, and give the time you have wasted in devotions to exercise and fresh air. If we are all doomed to hell, you can't turn the earth out of its track by bodily maceration. Evil plus evil doesn't equal good."

Mariana ceased praying and went out to walk. She was conscious of strange quickenings of sympathy. She loved the world and the people that passed her and the children laughing in the gutter. She bought a pot of primroses from the flower-stall at the corner, and, having spent a week's car-fare, walked a couple of miles in the sun to carry them to a rheumatic old lady who had once been kind to her. With patient good-humor she sat an hour in the sick-room, and, when she left, the rheumatic old lady kissed and blessed her.

The praise stirred her pulses with pleasure. She wondered if she might not become a Sister of Charity and spend her life in ministering to others, and when a ragged boot-black in the street begged for a dime she gave him the money she had saved for a pair of gloves, and glorified the sacrifice by the smile of a Saint Elizabeth. She felt that she would like to give some one the coat from her back, and, as she passed in and out of the crowd around her, her heart stirred in imaginative sympathy for humanity. That vital recognition of the fellowship of man which is as transient as it is inspiring, uplifted her. She wished that some one from the crowd would single her out, saying, "I am wretched, comfort me!" or, "I am starving, feed me!"

But no one did so. They looked at her with indifferent eyes, and her impulses recoiled upon themselves. At that moment she felt capable of complete self-abnegation in the cause of mankind, and even commonplace goodness possessed an attraction. But she realized that the desire to sacrifice is short-lived, and that, after all, it is easier to lay down one's life for the human race than to endure the idiosyncrasies of its atoms.

To us who adopt the proprieties as a profession and wear respectability for a mantle, unauthorized impulses in any form are to be contemned, and Mariana, flushed with generous desires, was as unacceptable as Mariana submerged in self.

After paying a couple of calls the girl's spirit of altruism evaporated. It was warm and close, and the sun made her head ache, while the fatigue from the unusual exercise produced a fit of ill-humor. She wondered why she had left her room, and then looked at her soiled gloves and regretted her encounter with the boot-black. The recollection of the pot of primroses and the week's car-fare caused her even more annoyance.

A block from The Gotham she ran upon Jerome Ardly, and her irritation vanished.

"Hello!" he ejaculated, "you are as white as a sheet. Too much September sun. Had luncheon?"

"Yes," responded Mariana; and she added, plaintively, "I am so tired. I have walked myself to death—and all for nothing."

"Form of monomania?" he inquired, sympathetically. "Nothing short of arrant idiocy would take any one out for nothing on a day like this."

Mariana looked at him and laughed. "I have been paying calls," she said. "I went to see Mrs. Simpson and she told me all about the rights of women. It was very instructive."

"If they resemble the rights of man," remarked Ardly, "they are not to be seen, heard, or felt."

"Ah, but it is all the fault of men," responded Mariana; "she told me so. She said that men were the only things that kept us back."

Ardly laughed.

"And you?" he inquired.

"I! Oh, I agreed with her! I told her that if men hindered us we would stamp them out."

"The devil you did!" retorted Ardly. "I know of no one better fitted for the job. You will begin on your fellow-lodgers, I suppose. As if you had not been treading on our hearts for the last year!"

Mariana lowered her parasol and entered The Gotham. As she mounted the stairs she turned towards him. The time had been when the presence of Jerome Ardly had caused a flutter among the tremulous strings of her heart, but that had been before Anthony crossed her horizon. And yet coquetry was not extinguished. "*Our?*" she emphasized, smiling.

PHASES OF AN INFERIOR PLANET

Ardly grasped at the hand which lay upon the railing, but Mariana eluded him.

"Why, all of us," he returned, with unabashed good-nature—"poor devils that we are! Myself, Nevins, Mr. Paul, to say nothing of Algarcife."

Mariana's color rose swiftly. "Oh, nonsense!" she laughed, and sped upward.

Upon the landing Mr. Nevins opened the door of his studio and greeted them.

"I say, Miss Musin, won't you come and have a look at 'Andromeda'?"

Mariana entered the studio, and Ardly followed her. In the centre of the room a tea-table was spread, and Miss Freighley, a smear of yellow ochre on the sleeve where she had accidentally wiped her brush, was engaged in brewing the beverage. Upon the hearth-rug Juliet Hill was standing, her tall, undeveloped figure and vivid hair relieved against a dull-brown hanging, and around the "Andromeda" a group of youthful artists were gathered.

"How delightful!" exclaimed Mariana, genially. She kissed Miss Freighley, and pressed the extended hands of the others with demonstrative cordiality.

"Oh, if I could only paint!" she said to Miss Freighley, in affectionate undertones. "If I could only go about with a box of brushes, without feeling silly, and wear a smudge of paint upon my sleeve without being dishonest." And she wiped Miss Freighley's sleeve upon her handkerchief.

"Thanks," responded that young lady, amiably; "but you can carry a music-roll, you know, which is much handier and a good deal tidier."

Mariana had turned to the "Andromeda." "Oh, Mr. Ponsonby!" she remarked, to one of the group surrounding it, "don't you uphold me in thinking the shadows upon the throat too heavy?"

Mr. Ponsonby protested that he would uphold her

in any statement she might choose to make, so long as he was not expected to agree with her. Mariana appealed to Mr. Nevins, who declared that he would agree with her in any matter whatsoever, so long as he was not expected to change his "Andromeda."

Mariana frowned. "Mr. Ardly thinks as I do—now don't you?"

Ardly sauntered over to them.

"Why, of course," he assented. "That shadow was put on with a pitchfork. I am positively surprised at you, Nevins."

"On your conscience?" demanded Mariana.

"Haven't any," protested Ardly, indolently. "Left it in Boston. It is indigenous to the soil, and won't bear transplanting."

"Miss Ramsey brought hers with her," replied Mariana, with a smile. "It worries her dreadfully. It is just like a ball on the leg of a convict. She has to drag it wherever she goes, and it makes her awfully tired sometimes."

"A good Bohemian conscience is the only variety worth possessing," observed Mr. Nevins. "It changes color with every change of scene and revolves upon an axis. Hurrah for Bohemia!"

"Hear! hear!" cried Mariana, gayly. She lifted a glass of sherry, and, lighting a cigarette, sprang upon the music-stool. Mr. Ponsonby drew up a chair and seated himself at the piano, and, blowing a cloud of smoke about her head, Mariana sang a rollicking song of the street.

As she finished, the door opened and Algarcife stood upon the threshold. For a moment he gazed at the scene—at Mariana poised upon the music-stool with upraised arms, her hat hanging by an elastic from her shoulder, her head circled by wreaths of cigarette smoke, her eyes reckless. His look was expressive of absolute amazement. Innocent as the scene was in reality, to him it seemed an orgy of abandon, and there was not a man in the room who would not have understood Mariana at that moment better than he did.

"I beg your pardon, Nevins," he said, abruptly. "No, I won't come in." And the door closed.

But Mariana had seen his face, and, with a flutter of impulse and a precipitate rush, she was after him.

"Mr. Algarcife!" Her voice broke.

He turned and faced her.

"What is it?"

"You—you looked so shocked!" she cried.

She stood before him, breathless and warm, the smoking cigarette still in her hand.

"Throw that away!" he said.

She took a step forward, struggling like a netted bird beneath the spell of his power.

"How absurd!" she said, softly. The cigarette dropped from her fingers to the floor.

He laughed. His eyes burned steadily upon her. Before his gaze her lashes wavered and fell, but not until she had seen the flashing of latent impulse in his face.

"But you dropped it," he said.

"Yes."

"Why did you?"

Mariana made a desperate effort at her old fearlessness. It failed her. Her eyes were upon the floor, but she felt his gaze piercing her fallen lids. She spoke hurriedly.

"Because—because I did," she answered.

He came a step nearer. She felt that the passion in his glance was straining at the leash of self-control. She did not know that desire was insurgent against the dominion of will, and was waging a combat with fire and sword.

She put up her hands.

"You are my friend," she said. Her tones faltered. The haze of idealism with which he had surrounded her was suffused with a roseate glow. He caught her hands. His face had grown dark and set, and the lines upon his forehead seemed ineffaceable.

Mariana was conscious of a sudden uplifting within her. It was as if her heart had broken into song. She stood motionless, her hands closing upon his detaining ones. Her face was vivid with animation, and there was a suggestion of frank surrender in her attitude. He caught his breath sharply. Then his accustomed composure fell upon him. His mouth relaxed its nervous tension, and the electric current which had burned his fingers was dissipated.

At the other end of the corridor a door opened and shut, and some one came whistling along the hall.

"It is Mr. Sellars," said Mariana, smiling. "I recognize his whistling two blocks away, because it is always out of tune. He thinks he is whistling 'Robin Hood,' but he is mistaken."

"Is he?" asked Anthony, abstractedly. His mind was less agile than Mariana's, and he found more difficulty in spanning the space between sentiment and comic opera.

Mr. Sellars greeted them cheerfully and passed on.

"I must go," said Mariana. "I promised to dine with Miss Ramsey."

There was an aggrieved note in her voice, but it had no connection with Anthony. With the passing of the enjoyment of emotion for the sake of the mental exaltation which accompanied it, the dramatic instinct reasserted itself. She even experienced a mild resentment against fate that the emotional altitude she had craved should have been revealed to her in the damp and unventilated corridor of The Gotham apartment-house. At a glance from Anthony the resentment would have vanished, and Mariana have been swept once more into a maze of romanticism. But he did not look at her, and the half-conscious demand for scenic effects was unsatisfied.

"Yes," said Anthony, "it is late." His voice sounded hushed and constrained, and, as he stood aside to allow her to pass, he looked beyond and not at the girl.

She turned from him and entered her room.

CHAPTER X

MARIANA found Miss Ramsey lying at length upon the hearth-rug in her tiny sitting-room, her head resting upon an eider-down cushion.

At the girl's entrance she looked up nervously. "I can't rest," she said, with a plaintive intonation, "and I am so tired. But when I shut my eyes I see spread before me all the work I've got to do to-morrow."

She sat up, passing her hand restlessly across her forehead. In her appearance there might be detected an almost fierce renunciation of youth. Her gown was exaggerated in severity, and her colorless and uncurled hair was strained from her forehead and worn in a tight knot upon the crown of her head. The prettiness of her face was almost aggressive amid contrasting disfigurements.

Miss Ramsey belonged to that numerous army of women who fulfil life as they fulfil an appointment at the dentist's—with a desperate sense of duty and shaken nerves. And beside such commonplace tragedies all dramatic climaxes show purposeless. The saints of old, who were sanctified by fire and sword, might well shrink from the martyrdom sustained, smiling, by many who have endured the rack of daily despair. To be a martyr for an hour is so much less heroic than to be a man for a lifetime.

But in Miss Ramsey's worn little body, incased in its network of nerves, there was the passionless determination of her Puritan ancestors. Life had been thrust upon her, and she accepted it. In much the same spirit she would have accepted hell. Perhaps, in meeting the latter, a little cheerfulness might have been added to positive pain—since of all tragedies her present tragedy of unfulfilment was the most tragic of all.

Mariana knelt beside her and kissed her with quick sympathy.

"I can't rest," repeated the elder woman, fretfully. "I can't rest for thinking of the work I must do to-morrow."

"Don't think of it," remonstrated Mariana. "This isn't to-morrow, so there is no use thinking of it."

In Miss Ramsey's eyes there shone a flicker of girlishness which, had fate willed it, might have irradiated her whole face.

"I have been wondering," added Mariana, softly, "what you need, and I believe it is a canary. I will buy you a canary when my allowance comes."

For the girl had looked into her own heart and had read an unwritten law. She had seen sanctification through love, and she felt that a woman may owe her salvation to a canary.

"How could I care for it?" asked the other, a little wistfully. "I have no time. But it would be nice to own something."

Then they left the hearth-rug and ate dinner, and Mariana drove the overhanging cloud from Miss Ramsey's eyes. The desire to be first with all who surrounded her had prompted her to ingratiate herself in every heart that throbbed and ached within The Gotham, from little, overworked Miss Ramsey to the smaller and more overworked maid who dusted her chamber.

After dinner, when Mariana returned to her room, she found a letter awaiting her. It was from her father, and, as was usual with his utterances, it was straight and to the mark.

"I have met with reverses," it stated, "and the family is growing large. In my present position I find it impossible to continue your allowance, and I think that, on the whole, your duty is at home. My wife has much care with the children, and you would be of service in educating them."

Mariana dropped the letter and sat motionless. In a flash she realized all that it meant. It meant returning to drudgery and hideous monotony. It meant returning to the house she hated and to the atmosphere that stifled her. It meant a colorless life of poverty and sordid self-denial. It meant relinquishing her art and Anthony.

With a rush of impulse she stepped out upon the fire-escape, the letter fluttering in her hand.

"Mr. Algarcife!" she called, softly.

As his figure darkened the lighted space between the window-sashes she went towards him. He faced her in surprise. "What is it?" he inquired, abruptly.

Mariana held out the letter, and then followed him as he re-entered his room.

"I cannot do it!" she said, passionately. "I cannot! I cannot!"

Without heeding her, Anthony unfolded the letter, read it and reread it with judicial composure; after which he folded it again, placed it in the envelope, and stood holding it in his right hand. The only visible effect it produced upon him was a nervous twitching of his thin lips.

"And what have you decided?" he asked, slowly.

Mariana interlaced her fingers impatiently. She looked small and white, and excitement caused her eyes to appear abnormally large. Her features quivered and her tone was tremulous.

"I will not go back," she protested. "I will not! Oh, I will not!"

"Is it so bad?" He still held the letter.

PHASES OF AN INFERIOR PLANET

"Bad! It is worse than—than anything. If I had stayed there I should have gone mad. It was paralyzing me inch by inch. Oh, if you could only know what it is—a dusty, dirty little house, smelling of cabbage, a troop of screaming children, and quarrels all day long."

He met her outburst with a remonstrative gesture, but there was a mellow light in his eyes and his face had softened. As if resenting a voluntary restraint, he shook back a lock of hair that had fallen upon his forehead.

"But your father?"

Mariana looked at him as if he represented the bar of judgment and she were pleading her cause. She spoke with feverish conviction.

"Oh, he doesn't want me! If you only knew what a relief it was to him when I came away. Things were so much quieter. He likes his wife and I hate her, so we don't agree. There is never any peace when I am there—never."

"And the children?" His eyes met Mariana's, and again his lips twitched nervously. He held the check-rein of desire with a relentless hand, but the struggle told.

"They are horrid," responded Mariana, insistently. "They are all hers. If they had really belonged to me, I wouldn't have left them, but they didn't, not one. And I won't teach them. I'd rather teach the children of that shoemaker across the way. I'd rather scrub the streets."

Anthony smiled, and the tenderness in his eyes rained upon her. The fact that she had thrown herself upon his sympathy completed the charm she exercised over him.

Still he held himself in hand.

"You know of nothing that could call you back?" he asked.

"Nothing," answered Mariana. "I shouldn't like to starve, but I'd almost as soon starve as live on cabbage." Then she faced him tragically. "My father's wife is a very coarse woman. She has cabbage one day and onions the next."

The smile in Anthony's eyes deepened. "It would be impossible to select a more wholesome article of food than the latter," he observed.

But Mariana was unmoved.

"Before I left, it was horrible," she continued. "Whenever onions were served I would leave the table. My father's wife would get angry and that would make me angry."

"A congenial family."

"But when we get angry we quarrel. It is our nature to do so." She lifted her lashes. "And when we quarrel we talk a great deal, and some of us talk very loud. That is unpleasant, isn't it?"

"Very," Algarcife commented. "I find, by the way, that I am beginning to harbor a sympathy for your father's wife."

Mariana stared at him and shook her head.

"I wasn't nice to her," she admitted, "but she is such a loud woman. I am never nice to people I dislike—but I don't dislike many."

She smiled. Algarcife took a step forward, but checked himself. "We will talk it over—to-morrow," he said, and his voice sounded cold from constraint.

"I won't go back," protested Mariana. "I—I will marry Mr. Paul first."

He held out his hand, and it closed firmly over the one she gave him. "You will not do that, at all events," he said; "for Mr. Paul's sake, as well as your own."

Then he drew aside, and Mariana went back to her room.

Anthony recrossed the window-sill and paced slowly

PHASES OF AN INFERIOR PLANET

up and down the uncarpeted floor. His head was bent and his gaze preoccupied, but there was composure in his bearing. He had sent the girl away that he might think before acting. Not that he was not fully aware what the result of his meditation would be, but that for six years he had been in training to resist impulse, and the habit was strong. But there are things stronger than habit, and emotion is among them. In a man who has neither squandered feeling in excesses nor succumbed to the allurement of the senses, passion, when once aroused, is trebly puissant, and is apt to sweep all lesser desires as chaff before the whirlwind. In the love of such a man there is of necessity the freshness of adolescence and the tenacity of maturity. When one has not expended lightly the fulness of desire, the supply is constantly augmented, and its force will be in proportion to the force of the pressure by which it has been restrained. Algarcife, pacing to and fro between his book-lined walls, felt the current of his being straining towards emotion, and knew that the dominance of will was over. In the realization there existed a tinge of regret, and with the rationality which characterized his mental attitude he lamented that the pulseless sanity of his past was broken. And yet he loved Mariana—loved her with a love that would grow with his growth and strengthen with his weakness. He bowed his head, and his hands clinched, while the edge of his blood was sharpened. He beheld her eyes, curtains veiling formless purity—he felt the touch of her hands, the breath of her lips—he heard the rustle of her skirts—and the virginal femininity of her hovered like an atmosphere about him.

Presently he crossed to the fire-escape, stepped outside, hesitated an instant, and then went to Mariana's window. The shutters were closed, but the light burned behind them.

"Mariana!" he called; and again, "Mariana!"

Through the slats of the shutters the figure of Mariana was visible in high relief against the brightness.

"What is it?" she asked, coming nearer.

He spoke slowly and with constraint.

"Mariana, you will not marry Mr. Paul."

She laughed. The sound was like wine in his blood, and constraint was shattered.

"Is there any obstacle?" she inquired.

"There will be," he answered, and his voice rang clear.

"What?" She was leaning against the shutters. He felt her breath upon his brow.

"You will marry me."

"Oh!" gasped Mariana, and was silent.

Suddenly he surrendered self-control. "Open the shutters," he said.

The shutters were unfastened, they swung back, and Mariana came out. She looked very young, her hair hung about her shoulders, and in the dim light her face showed small and white. For a moment they stood motionless, each dumb before the knowledge of the other's dominance. Anthony looked at her in heated silence. His face was pale, his eyes glowing.

"Mariana!" He did not move nearer, but his voice thrilled her like a caress. She shrank from him, and a heavy shadow fell between them.

"Mariana, you will marry me?" In the stillness following his words she heard the sharpness of his breathing.

"I—I am not good enough," said Mariana.

"My saint!"

As if impelled, she leaned towards him, and he caught her in his arms. Beneath them the noise of traffic went on, and with it the hunger and the thirst and the weariness, but they stood above it all, and he felt the beating of her pulses as he held her.

PHASES OF AN INFERIOR PLANET

"Say you love me," he pleaded — "say it." His breath burned her forehead.

"Oh, don't you see?" she asked — "don't you see?"

She lifted her head and he took her hands and drew her from the darkness into the light and looked into her eyes. They shone like lamps illuminating an altar, and the altar was his own.

"Yes," he said; "but say it."

Mariana was silent for an instant, and when she spoke her voice was vibrant with passion.

"You are my love, and I love you," she answered. "And I?"

"The desire of my eyes."

She came nearer, laying one hand upon his arm. He did not move, and his arm hung motionless, but his eyes were hot.

"I am yours," she said, slowly, "for ever and ever, to have and to hold, to leave or to take — yours utterly."

CHAPTER XI

The news of Mariana's engagement was received without enthusiasm in The Gotham. A resentment against innovations of so sweeping an order was visible in the bearing of a number of the lodgers, and Mr. Nevins was heard publicly expressing his disapproval. "I never got comfortably settled anywhere in my life," he announced, "that somebody didn't step in and disarrange matters. At the last place the head waiter married the cook, and now Algarcife is marrying Mariana. After our discovering her, too. I say, it's a beastly shame!"

Mr. Ardly was of one mind with him; so was Mr. Morris. Alone, of all the table, Mr. Paul stood firm upon the opposite side. An hour after the news was out he encountered Algarcife upon the stairs and smiled compassionately.

"I have heard with concern," he began, stiffly, "that you contemplate taking a serious step."

"Indeed?" returned Anthony, with embarrassment. "I believe I do contemplate something of the kind, but I had hoped to get it over before anybody heard of it."

"Such things travel fast," commented Mr. Paul, cheerfully. "I think I may say that I was in possession of the fact five minutes after your ultimate decision was reached. It is a serious step, as I have said. As for the young woman, I have no doubt of her worthiness, though I have heard contrary opinions—"

"Who has dared?" demanded Anthony.

PHASES OF AN INFERIOR PLANET

"Merely opinions, my dear sir, and the right of private judgment is what we stand on. But, I repeat, I have no doubt of her uprightness. It is not the individual, sir, but the office. It is the office that is at fault."

Mr. Paul passed on, and upon the next landing Algarcife found Mr. Nevins in wait.

"Look here, Algarcife," he remonstrated, "I don't call this fair play, you know! I've had my eye on Mariana for the last twelve months!"

A thunder-cloud broke upon Anthony's brow. "Then you will be kind enough to remove it!" he retorted, angrily.

"Oh, come off!" protested Mr. Nevins. "Why, Mariana and I were chums before you darkened this blessed Gotham! She'd have married me long ago if I'd had the funds."

"Confound you!" exclaimed Anthony. "Can't you hold your tongue?"

Mr. Nevins smiled amiably and spread out his hands.

"No, I cannot," he answered, imperturbably. "Say, old man, don't get riled! You'll let me appear at the wedding, won't you?"

Algarcife strode on in a rage, which was not appeased by Ardly's voice singing out from his open door.

"Congratulations, Algarcife! You are a lucky dog! Like to change shoes."

Upon the balcony he found Mariana, with a blossom of scarlet geranium in her hair. She stretched out both hands and flashed him a smile like a caress. "You look positively furious," she observed.

Algarcife's sensitiveness had caused him to treat Mariana much as he would have treated a Galatea in Dresden, had one been in his possession. But Claude Nevins had annoyed him, and he spoke irritably.

"I wish you would have nothing to do with that fellow Nevins," he said.

"Why, what has he done?"

"Done? Why, he's an ass—a consummate ass! He told me he had his eye on you!"

Mariana's laugh pealed out. She raised her hand and brushed the heavy hair from his forehead. Then she tried to brush the lines from his brow, but they would not go.

"Why, he's going to give me a supper the night before our marriage," she said; "that is, they all are—Mr. Ardly, Mr. Sellars, and the rest. They made a pot of money for it, and each one of them contributed a share, and it is quite a large pot. We are to have champagne, and I am to sing, and so will Mr. Nevins. I wanted them to ask you, but Mr. Nevins said you'd be a damper, and Mr. Ardly said you would be bored."

"Probably," interpolated Anthony.

"But I insisted I wanted you, so Mr. Ardly said they would have to have you, and Mr. Nevins said they'd have Mr. Paul, if I made a point of it; but they thought I might give them one jolly evening before settling down, so I said I would."

"You will do nothing of the kind," retorted Algarcife.

"But they are so anxious. It will be such a dreadful disappointment to them."

"I will not have it."

"But I've done it before."

"Don't tell me of it. You want to go, and without me?"

"Of course I'd rather you should be there, but it is cruel to disappoint them," Mariana objected, "when they have made such a nice pot of money."

"But I do not like it," said Anthony.

Mariana laughed into his eyes. "Then you sha'n't have it," she said, and leaned against the railing and touched his arm with her fingers. "Say you love me, and I will not go," she added.

PHASES OF AN INFERIOR PLANET

Anthony did not touch the hand that lay upon his arm. His mood was too deep for caresses.

"If you knew how I love you," he said, slowly—"if you only knew! There is no happiness in it; it is agony. I am afraid—afraid for the first time in my life—afraid of losing you."

"You shall never lose me."

"It is a horrible thing, this fear—this fear for something outside of yourself!" He spoke with a sudden, half-fierce possession. "You are mine," he said, "and you love me!"

Mariana pressed closer to his side. "If I had not come," she began, softly, "you would have read and worked and fed the sparrows, and you would never have known it."

"But you came." The hand upon the railing relaxed. "My mother was a Creole," he continued. "She came from New Orleans to marry my father, and died because the North was cold and her heart was in the South. You are my South, and the world is cold, for my heart is in you."

"I have wanted love all my life," said Mariana, "and now I have found it. I have thought before that I had it, but it was only a shadow. This is real. As real as myself—as real as this railing. I feel glad—oh, so glad!—and I feel tender. I should like to pray and go softly. I should like to make that old woman at the flower-stall happy and to freshen the withered flowers. I should like to kiss the children playing on the sidewalk. See how merry they look," and she leaned far over. "I should like to pat the head of that yellow dog in the gutter. I should like to make the whole world glad—because of you."

"Mariana!"

"The world is beautiful, and I love you; but I am sorry—oh, so sorry!—for the people in the street."

"Forget them, beloved, and think of me."

"But you taught me to think of them."

"I will teach you to think of me."

"That I have learned by heart."

"Mariana!"

They stood with locked hands upon the balcony, and the roar of the elevated road came up to them, and the old flower-woman put up her withered flowers and went her way, and the children's laughter grew fainter upon the air, and the yellow dog gnawed at a rock that it took for a bone; and the great, great wheel ground on, grinding to each man and to each dog according to his kind his share of the things written and unwritten in the book of life.

A week later they were married. Mariana had coveted a church ceremony, and Anthony had desired a registrar's office, so they compromised, and the service was read in Mr. Speares's study.

"I should have dearly liked the 'Lohengrin March' and stained-glass windows," remarked Mariana, a little regretfully, as they walked homeward. "It seems as if something were missing. I can't tell just what."

"What does it matter?" asked Algarcife, cheerfully. "A street corner and an organ-grinder would have answered my purpose, had he been legally empowered to pronounce the blessing. It is all rot, I suppose, but I'd face every priest and rabbi in New York if they could bind us closer."

He smiled at Mariana. His eager face looked almost boyish, and he walked with the confident air of one who is sure of his pathway.

"But they could not," added Mariana, and they both laughed, because they were young and life was before them.

They retained the rooms in The Gotham with the fire-escape outside the windows, though Anthony found that his income, after deducting a portion for Mariana's expenses, was barely sufficient. He had not realized before how complete was his reliance for existence upon the Bodley College. Even in the thrill of his first happiness there was a haunting vision of Mariana reduced to poverty and himself powerless. He endeavored to insure an independent livelihood by contributing semi-scientific articles to various reviews, but the work was uncongenial, and he felt it to be a failure. The basis of his mental attitude was too firmly embedded to yield superficial product, and he tasted the knowledge that, had he known less, he might have lived easier.

At this time his great work was laid aside, a sacrifice to necessity, and he spent his days and nights in unmurmuring toil for the sake of Mariana. He was willing to labor, so long as he might love in the intervals of rest.

As for Mariana, she was vividly alive. Beneath the warmth of emotion her nature expanded into fulfilment, and with fulfilment awoke the subtle charm of her personality.

"Have you seen Mariana?" inquired Nevins of Ardly one day. "If so, you have seen a woman in love."

Ardly smiled and flicked the ashes from his cigar.

"Is she?" he asked, cynically; "or is it that the froth of sentiment above her heart is troubled and she believes the depth of passion is stirred? I have lived, my dear fellow, as you probably know, and I have seen strange things, but the strangest of these is the way of a maid with a man."

"Be that as it may, she is charming," returned Nevins. "And Algarcife ought to thank his stars, though why she married him is a mystery I relegate to the general unravelling of judgment-day."

"She probably had sense enough to appreciate the most brilliant man in New York," concluded Ardly, loyally, as he took up a volume of Maupassant and departed.

And that Mariana did appreciate Algarcife was not to be questioned. She threw herself into the worship of him with absolute disregard of all retarding interests. When he was near, she lavished demonstrations upon him; when he was away, she sat with folded hands and dreamed day-dreams. She had given up her music, and she even went so far as to declare that she would give up her acquaintances, that they might be sufficient unto each other. For his sake she discussed theories which she did not understand, and accepted doctrines of which she had once been intolerant. That emotional energy which had led her imagination into devious ways had at last, she told herself, found its appropriate channel. Even the stringent economy which was forced upon them was turned into merriment by the play of Mariana's humor.

"Life must only be taken seriously," she said, "when it has ceased to be a jest, and that will be when one has grown too dull to see the point—for the point is always there."

"And sometimes it pricks," laughed Anthony.

CHAPTER XII

In an up-town block, a stone's-throw west of Fifth Avenue, stands the Church of the Immaculate Conception. It is a newly erected structure of gray stone, between two rows of expressionless tenements, and, despite the aggressive finality emphasized in its architecture, wearing a general air of holding its ground by sheer force of stolidity.

The interior of the church is less suggestive of modernity, and bears, on the whole, a surface relationship to a mediæval cathedral. The purple light filtering through the stained-glass windows is, in its essential quality, a European importation, and the altar-piece is a passable reproduction of a painting of Murillo's.

More than fifty years ago the church, then an unpretentious building of red brick, endowed neither with rood-screen nor waxen candles, had called to its rectorship the Reverend Clement Speares, a youthful leader of the ritualistic element in Episcopalianism. Father Speares heard the call and accepted the charge, and within a dozen years he had succeeded in trebling the number of his congregation, and in exchanging the red-brick building for the present Church of the Immaculate Conception, with its mystic light of mediævalism.

The congregation, of that class who toil not, neither spin, but before whose raiment Easter lilies falter, was fashionable, and also wealthy. The single-hearted zeal which its priest had put into fifty years of service had failed to wean his flock from a taste for the flesh-pots.

PHASES OF AN INFERIOR PLANET

In return for the generosity with which they supported their place of worship and its appurtenances, they claimed the indefeasible right to regulate their own attire and to reserve their pews from the encroachment of aliens. They were willing to erect a mission chapel in the slums, but they submitted to no trespassing upon the exclusiveness of their accustomed preserves.

Father Speares, who, had his temporal power been in proportion to his ecclesiastical influence, would have thrown open the Holy of Holies to the beggar in the street, and have knelt with equal charity between the Pharisees and Publicans, resigned himself to the recognition of spiritual caste, and devoted his days to Fifth Avenue and his evenings to the Bowery.

To his honor be it said that he made no more valiant stand for the salvation of the one than of the other. A soul was a soul to him, and personal cleanliness a matter of taste.

He was a man of resolute convictions and unswerving purpose. If he did not possess eloquence of speech, he possessed sincerity of mind, which is quite as rare, and very nearly as effective. He had a benevolent countenance combined with a sympathetic manner, and the combination exercised a charm over those of his hearers who attended his church in the endeavor to narcotize troublesome nerves. Unconsciously, by his adoption of celibacy from the mother church, he had borrowed from the elder faith the powerful weapon of romanticism, exciting the imaginative qualities, while he emphasized the maxim of the right of private judgment by rejecting the dogma of papal infallibility.

But since the Church of the Immaculate Conception had risen into being with Father Speares, there was an Ishmaelitish rumor afloat that with Father Speares it would pass away. Father Speares himself was not in-

PHASES OF AN INFERIOR PLANET

sensible to the danger, and with the fervor of an enthusiast he labored to perpetuate the ceremonials his soul loved. With the force of a revelation there was borne upon him the conception that on him and his successors rested the mission to impel the conservative wing of Episcopalianism into that assimilation to Roman Catholicism whose resultant is the Ritualistic movement. Unto this end he had spent more than fifty years of labor. At the close of the nineteenth century he stood a picturesque and pathetic figure, combating with a mediæval eloquence the advancing spirit of his time, a representative of the lost age of faith lingering far into the new-found age of rationalism.

When Anthony Algarcife, a young orphan, had been sent to him, he had taken the child into his confidence.

"I will help you," the boy had said, enthusiastically—"I will help you." And he rolled up his little shirt-sleeves in the desire to settle spiritual differences in the good old fashion of physical force.

Father Speares had smiled and patted him upon the shoulder. "Please God, you shall, my boy!" he had answered, and had made the child a white-robed acolyte, that he might ignite by youthful hands the fires of faith.

Anthony had been a disappointment, he had said, but of the bitterness of the disappointment he had made no mention. Beneath his teaching he had seen the young mind unfold and expand strenuously, and then, while his eager eyes were watching, he had seen it shoot from him and beyond his grasp, trampling his cherished convictions beneath ruthless feet.

"It is all rubbish," Anthony had declared in the first intolerance of his youth. "The mental world is filled with a lot of decaying theology, which has been accumulating for centuries. It remains for us to sweep it away."

"And you would sweep me with it," said Father Speares, a little bitterly.

"The ground must be cleared," returned Anthony. "You are sitting upon the rubbish, as a miser in Pompeii might have sat upon his gold while Vesuvius overflowed. It is wiser to flee and leave hoarded treasure to be ingulfed. That rubbish was once sound theology, I grant, but it has crumbled, and its usefulness of a thousand years ago will not it save from the ash-heap of outgrown ideas to-day."

Father Speares sighed and set his lips. "The boy is young," he said, with the yearning self-deception of age. "It will pass, and he will return the stronger for his wandering."

But the event had not borne out his prophecy. It did not pass, and Anthony did not return.

"It is my head," he explained, half irritably. "There is a wall of scepticism surrounding my brain, through which only the toughest facts may penetrate. I am minus the faculty of credulity."

"Or reverence," Father Speares added, reproachfully. "You regard spiritual things as a deaf man regards sound or a blind man sight."

Anthony's irritation triumphed.

"Or as a man awake regards a dream," he suggested. "The film of superstition has cleared from my eyes, and I see. The truth is that I regard all religions exactly as you regard all except the one which you inherited. An accident of birth has made you a Christian instead of a Moslem or a Brahman, that is all."

"And a twist of the mind has made you an atheist."

"As you please — atheist, agnostic, sceptic, what you will. It only means that you offer me an irrational assumption, and I reject it. It is the custom of you theologians to fit ugly epithets to your opponents, whereas the denial of Christianity no more argues atheism than the denial of Confucianism does. It merely proves that a man refuses to acknowledge any one of the gods which men have created, and that he leaves the ultimate essence outside his generalizations. Such a man has learned the first lesson in knowledge—the lesson of his own ignorance."

"And has missed the greater lesson of the wisdom of God."

Algarcife shrugged his shoulders.

"It is no use," he said; "I can't believe, and I wouldn't if I could."

So he had gone from Father Speares into the world. Virile, strenuous, and possessed with intellectual passion, he had closed the doors of his mind upon commonplaces, and with the improvidence from which mental stamina failed to redeem him had wedded himself to poverty and science.

Five years after leaving Father Speares's roof he returned with Mariana at his side.

"We have come to be married," he announced.

Father Speares gasped and suggested prudence. "It is unwise," he remonstrated—"it is utterly unwise."

"I agree with you," admitted Anthony. "It is unwise, and we know it; but there is nothing else to be done—is there, Mariana?"

Mariana looked into Father Speares's face and smiled.

"Of course you are right," she said, "and we are very foolish, but—but there really isn't anything else to do."

And Father Speares was silenced. He looked at the license a little ruefully, read the service, and sent them off with a benediction.

"God knows, I wish you happiness," he assured Mariana when she kissed him.

Several months later, meeting Algarcife on Broadway, he repeated the words.

"I am happy," returned Algarcife, emphatically. "Mariana is an angel."

"I am glad to hear it," said Father Speares, and he sighed irrelevantly. "A good woman is a jewel of rare value."

The term "good woman," applied to Mariana, gave Anthony a sense of unfitness. Mariana was certainly a jewel, but, somehow, it had never occurred to him to look upon her as a "good woman."

"She is very charming," he remarked, quietly.

Father Speares was regarding him critically. "You are not looking well," he said. "Is it work or worry?"

Algarcife shook his head impatiently. "I—oh, I am all right," he rejoined. "A little extra work, that's all."

"Your book?"

Algarcife's face contracted, and the harassed expression about his mouth deepened.

"No, not my book," he answered, hastily. "I've put that aside for a while. I am trying a hand at bread-winning."

"With satisfactory results, I hope."

Anthony's laugh was slightly constrained.

"Why, certainly! Am I the man to fail?"

"I don't know," commented Father Speares—"I don't know. I never thought of you in that light, somehow. But if I can help you, remember that you were once my boy."

Anthony held out his hand quickly, his voice trembling.

"You are generous—generous as you have always been, but—I am all right."

They parted, Algarcife turning into a cross street. He walked slowly, and the harassed lines did not fade from his mouth. He seemed to have grown older within the last few months, and the fight he was making had bowed his shoulders and sown the seeds of future furrows upon his face.

PHASES OF AN INFERIOR PLANET

At the corner he bought a box of sardines and a pound of crackers for Mariana, who liked a late supper. Then he crossed to The Gotham and ascended the stairs.

He found Mariana in a dressing-sack of pink flannel, sitting upon the bed, and engaged in manufacturing an opera-bonnet out of a bit of black gauze and a few pink rosebuds. She was trying it on as he entered, and, catching sight of him, did not remove it as she raised her hand warningly. "Tell me if it is becoming before you kiss me," she commanded, pressing her thimble against her lips.

Anthony drew back and surveyed her.

"Of course it is," he replied; "but what is it, anyway?"

Mariana laughed and leaned towards him.

"A bonnet, of course; not a coal-scuttle or a lamp-shade."

Then she took it from her head and held it before her, turning it critically from side to side.

"Don't you think it might have a few violets against the hair, just above the left temple? I am sure I could take some out of my last summer's hat."

She left the bed and stood upon a chair, to place the bonnet in a box upon the top of the wardrobe. "As a scientific problem it should interest you," she observed. "I created it out of nothing."

Anthony caught her as she descended from the chair.

"As a possible adornment for your head it interests me still more," he replied.

"Because you haven't been married long enough to discover what an empty little head it is?"

"Because it is the dearest head in the world, and the wisest. But what a thriftless house-keeper, not to have set the table!" A door had been cut into his study, and he glanced through. "Do you think you are still below Mason and Dixon's line, where time is not recognized?"

"I forgot it," said Mariana; "but there isn't any bread, so you must go after it. Oh, you didn't get sardines again, did you? I said potted ham—and it is really a very small chicken they sent us."

"Well, no matter. It might have been a chop. By the way, I met Mr. Speares—"

"Father Speares," corrected Mariana.

"Mr. or Father, he's a nice old chap, isn't he?"

"He's a saint," said Mariana. Then she grew serious. "If you could have gone into the Church— honestly, I mean — how pleased he would have been, dearest."

"Yes; but I couldn't, you know, and if I had I could not have married you. He is High Church, you see. Celibacy is his pet institution."

Mariana colored. "Then I am glad you didn't." She flung herself upon him; then, drawing back, added, wistfully, "But you wouldn't have been poor."

"Do you find it so hard?"

"I hate it — for you. You work so hard. And I can't help you."

"My beloved!"

"I mind it most for you. But, of course, I feel badly when the washer-woman comes and there isn't any money—and I should like to have some gloves—"

"You shall have them, my darling. Why didn't you tell me?"

Mariana leaned upon his breast and swept her loosened hair across his arm. "It doesn't matter very much," she answered. "If I were starving and you kissed me I should forget it." And she added, with characteristic inconsequence: "Only I haven't been out for several days because I didn't have any."

"You shall have them to-morrow. Is there anything else, dearest?"

PHASES OF AN INFERIOR PLANET

"Nothing!" laughed Mariana.

She went to the mirror and began coiling her hair. From the glass her eyes met Anthony's, and she threw him a smiling glance.

I have been reading one of your books," she said, pointing with the brush; "there it is."

Anthony lifted the volume from the bureau and grew serious. "Mill?" he observed. "It is a good start. Every woman should know political economy. I am glad it interests you."

"I haven't gone beyond the first page yet," returned Mariana, putting up both hands to fluff her aureole, and pausing to run her fingers over her eyebrows in the attempt to narrow them. "There was something in the first page about 'a web of muslin,' and, somehow, it suggested to me the idea of making that bonnet. Odd, wasn't it? And I am so glad I read it, for I am sure I should never have thought of the bonnet otherwise—and it *is* becoming."

"But you like Mill?"

"Oh yes," said Mariana; "I find him very suggestive."

CHAPTER XIII

Anthony and Mariana founded their life together upon well-worn principles. They accepted in its entirety the fallacy that love is a self-sustaining force, independent of material conditions.

"So long as we love each other," Mariana declared, "nothing matters."

And Anthony upheld this declaration. To Algarcife those first months of intimate association were inexpressibly fresh and inspiring. That acute sense of nearness to Mariana supplied what had been a void in his existence, and he looked back upon the time he had spent without her as a colorless stretch of undifferentiated days.

And yet, with a feminine presence beside him, work was less easy. In the evenings, when Mariana followed him to his study and seated herself in a rocking-chair beneath the lamplight, he sometimes experienced a vague recognition of its inappropriateness. He found the old absorption to have grown intractable, and the creak of Mariana's rocker, or the low humming of her voice, was sufficient to surprise in him that repressed irascibility from which he had never been able to shake himself free. Even in the midst of his passionate delight in her, a profound melancholy would seize him at times, and he would find the cravings of his intellectual nature harassed by the superficial tenor of his daily employment. Again, as Mariana sat in the lamplight, her swift fingers busy with some useless bit of millinery, he would regard her with a sudden tightening of his pulses, and a thrill of fear at the prospect of a coming separation. The droop of her head, the contour of her face where the bone of her chin was accentuated by thinness, the soft line of throat above the full collar, the nimbus of hair shining in the light, the fall of her skirt, the slender slippered feet, aroused in him a tumultuous sense of possession. He would turn from his writing to rest upon her a warm and magnetic glance, before which her lowered lashes would be lifted, her pensive lips break into a smile.

Then, again, the instinct for solitude, which his years of study had intensified, would reawaken, and the creaking of the rocker would act as an irritant upon his nerves.

It was at such a moment that Mariana had looked up and spoken, the bright inflection of her voice aggravating the interruption.

"Anthony!"

Algarcife turned towards her, his pen raised as if in self-defence.

"When did you begin to love me?"

The pen was lowered, Algarcife smiled. "In the beginning," he answered; then he frowned, his tone grew captious. "I can't, Mariana," he protested—"I really can't. I must get this work over."

"You are always working."

"Heaven knows, I am! If I weren't, we would starve."

"It is horrible to be poor."

"We don't improve matters by exclaiming over them. On the contrary, you will prevent my getting this article off to-night, and we will be a few dollars the poorer."

"You never talk to me. You are always working."

She spoke pettishly, with an impulse to exasperate.

"Mariana!"

Mariana threw aside her work and clasped her hands.

Her face was upturned, her head supported by the back of the chair. He could see the violet shadow which rested like a faint suffusion where the heavy hair swept from behind her ear.

Suddenly her head was lowered, and the mellow lamplight irradiated across the pallor of her face.

"Of course I know you are working for me," she said, "but I had rather have less labor and more love."

"I love you as much when I am working for you as when I am shouting it in your ear."

"But I like to hear it."

"I love you. Now be quiet."

Mariana came and leaned over him. She put her arms about his shoulders and rested her head upon them. There was a sob in her voice. "Let me help you," she said. "It is so hard to sit still and do nothing, while you are killing yourself. Let me help you."

Anthony turned and caught her, and she lay limp and motionless in his embrace. He kissed her with sudden passion.

"You help me by living," he said, "by breathing, by being near me, by giving yourself to me unreservedly. Without you I lived but half a life—without you, now that I have had you, I should go to pieces—absolutely. I love you as a man loves once in a thousand years. But we must live, and I must work."

He released her and went back to his writing, while Mariana, in passionate elation, picked up Mill's *Political Economy*, and fell to studying.

It was shortly after this that she sought to turn her own talents to financial results. With this end in view she invested her pocket-money in a yard or so of white linen and a mass of colored silks, and wove a garland of nasturtiums around a centre-piece intended to decorate a dinner-table. When it was finished she was seized with a fit of sanguineness, and as she rinsed it in a dozen different waters to insure whiteness, she calculated what the annual products of her labor would amount to. "If I manage to do one a month," she remarked, pressing the centre-piece lightly between her moistened hands, "and say I get about fifteen dollars for each one, I should soon have quite a little income; twelve times fifteen is—how much, Anthony?"

"More than I am going to let you work for," replied Algarcife. "Your eyes have been red ever since you started that confounded table-cover. It is the very last."

Mariana placed one finger to her lips, and then applied it lightly to the iron she held in her hand. "I do hope I won't scorch it," she observed. "Oh, do give me that blanket! It must be ironed on a blanket to make the flowers stand out. Aren't they natural?"

She lifted her heated face and glanced at him for approbation.

"I feel like plucking them," returned Algarcife. "Don't tire yourself. Good-bye." And he passed into the next room and closed the door.

Mariana ironed the centre-piece, wrapped it in yellow tissue-paper, and carried it to an exchange for women's work around the corner. It was placed in a glass-case amid a confusion of similar articles, where it languished for the space of several months. At the end of that time she redeemed it.

The failure of the enterprise precipitated an attack of hysteria, which spent itself in Anthony's arms and left her resigned and exhausted.

"I can't do anything to help you," she observed, hopelessly. "I hoped to clear at least fifteen dollars from that centre-piece, and, instead, I lost five. I shall always be an encumbrance."

"You are my beloved counsellor."

"My love isn't of much use, and you never take my advice."

"But I like to listen to it."

Mariana rested her head upon his shoulder and closed her eyes.

"I am only a luxury," she said, "like wine or cigars, but it wouldn't be pleasant to dispense with me, would it?"

"It would be death."

She sighed contentedly, her hand wandered across his brow. There was a faint, magnetic force in her finger-tips which left a burning sensation like that caused by a slightly charged electric current.

"I made you marry me, you know," she remarked, complacently, "so I am glad you don't regret it."

"Nonsense," remonstrated Algarcife, his lips upon her hair, the warm contact of her body inducing a sense of nearness. "I married you by force. I quite took your breath away. If you had resisted, I should have had you whether or no."

"Oh, but I did make you," returned Mariana. "But there was nothing else to do. I couldn't possibly have gone home, and I did love you so distractedly."

"As you do now."

"As I do now. Of course I must have known that rushing to you that night with the letter was just like a proposal of marriage."

"It was, rather," concluded Algarcife.

"But you needn't have married me unless you wanted to," urged Mariana. "There was Mr. Paul—"

Anthony laughed. "I was a vicarious sacrifice," he declared, "to insure the peace of Mr. Paul."

The next day Algarcife received an unexpected sum of money, and they agreed to celebrate their rising fortunes by a night at the opera. It was "Tannhauser," and Mariana craved music.

"I am afraid it is improvident," Anthony, whom the

PHASES OF AN INFERIOR PLANET

opera bored, remarked, dubiously; then looking into Mariana's wistful face, he recanted. "It doesn't matter," he added. "A little extravagance won't affect the probability of future starvation. We will go."

And they went. Mariana wore her freshest gown and the little bonnet with the knot of violets above the left temple. She was in her gayest mood, which was only dampened in a slight degree by the odor of the benzine clinging to her newly cleaned gloves.

As she leaned against the railing in the fifth gallery, gazing plaintively down into the pit, she looked subtle and seductive—like a creation in half-tones, swept by fugitive lights and shadows. The pallor of her face was intensified, her radiant lips compressed, and the green flame in her glance scintillated beneath luxurious lashes. Anthony, fastening upon her contented eyes, wondered at the singular charm which she radiated. Small, slight, insignificant, and charged with imperfections as she was, her very imperfections possessed the fascination of elusiveness. Her radiance was intensified in the memory by the plainness succeeding it; the sensitive curve of her nostrils was heightened in effect by the irregularity of feature, and the angular distinctness of the bones of her chin emphasized the faint violet shadows suffusing the hollows. Had her charm been less impalpable it would have lost its power. The desire of beauty might have satiated itself in a dozen women, or of amativeness in a dozen others, but Mariana fascinated instinctively, and her spell was without beginning in a single attribute and without end in possession.

As she sat there in the fifth gallery, drinking with insatiable thirst the swelling harmony, her emotional nature, which association with Algarcife had somewhat subdued, was revivified, and she pressed Anthony's responsive hand in exaltation. The music reverberating round her brought in its train all those lurid dreams which she had half forgotten, and the dramatic passion awoke and burned her pulses. She felt herself invigorated, swept from the moorings of the commonplace, and subverted by the scenic intensity before her. She felt taller, stronger, fuller of unimpregnated germs of power, and, like an infusion of splendid barbaric blood, there surged through her veins a flame of color. With a triumphant crash of harmonious discord, she felt that the artistic instinct was stimulated from its supineness, and the desire to achieve was aglow within her. The electric lights beneath the brilliant ceiling, the odor of hot-house flowers, the music sweeping upward and bearing her on its swelling tide, acted upon her overwrought sensibilities like an intoxicant. She drew near to Anthony; her lips quivered.

"Oh, if it would last," she said—"if it would last!"

But it did not last, and when it was over Mariana pressed her hand to her brow like one in pain. The return to reality jarred upon her vibrant nerves, and she became aware of shooting throbs in her temples, and of the depressing moisture in the atmosphere.

"I am faint," she complained. "I must have something—anything."

"It is all that clashing and banging," responded Anthony. "What a relief silence is!"

They bought ale and cheese and crackers from a grocery at the corner, and carried the parcels to their room. Mariana let down her hair, put on her dressing-gown, and threw herself upon the hearth-rug. She felt weak and hungry. "If there were only a fire," she lamented regretfully, stretching her hands towards the register; after which she opened the paper-bags and ate ravenously.

In the night she awoke with a start and a sob. She reached out moaningly in the darkness. Her hands were trembling and the neck of her gown was damp

PHASES OF AN INFERIOR PLANET

and chill. "I believe I shall go mad," she said, desperately.

Anthony struck a match, lighted the candle, and looked at her. He laid a cool hand upon her forehead. "What is it?" he asked. "Are you nervous? Have you been dreaming?"

"No, no," cried Mariana, rolling her head upon the pillow, "but I want music. I want art. There is so much that is beautiful, and I want something."

She wept hysterically. Anthony got up and made her a cup of tea, which she could not drink because it was smoked.

But on the morrow she was herself again. As she was arranging her hair she laughed and chattered gayly, and the effect of the previous evening was shown only in a tendency to break into song. Before drinking her coffee she turned to the piano and trilled an Italian aria, the fingers of one hand wandering over the key-board in a careless accompaniment.

During the day her buoyancy was unfailing. She took up her studies zealously, and the morning devoted to Mill was rich in results. Her acuteness of apprehension was a continual marvel to Algarcife's steadier perception, and he regarded with deference the quickness with which she grasped the general drift of unstudied social problems. An exaggerated example of feminine intuition he ascribed unhesitatingly to a profundity of intellectual ability. That Mariana was adapting herself to his theories of life, he recognized and accepted. There was relief in the thought that his influence over her was weightier than the appeal of her art. With adolescent egotism, he convinced himself that he was shaping and perfecting a mental energy into channels other than the predestined ones; and while Mariana was matured into a palpitant reflection of his own image, he believed that he was liberating an intellect enthralled by superficialities. But,

PHASES OF AN INFERIOR PLANET

in truth, the stronger force was assimilating to itself the weaker, and the comradeship existing in their love was perfect in smoothness and finish. The opinions which Anthony radiated Mariana reflected, and they presented to the world proof of a domestic unity complete in its harmony.

CHAPTER XIV

One evening in March, Mr. Nevins gave a supper in his studio.

Anthony had come in that morning looking somewhat perplexed. " Nevins wants us to-night," he said to Mariana, " and I couldn't get out of it."

Mariana looked up eagerly from her practising. " Oh, it is the 'Andromeda,'" she replied. " He said he would celebrate it. So it has been accepted."

" But it hasn't been. It is the rejection he is celebrating. He told me so. I feel sorry for the fellow, so I said we would go."

" Of course we will !" exclaimed Mariana. " But I'm afraid he'll be gloomy."

"On the contrary, he has just come off a spree, and has a patch over his left eye. His hilarity is positively annoying. He and Ardly are smashing everything in their rooms. The pitcher went as I passed."

"Oh, it is his way of expressing feeling," returned Mariana, sympathetically. " Listen to this new air. It goes tra la la, tra—"

Anthony cut her short.

" My dear girl, I'm in an awful hurry. Would you mind being quiet awhile?" And he entered his study, closing the door after him. Mariana left the piano and sat with folded hands looking down into the street below. A fine rain was falling, and the streets were sloppy with a whitish slime. The women that passed held their skirts well above their ankles, revealing all shapes and varieties of feet. She noticed that they carried their skirts awkwardly, with a curious hitch upon the right hip. They were workingwomen for the most part, and their gowns were neither well made nor well cut, but they walked aggressively, with an uneven, almost masculine, swagger.

Mariana yawned and sighed. She would have liked to go back to the piano and bang a march or some stirring strain of martial music, but she recalled Anthony's injunction and yawned again. She remembered suddenly that her practising had become uncertain of late, and that Anthony's objection seemed to lie like a drawn sword between her and her art. An involuntary smile crossed her lips, that she who had pledged herself to the pursuit of music had also given herself to a man to whom Wagner was as Rossini. She dwelt upon her changed conditions almost unconsciously. It was not that her devotion to art had cooled since her marriage, but that something was forever preventing the expression of it. That Anthony regarded it as one of the trivialities of life, she saw clearly, and there was an aggrieved note in her regret. To her, in whom the artistic instinct was bone of her bone and blood of her blood, the sacrifice of a professional career was less slight than Algarcife believed, and in the depths of her heart there still lurked the hope that in time Anthony's impassioned opposition to a stage life would wear itself out. When the moment came, she dreamed of a final reinspiration of the slumbering fires of her ambition. Now, as she sat beside the window, she became aware of the awakening. Once again she allowed her mind to hover above the distant future and to illuminate its neutral canvas with garish colors. In the future anything and everything was possible. Some weeks ago Signor Morani had sent for her and offered her tuition, and she had accepted. "If you achieve success you can repay me," he had said, adding, with philosophic

PHASES OF AN INFERIOR PLANET

intention, "If not, I shall have lost nothing that was my own."

Mariana, in a burst of gratitude, had wept upon his shoulder, and he had smiled as he patted her prostrate head.

"Remember," he said, "that you are an artist first, and a wife and mother afterwards, and you will succeed."

Sitting beside the window and staring at the expressionless tenements across the way, she laughed with soft insistence at the professor's warning. What a consuming force was love, that it had destroyed her old mad longing for the stage! Was it all love, or was it only the love of Anthony?

Then before her, in the train of her thoughts, the sentiments of her life were limned vividly, and she remembered the young highwayman whose picture she had seen. She saw the bold, Byronic countenance, with the shadow of evil upon the lips and the uncultured eyes. She recalled the blur by which the printer had obscured the chin, and she felt again the tremor with which she had awaited the sentence of the court. She thought of Edgardo, the romantic tenor, of his impassioned arias, and then of his fat and immobile face, of his red-cheeked German wife, to whom he was a faithful husband, and of his red-cheeked German children, to whom he was a devoted father. She laughed again as she remembered the tears with which she had bedewed her pillow, and the spasm of jealousy in which she had mentally attacked the prima donna. Last of all she thought of Jerome Ardly, as she had seen him upon the night of her arrival, sitting in indolent discussion of his dinner, the *Evening Post* spread out upon his knee. She experienced in memory the thrill which had seized her at his voice. She remembered how strong and masterful he had looked with the glow of heart disease, which she had thought the glow of health, upon his face. Then her thoughts

PHASES OF AN INFERIOR PLANET

returned to Anthony and settled to rest. To dwell upon him was as if she had laid her head upon his arm and felt his hand above her heart; as if she had anchored herself in deep waters, far beyond the breakers and shallows of life.

In the next room she knew that Anthony was at work, that he had probably, for the time being, forgotten her existence. The knowledge caused her a twinge of pain, and she went to the door, opened it, and looked in.

Algarcife glanced up absently.

"You don't wish anything, do you?" he inquired, and she saw that an irritable mood was upon him. "I can't be interrupted."

"It is nothing," answered Mariana as she closed the door, but she felt a sudden tightening of the heart, and, as she gathered up several loose sheets of music lying upon the floor, she thought, with a spasm of regretful pain, of the practising she had given up. "He does not know," she said, and a few tears fell upon the key-board.

That night, when she was dressing for Nevins's supper, she noticed that there was a faint flush in her cheeks and her hands were hot.

"We lead such a quiet life," she said, laughing, "that a very little thing excites me."

Algarcife, who was shaving, put down his razor and came towards her. He was in his shirt-sleeves, and she noticed that he looked paler and more haggard than usual.

"Look here, Mariana," he began, "don't talk too much to Nevins; I don't like it."

Mariana confronted him smilingly.

"You are positively the green-eyed monster himself," she said. "But why don't you say Ardly, and come nearer the truth? I was in love with him once, you know."

"Hush!" said Anthony, savagely; "you oughtn't to joke about such things; it isn't decent."

"Oh, it didn't go as far as that!" returned Mariana, with audacity.

"How dare you!" exclaimed Algarcife, and they flung themselves into each other's arms.

"How absurd you are!" said Mariana, looking up. "You haven't one little atom of common-sense—not one."

Then they finished dressing, lowered the lights, and went down-stairs.

Mr. Nevins greeted them effusively. He was standing in the centre of a small group composed of Miss Freighley, Mr. Sellars, and Mr. Paul, and the patch above his left eye, as well as his general unsteadiness, bore evidence to his need of the moral suasion to which Mr. Paul was giving utterance. In a corner of the room the "Andromeda" was revealed naked to her friends as well as to her enemies, and at the moment of Anthony's and Mariana's entrance Mr. Ardly was engaged in crowning her with a majestic wreath of willow.

He looked up from his task to bestow a morose greeting.

"We have invited you to weep with us," he remarked. "The gentle pronoun 'us,' which you may have observed, is due, not to my sympathetic nature, but to the fact that I have lost a wager upon the rejected one to Mr. Paul—"

"Who is also among the prophets," broke in Mr. Nevins, with a declamatory wave of his hand. "For behold, he prophesied, and his prophecy it came to pass! For he spake, saying, 'The "Andromeda," she shall be barren of honor, and lo! in one hour shall she be made desolate, and her creator shall put dust upon his head and rend his clothes, yet shall it avail not—'"

PHASES OF AN INFERIOR PLANET

"Shut up, Nevins!" roared Ardly, seating himself at the table beside Mariana. "As if everybody didn't know that Mr. Paul's prophecy was obliged to come to pass! Did you ever see a pessimist who wasn't infallible as a soothsayer? It beats a special revelation all hollow."

"Please don't be irreverent," remonstrated Mariana. "I am sure I am awfully sorry about the 'Andromeda,' and I believe that if Mr. Nevins had taken my advice and lightened those shadows—"

"Or mine, and lengthened that thigh," broke in Ardly.

"Or mine, and shortened the fingers," added Miss Freighley.

"Or mine, and never painted it," in a savage whisper from Algarcife.

Mr. Nevins silenced the quartet with promptness. "Hang it all!" he exclaimed, crossly; "between most of your suggestions for art's sake, and Mr. Paul's suggestions for decency's sake, there wouldn't be a blamed rag of her left."

"On the contrary," commented Mr. Paul, "an additional rag or two would be decidedly advantageous."

Mariana raised her finger, with an admonishing shake of the head.

"Out upon you for a Philistine!" she said. "I haven't heard such profanity since I showed my colored mammy a 'Venus de Milo,' and her criticism was, 'Lor', child! nakedness ain't no treat to me!'"

Mr. Nevins laughed uproariously, and filled Mariana's glass, while Algarcife glared from across the table.

"I should like to paste that motto in every studio in New York," returned Mr. Paul. "It was the healthful sentiment of a mind undepraved by civilization."

"What a first-rate censor you would make!" smiled Ardly, good-naturedly—"the fitting exponent of a people who see nastiness in a box of colors and evil in everything."

Mr. Paul bore the charge with gravity. "Yes, I keep my eyes well open," he responded, complacently.

Algarcife leaned across the table, and discussed woman's suffrage with Miss Ramsey. Mariana flushed and smiled, and glanced from Nevins to Ardly and back again.

Mr. Sellars, who had been engrossed by his salad, took up the cue.

"Oh, the world isn't to blame if we see it through a fog!" he said. "Excellent salad."

"Thanks," drawled Mr. Nevins, amicably. "I cut it up, and Ardly made the dressing. The cutting up is the part that tells."

"But why didn't you bring it to me?" asked Mariana. "I should have liked to help you." Then she raised her glass. "Health to 'Andromeda' and confusion to her enemies!"

There followed a wild clashing of glasses and a series of hoarse hurrahs from Mr. Nevins. After which Mariana was borne tumultuously to the piano, where she sang a little French song about love and fame.

Then Mr. Sellars sang an Irish ballad, and Nevins volunteered the statement that, after hearing Ardly, anybody who didn't mistake his nose for his mouth would be a relief.

"You don't listen," protested Ardly. "We have an excellent system," he explained. "We sometimes spend a musical evening, and when Nevins sings I look through the portfolio for my pieces, and when I sing he looks for his."

That night when Mariana went up to her room she was in exuberant spirits. In a whirl of energy she pirouetted before the mirror. Then she stopped suddenly, grew white, and swayed forward.

"I can't stand excitement," she said, and before

Anthony could reach her she fell a limp heap upon the floor. Algarcife dashed into the adjoining room and returned with a flask of brandy. Then he undressed her, wrapped her in a dressing-gown, and, drawing off her shoes and stockings, chafed her cold feet. Mariana was too exhausted to protest, and allowed herself to be lulled to sleep like a child.

For several weeks after this she was nervous and unstrung. She grew hollow-eyed, the shadows deepened, and her sunniness of temper gave place to an unaccustomed melancholy. She had learned that a new life was quickening within her, and she experienced a blind and passionate fear of inevitable agony. She feared herself, she feared suffering, and she feared the fate of the unborn life. One evening she threw herself into Anthony's arms. "It is the inevitableness," she said. "If I knew that it might not happen, I could bear it better. But nothing can prevent it, and I am afraid—afraid."

Algarcife grew white. "I am afraid for you," he answered.

"And the child? We shall be responsible for it. The thought maddens me. We are so poor, and it seems to me that it is wrong. I feel as if I had committed a sin—as if I were forcing something into the world to fight with poverty and discomforts. It may even hate us for bringing it. I almost hope it will die."

"We will make it a happy child."

"But doesn't it frighten you?"

Algarcife smiled. "Not as much as you do, you bodiless bit of eccentricity."

"All the same, I feel as if it were a sin," said Mariana. "Mill says—"

Anthony laughed aloud and caught her to him. "So you are turning my own weapons upon me," he said. "For the sake of domestic harmony, don't quote Mill to me, Mariana."

CHAPTER XV

IN the autumn the child was born. Mariana, dissolved in nervous hysteria in the beginning, rallied when the time drew on, and faced the final throes triumphantly. For several months beforehand she sat and waited with desperate resignation. Her existence, hedged in by the four walls of her room and broken only by the strolls she took with Algarcife after nightfall, exasperated her resentment against social enactments, and she protested bitterly.

"A woman is treated as if she were in disgrace," she said, "and forced to shun the light, when, in reality, she is sacrificing herself for the continuance of the race, and should be respected and allowed to go about in a right and natural manner. I believe all this indecency started with those old scriptural purifications, and I wish it hadn't."

But when the days passed, her lamentations gave place to serenity of speech, and her expression became almost matronly. Dramatically she was stifling her æsthetic aversion and adjusting herself to her part.

When it was over, and she lay still and etherealized among the pillows, she was conscious only of an infinite restfulness. It was as if the travail through which she had passed had purged her of all capacity for sensation, and the crying of the new-born child fell upon her ear like the breaking of faint and far-off waves of sound.

From Anthony's caress she turned with a gesture of annoyance, and, in a vague association of ideas, she wondered if a man who had climbed from hell to heaven would be gratified by a draught of milk-and-water. She seemed to stand aloof and far off upon some ice-crowned summit, where the air was too rarefied to support the growth of human passions. She felt that she had become a pure intelligence, and that the appeal of her flesh no longer retarded her ascent. The elemental values of life were obscured by the shadows of indifference. Love existed only as an intangible and forced illusion, passion as a disease of the blood. While her still and inert body lay freed from pain, her mind was singularly strong and clear. The limitations of a personality seemed no longer to encompass her. She imagined she saw as God saw, sustained by pulseless repose, seeing, not feeling, the swing of the universe. She wondered if the time would ever come when she would descend from this altitude and take up again the substance of self, when her senses would again enmesh her.

Some one came across the room and laid a bundle upon the bed beside her, but she did not look at it. Then her hand was lifted and a glass put to her lips, and the faint odor of chloroform which hung about her faded before the fresher odor of digitalis. The child cried at her side, and the first sensation she felt was one of irritation.

"Take it away," she said, fretfully, and fainted.

With her returning vigor, Mariana's normal nature reasserted itself. The first day that she was able to sit propped up among the pillows she had the child brought to her, and looked at it critically, half in curiosity, half in tenderness.

"Did you ever see one with quite such a screwed-up face?" she inquired, dubiously, of the nurse who hovered about.

"Plenty, ma'am ; most of 'em are like that—all puckers and wrinkles."

PHASES OF AN INFERIOR PLANET

"It might be a thousand years old," continued Mariana, "or a hickory-nut." Then she added: "I don't feel as if it belonged to me at all. I don't care for it in the least."

"That 'll come."

"I hope so," answered Mariana, "and I am sorry that it is a girl. It will have so much to bear. I wonder if I looked like that when I was a baby. I declare, it is positively green. What is the matter with it?"

"Just the shadow from the blind, ma'am."

The baby lay upon its back, with half-closed, indistinguishable eyes, slobbering over one red fist. It looked old and wizened, as if oppressed by the understanding that it had entered upon the most perilous of mundane transmigrations. It had cried only once, and that was upon its entrance into the predestined conditions. There was something almost uncanny in its imperturbability, suggesting, as it did, that it had been awed into silence by the warning finger of fate.

"Poor little thing," said Mariana. She leaned over it and stroked the smooth, round head, from which the soft hair was rubbing off, leaving it preternaturally bald. "What a mite!" She encircled it within the curve of her arm and lay looking up at the ceiling. "How strange it all is!" she thought. "It was only yesterday that I was a child myself—and now my first and last and only born is here alive." Then she frowned. It seemed inexplicable to her that women went on travailing and giving birth. That a woman who had once known the agony of maternity should consent to bear a second or third or fourth child struck her as ridiculous. She closed her eyes and laughed. Suddenly she felt a clammy clutch upon her finger and looked down. The baby's eyes were open, and it was staring straight ahead at the cloud of dust and sunshine that flooded the room. The red fist had left its mouth and fastened upon her hand.

Mariana smiled.

"Its eyes are blue!" she cried, "just like turquoises. Look, nurse! Oh, my dear, poor, ugly little baby!"

A rush of tenderness choked her words, and she lay silent and rapt, her hand responding to the weak grasp upon her finger. In some way she felt changed and tremulous. That invincible instinct of motherhood, which was a forced and abnormal product of her temperament, pulsed from her heart to her answering veins. She experienced in its fulness the sense of guardianship upon which rests the first intuitive recognition of the maternal responsibility. Her emotion welled forth to meet the appeal of the helplessness beside her, and she extended her fragile arm as if in the act of giving shelter. When Algarcife came in some hours later he found her lying asleep, her hand still upon the small, soft head of the child. In the noonday light the intense, opaline pallor of her face was startling.

In quick alarm he leaned over her, listening for the rise and fall of her breathing. It came softly, with a still insistence, like the ripple of a faint wind upon rose leaves. The heavy lashes resting upon her cheeks accentuated the entire absence of color, and the violet tones rising in the shadows of mouth and chin lent to her face the look of one in a trance or in death. It was as if the scarlet current in her blood had, by some necromancer's magic, been transfused from pale violets. Her gown was open at the throat, and he marked the same bloodlessness and hints of bluish shadows in her cold breast. He saw it also in the fragile curve of her uncovered arm and in the marble-like beauty of her hands.

"Mariana," he whispered.

She turned slowly towards him and unclosed her eyes.

"Give me something," she said; "brandy—a great deal."

He brought it to her and raised her on his arm as she drank it.

"I was dreaming," she said, fretfully. "I dreamed that I was falling—falling past the earth, past millions of worlds—past a great many apple orchards, and they were all in bloom. But, somehow, I never reached the bottom. There wasn't any bottom."

"You are stronger now?" he questioned, almost wistfully.

"Not a bit," returned Mariana, peevishly. "I am so — so — so weak." Then she laughed softly. "Do you know that brandy makes me think of my childhood, and a great goblet of mint-julep, with the crushed ice all frosted on the glass. My father was famous for his mint-juleps. I wish I had one now."

"Shall I make it for you?"

"Oh, it wouldn't be the same! I should never like one that didn't have the ice frosted on the glass." She grew weakly reminiscent. "Once, when I was a little child," she said, "I was dressed up in a nice white frock and red sash, and sent out on the sidewalk to play, and I grew tired and wandered off and got lost. I went a long way, and at last I came to the city almshouse. I was going up the steps when I looked into a bar-room across the way, and saw a gentleman with a very red face drinking a toddy. I went over and asked him if he were related to my father, and he said he supposed not, but he took me in behind the screen and sat me upon a table and offered me a taste of toddy, and I said, 'No, thank you. I have plenty of that at home.'"

Then she turned over and went to sleep, while Algarcife sat beside her and held her hand. His gaze ravished her with its fierce tenderness. His life and heart and brain seemed bound up and enshrined in the sleeping woman who lay in that death-like pallor, with the child at her side. He followed the sweep of the loosened and disordered hair that fell in a heavy braid across the pillow. He lingered, unsatisfied, upon the worn and emaciated face, in which there was none of the material beauty of flesh and blood. With an impassioned ardor he studied the defects of outline, the thin and irregular features, the hollows of the blue-veined temples, the firm and accentuated chin. Now there was none of that bewildering illumination of expression left, which in moments of intensity was like a fleeting search-light thrown across her face, forever changing in tone and color. She lay rapt and wan and pallid—a woman overthrown.

His glance fell upon the child in the hollow of her arm, and he bent to look at it. He was conscious of no feeling for it as his own, but of a general feeling of pity for it as a helpless animal. He supposed the other would come later, and in the meantime Mariana was sufficient.

Then, as he sat there, a harassed look crept into his eyes, and he frowned impatiently. Mariana's illness had entirely exhausted the small fund he had accumulated, and he knew that the next few years would bring a hand-to-hand, disastrous conflict with want. For himself he cared little, but for Mariana and the child he experienced a blind and bitter disgust at his own impotence. Working night and day, as he did, and preserving his hold upon the Bodley College, which was at best an uncertain reef, he knew that he could manage to wring from the world but a bare subsistence. He felt resentful of the fact that all his knowledge, all his years of study, all his scientific value would weigh for nothing in the struggle for bread against a moderate capacity for fulfilling the dictates of other men. This ruthless waste of energy exasperated him in its inevitable assault upon his theories of

PHASES OF AN INFERIOR PLANET

life. He looked at his hands—thin and virile hands, with knotted knuckles and square-cut finger-tips—the hands of a nervous, impracticable temperament. Of a sudden he felt himself as helpless to contend with existing conditions as the baby lying within the crook of Mariana's arm. For an instant his natural irascibility of temper seemed to have overborne the bounds of his reserve. That extreme sensitiveness to minor irritants became painful in its acuteness. He saw in it the effects of the nervous exhaustion which followed in the wake of uncongenial mental work combined with the stress of financial worries, and withdrew the curb of will. For the moment he regretted his old life—regretted his freedom and the solitude which had surrounded him even amid the tumult of the city. He reproached himself that he had not allowed Mariana to live her life as it pleased her, unhampered by the obligations he had permitted her to assume. Then he recalled her as she came to him that September night, the letter fluttering in her hand, and it seemed to him that he was not wholly responsible—that something mightier than himself had manipulated their destinies. To his dark and embittered mood there appeared a certain humor in the thought that they were puppets in the hands of the grim comedian Time. And then the scientific tenor of his mind, which contrasted saliently with his nervous temperament, reasserted itself, and he traced in vague outline the inviolable sequence of cause and effect, upon which his own and the world's revolutions hung. Again he fortified himself with a philosophic acceptance of the authoritative "must" of those unconquerable forces which we call fate.

With a returning gentleness he loosened Mariana's hand and went back to his work.

When Mariana grew strong enough to wear a blue wrapper and sit in a rocking-chair beside the window, she began working upon dainty garments for the baby.

With characteristic extravagance she embroidered a hundred roses upon a white carriage-robe which would probably not survive the first laundering. She made tiny bags for powdered orris-root, and scattered them among the tucked and ruffled cambric, and that faint suggestion of fresh violets was extended from herself to the child.

One day, Miss Ramsey, coming in on her way upstairs, found her tearing up a linen petticoat to make night-slips for the baby, whom she had called "Isolde."

Miss Ramsey remonstrated. She had been a faithful servitor during Mariana's convalescence, and she felt that she had earned the right to interpose. "My dear Mariana," she said, "what are you doing? Cotton at ten cents a yard would do equally well."

"But I couldn't make the little thing sleep in cotton," answered Mariana, "and I haven't any money, so I cut up a few of my things. It must be well cared for. I really couldn't have a child that wasn't nice and clean."

Miss Ramsey smiled.

"Do you think," she asked, "that it would know the difference between cotton and linen? Besides, I've always heard that cotton was more healthful."

Mariana threaded her needle and bent her head.

"It is in the blood," she returned. "My grandmother couldn't bear to be touched by anything but silk. She lived upon her plantations and owned a great many slaves, and she could afford it. Everything, from her night-caps to her chemises, was made of soft white silk. I have one of her chemises, and it is all hand-sewed, with a fall of real lace around the bosom. My mother inherited the taste, and she never wore cotton stockings, even when she couldn't afford meat but twice a week. I am just like her, only she was proud of it and I am ashamed of it."

"But you have overcome it," said Miss Ramsey.

PHASES OF AN INFERIOR PLANET

Mariana laughed.

"I can't. Anthony says luxury is bred in my bone, but then he doesn't even care for comforts. I believe he had just as soon eat turnip-salad on a plain deal table as sweetbreads on Irish damask."

"Life teaches us the pettiness of such things," said Miss Ramsey. "When one isn't sure one will get a dinner at all, one is not apt to worry about the possible serving. By-the-way, Mr. Nevins wants to paint the baby when it gets a little larger."

Mariana looked delighted.

"Of course he shall," she said; then she took the child from the nurse's arms and gave it into Miss Ramsey's. "Feel how light she is," she continued. "I know she isn't very pretty, but she is beautifully formed — nurse says so — and did you ever see one with quite so much expression?"

Miss Ramsey held it upon her knee, patting its flexible back with one timid hand. "I really believe it notices things," she said. "It is looking straight at you."

"Of course it does," Mariana answered. "Of course it knows its own blessed little mamma—doesn't it, Isolde?"

The child whimpered and squirmed upon Miss Ramsey's knee.

"Take it, nurse," said Mariana. "It doesn't look nice when it cries."

A week later Mr. Speares came, and was introduced to the baby as it lay in its crib. He leaned over it in the helpless inattention of a man who has a mortal terror of a human being during the first stages of its development.

"It looks very pleasant," he said, finally.

Mariana lifted the child and held it against her shoulder. Had Mr. Nevins seen her in her light-blue gown, with the soft look in her eyes, he would have seized the opportunity and used it to advantage.

PHASES OF AN INFERIOR PLANET

"Look at her eyes," she said. "Is she like Anthony used to be?"

Mr. Speares examined it critically. "I don't observe it," he replied; "but I don't suppose its features are quite formed as yet. It will be easier to trace a likeness later on."

Mariana laughed and smoothed the long dress with her frail, blue-veined hand. "The nurse says it is like me," she returned, good-humoredly. "I say it is like Anthony, and Anthony says it is like the original primate."

CHAPTER XVI

"I AM getting old," said Mariana. She was sitting before the mirror, and as she spoke she rose and leaned forward in closer inspection. "This line," she added, dolefully, rubbing her forehead, "is caused by the laundress, this by the departure of the nurse, and this by the curdling of the baby's milk."

Anthony crossed over and stood behind her. "I would give my right arm to smooth them away," he said.

Mariana fastened the collar of her breakfast sacque and looked back at him from the glass. She did not reply. Not that she would not have liked to say something affectionate, but that she felt the effort to be pleasant to be physically beyond her. Her life of the last few weeks had taught her that demonstrative expressions are an unnecessary waste of energy.

There was a rap at the door, and she opened it and took the milk-bottle from the dairy-man. After setting a cupful upon the little gas-stove, she raised the window and placed the remainder upon the fire-escape. "I am afraid," she remarked, "that I will have to try one of those innumerable infant foods. One can never be sure that the milk is quite fresh."

Anthony tied a cravat which was particularly worn, put on a coat which was particularly shiny across the shoulders, and went into the adjoining room to set the table. He boiled the coffee, took in the baker's rolls from a tray on the threshold, and put on a couple of eggs. Then he called Mariana.

She came, sat down at the table, and lifted the coffee-pot. She looked hollow-eyed and haggard, and her hand shook slightly. "I am so weak," she said, fretfully. "I can't get my strength. I just go dragging about."

Anthony looked at her in sudden pain. "If there were a speculating devil around who took stock in souls," he said, "I am sure we might offer him an investment. People are fools to think there is any happiness without money."

"Or any decency," added Mariana. Then the baby cried, and she took it up and brought it to the table, holding it upon her knee as she ate. Her appetite failed, and she pushed her plate away.

"The egg is so white," she said, pettishly, "I can't eat it." Then her voice choked. "I—I sometimes wish I were dead," she added, and went to pour the baby's milk into its bottle.

Mariana's strength did not return. As the months passed she grew more listless, her pallor deepened, and the shadows under her eyes darkened to a purplish cast. The incessant round of minor cares clouded her accustomed sunniness of temper, and her buoyant step gave place to a languid tread. It was as if the inexorable hand of poverty had crushed her beneath its weight.

Algarcife, coming in from his more systematic employment, would marvel vaguely at her unresponsiveness. His tenderness would recoil in pained surprise as he felt her indifference to his caress, and her long silences while he sat beside her. "Mariana," he would begin, "won't you talk to me?" and Mariana would rouse herself with a start. "But what is there to say?" she would ask, and sink back into stillness. It was, perhaps, impossible for him to understand that at such times she was but undergoing the inevitable reaction from long months of physical and mental suffering—

PHASES OF AN INFERIOR PLANET

that the energy which she had expended in supplying the drains upon her nature had left her incapable of further effort. He did not know that emotion with a woman is so largely regulated by nervous conditions, that complete exhaustion of body and mind is apt to repress, not the fund of affection, but its outward manifestations. In his passionate desire to shield Mariana, he had kept from her knowledge the financial stress into which her prolonged illness had plunged him. He had watched his growing indebtedness silently, and had reduced his personal expenses to a minimum while he sought to supply her with comforts. But from the immediate needs and anxieties of her own life he had not been able to guard her. The gnawing fears for the child, the nights when she awoke from needed sleep to lean over its crib and soothe it with lullabies, the weary hours in the day when she walked with aching head back and forth, he could not prevent, nor could he restore to her the health which she had lost. That the vein of iron which lay beneath the surface lightness of her nature had developed through responsibility, he saw clearly, but he also saw that she lived her life in apparent unrepining, not because of a rational acceptance of the order of things, but because illness and toil had for the time overthrown her æsthetic intuitions. To recall her as she had been during the first months of their marriage, white, fresh, and exquisite in attire, and then to look at her in a faded wrapper, her heavy hair disordered, her lips compressed, was to know that Mariana as she was to-day was not Mariana in a normal state. That it could not last, he knew. That with the first wave of returning vigor her longing for dramatic effects and the small requirements of existence would reawaken, he admitted unhesitatingly. She would grow vital again, she would demand with passionate desire the satisfaction of her senses—she would crave music, color, light, all the sensuous fulness of life. And where would she find it?

One day, as he came in to luncheon, he found her playing with the baby, a flash of brightness upon her face.

He looked at her and smiled.

"It is company for you, isn't it, dearest?"

Mariana's smile passed.

"I don't have time to think about that part," she returned. "I am always working. When I've got her all nice and fresh, and laid her on the bed, she begins to cry for her bottle. Then, while I am heating the milk, she cries to be walked, and, by the time the bottle is ready, she is so red in the face she can't drink it, and she spills it all over herself. Then I begin and go through it all again."

"What a little beast she is," said Algarcife, surveying the baby with parental displeasure. "What a pity she isn't a Japanese! Japanese babies never cry." Then he grew serious. "I sometimes wonder how you stand it," he added. "Here, give me the little devil!"

Mariana rescued the baby's rattle from its throat and laid it in the crib. It screamed, and she took it up again.

"There is a good deal in having to," she replied.

Algarcife walked to the window and stood looking down into the street. His brow was gloomy. Suddenly he faced her. "Are you sorry that you married me, Mariana?"

Mariana did not impulsively negative the question, as he had half expected. She even appeared to consider it. Then she slowly shook her head.

"I should have been more unhappy if I hadn't," she answered.

"It would have been a confounded sight better if you had never seen me."

PHASES OF AN INFERIOR PLANET

But Mariana put the child down and fell into his outstretched arms.

"No, no," she said; "but I am tired—so tired."

Anthony picked her up and laid her on the bed. Then he threw a shawl over her. "I am going to take an hour off and discipline your tyrant," he said. "Go to sleep." He lifted the baby and went towards the door. "You aren't such a black-hearted chap, after all, are you, Isolde?"

The baby cuddled against his shoulder, and he passed into the next room, closing the door after him.

Mariana lay upon the bed and thought. Her eyes were wide open, and she stared fixedly at the ceiling, watching the fluctuations of light that chased across its plastered surface. It was a relief to be absolutely alone, to be freed from the restraint which the presence of another thinking entity necessitated. She drew the shawl closer about her and pressed her cheek upon the pillow. The contact of the cotton was exciting to her fevered flesh. In the dim train of association it brought back to her an illness in her childhood, and she recalled her first sensations of headache and fatigue. They had come upon her as she was playing in an open meadow, and, before toiling to the house, she had stopped beside the reedy brook and knelt to drink, while the cool, fresh notes of the bobolinks sounded about her. She remembered it all now as she lay amid the noise of the city. The roar of the elevated road was silenced, and she heard the bobolinks again. She saw the emerald sweep of the wheat fields, undulating in golden lights and olive shadows. She saw the stagnant ice pond, with the overhanging branches of willows and the whir of the parti-colored insects. She smelt the pungent sweetness of the wild rose and the subtle odor of the trumpet-flower, glowing amid its luxuriant foliage like a heart of fire.

Then she raised her head and surveyed the room in

which she lay. She saw the garish daylight streaming in a flood of dust and sunshine through the narrow window. She saw the lack of grace that surrounded her, emphasized by a crowd of trivial details. She saw the tall, painted wardrobe with its bulging doors and the bandboxes upon the top, the cheap bureau with its gaping drawers, and the assortment of shoes half-hidden under it. She saw her work-basket, overflowing with stockings to be darned and small slips to be mended.

With a stifled sob she turned from it all, pressing her face against the pillow. The heritage of yearning for vivid beauty and sharp, sweet odors surged upon her. "I can't be poor!" she cried, passionately. "I can't be poor!"

But as the spring came, Mariana regained something of her old vigor, and it was in April of that year that Mr. Nevins painted the portrait which was exhibited some six months later, and with which began his rising fortunes. It represented her in the blue wrapper, holding the sleeping Isolde upon her knee, that soft and pensive stillness in her eyes. Within a couple of months after its appearance, Mr. Nevins had received orders for similar portraits from a dozen mothers, and had taken his position in the art world as the popular baby specialist.

Mariana had enjoyed the portrait and the sittings. They diverted her thoughts from the groove of the ordinary and gratified to a small extent her social instinct. When it was finished, and Mr. Nevins no longer came, she relapsed into listlessness. It was the friction of the outside world she needed. Hers was not the nature to develop through stagnation. In barren soil she wilted and grew colorless, while at the touch of sunshine she expanded and put forth her old radiance.

Anthony, watching her, would become oppressed at

times with the thought that this thin and fragile woman, dragging through her irksome round of duties, anæmic and hollow-eyed, might by the magic of wealth and ease mature into a passionate, lithe, and gracious creature, of which she was now the wraith—and yet which even now she suggested. For the furnace through which she had passed, in robbing her of freshness and bloom, had been unable to destroy her vague and ineffable charm.

"She is a woman ruined," he said, bitterly, and he said it with a dull aching in his heart. To him Mariana, emaciated and unresponsive, was still the Mariana to be possessed and held with burning desire. The small clashes of temper, the long silences, the apparent indifference, had been powerless to weaken the force of his love. It was still indomitable.

One night, upon going to his room, he found her in her night-gown kneeling on the hearth-rug. From her breathing he knew that she was asleep, and it was a moment before he aroused her. In the dim light she resembled a marble figure of prayer, her cheek resting upon her hand, the lashes fallen over the violet circles beneath her eyes.

Beside the bed, the baby lay in its little crib, the restless fists lying upon its breast, a fine moisture shining like dew upon the infantile face. He stood looking at it, a thrill shooting into his heart. For the first time he realized with acuteness a positive feeling for the child—realized that it was his as well as Mariana's, that it had a claim upon him other than the claim of Mariana, that he was not only the husband of a woman, but the father of a child.

Bending over the crib, he touched with one finger the crumpled rose-leaf hands, with the soft indentation around the wrist as if left by a tightly drawn cord.

He smiled slightly. Then he crossed over and kissed

PHASES OF AN INFERIOR PLANET

Mariana. She opened her eyes, yawned, stretched her arms above her head, and rose.

"I have really been asleep," she said.

"You were so tired," answered Algarcife, and his voice was limpid with tenderness. "It kills me that you should work so, Mariana."

Mariana rested against him for an instant. Then she went to the crib, and, raising the baby's head, smoothed its pillow. As she laid it down again she pressed the cover carefully over its arms; then, throwing herself into bed, she fell asleep with a sigh.

CHAPTER XVII

WITH the closing session, Algarcife lost his position at the Bodley College. He had published, for a mere pittance, a series of articles upon the origin of sex, and, as a result, he was requested to deliver his resignation to the principal of the institution. A man holding such views, it was argued, was an unsuitable instructor for sixty-one young women. So the instructorship was transferred to a divinity student who was casually looking into science, and Algarcife was dismissed.

Upon receiving his dismissal, he descended into the street and walked slowly homeward. His first sensation was one of anger—blind anger against the blindness of the universe. It seemed incredible that a premium should be set upon commonplaceness, that modern civilization should demand of a man that he shape his mind by an artificial process after the minds of semi-savage ancestors. Was thought to be forever prostrate beneath the feet of superstition? Was all boldness of inquiry, all mental advancement along other than given lines, to be branded in the nineteenth century by the *odium theologicum* as it had been branded in the time of Bruno?

Then there followed a wave of personal bitterness which in its turn was succeeded by a flood-tide of indifference.

Going home, he found Mariana in nervous despair. The baby, who had been unwell for several days, had been suddenly threatened with convulsions. Upon the doctor's arrival, he had predicted a dangerous teething, and had insisted upon Isolde leaving town before the beginning of hot weather.

"I am so miserable," said Mariana, moistening a towel to remove the traces of milk that she had upset upon her wrapper. "What can we do?" With a feverish gesture she brushed her heavy and disordered hair from her brow and shook her head helplessly. "Monday is the first of June," she added.

Anthony listened almost stolidly. When he spoke there was a dogged decision in his voice. "The money must be had," he answered. "God knows, I believe I'd steal it if I'd half a chance!"

"Then we'd all go to prison," remarked Mariana, ruefully, as she measured the coffee into the coffee-pot.

Algarcife smiled with a quick sense of humor. "At any rate, a livelihood would be insured," he returned. "Honest industry is the only thing that goes a-begging in this philanthropic century." Then, as Mariana returned to the baby, he drank his coffee in silence and went out. As a beginning, he secured an order to write hygienic articles for a Sunday newspaper. Then he called upon Father Speares and found that he was out of town, and even in his desperation was conscious of a sensation of relief at the thought that Father Speares was beyond appeal. But the sensation was reactionary, and, upon consulting the weather bulletin and finding that a change in temperature was expected, he wrote a letter, which he left at the clergyman's house.

"How is Isolde?" he asked of Mariana an hour later.

Mariana smiled and raised her finger warningly. "Much brighter to-day," she answered, "and sleeping sweetly."

Anthony bent over the crib, holding his breath as he watched the child. He noticed that she looked thinner; the blue veins showed in a delicate tracery upon the forehead, and the crease around the tiny wrists was less deep.

Mariana, serious and careworn, leaned upon the opposite side.

"What do you think?" she whispered.

"Only a little pale," he replied; "all children are when teething, I suppose."

They went into the next room and sat down, leaving the door ajar.

"The doctor was here again," began Mariana, playing with the folds of her gown. "June is the dangerous month—he says so."

Algarcife raised his eyes and looked at her.

"I wrote to Father Speares to-day," he said.

For a moment Mariana was silent, a flush rising to her brow. Then she rose and came over to his side, putting her arms about his neck.

"My poor love," she murmured. Anthony drew her down upon the sofa beside him.

"It was tough," he said, slowly, "but—how I hate to tell you, Mariana!—there is something else."

Mariana flinched sharply.

"Surely he has not refused?" she exclaimed.

"He is away, but the College has given me notice."

Mariana did not answer, but she grew white and her lips trembled. Then she flung her arms out upon the sofa and laid her head upon them. Her sobs came short and fast.

"Mariana!"

She lifted her head and choked back her tears, sitting cold and stiff beside him.

"If it were only ourselves," she said; "but the baby—what will become of the baby?"

There was a strained note of cheerfulness in Algarcife's voice.

"Don't cry," he said, laying his hand upon her shoulder. "I must get the money. Father Speares will lend it to me. We will pull through all right, never fear."

Mariana rested her head upon his arm and looked up at him.

"How ill you look!" she said. "My poor boy!"

Then the baby cried, and she went back to it. As Algarcife rose from the sofa, he was seized with a sudden swimming in his head, and, to steady himself, leaned against the mantel. The objects in the room seemed to whirl in a tangle before him, and his vision was obscured by a vaporous fog, while a tumultuous ringing sounded in his ears. But in a moment it passed, and he was himself again.

"Biliousness," he remarked, and started out in search of stray journalistic work. He found it easier to obtain than he had supposed, and, with his usual precision of method, calculated that by working fifteen hours a day he might, provided the supply of work continued, make up the amount which he would lose with the loss of the Bodley College.

After a week of such work, he became optimistic in mind and correspondingly depressed in body. "If my brains didn't get so sluggish," he said to Mariana, "the work would be nothing; but caffeine will remedy that." And he returned to the use of the drug, silencing Mariana's remonstrances with a laugh.

"My dear girl, if I didn't take something to keep me awake, I'd fall asleep in my chair at ten o'clock, and the subscribers to the evening issue would never learn the hygienic value of regular hours and a sufficient amount of recreation."

"But you will wreck yourself," urged Mariana.

"Nonsense. This caffeine is going to take Isolde and yourself to the country."

"And you?"

"I—oh, don't worry about me! I am all right."

And he would begin work with a pretence of alacrity, keeping to it until drowsiness warned him of physical exhaustion, when he would pause, stretch himself, measure his dose of caffeine, and, lifting his pen, dog away until past midnight.

It was an afternoon shortly after this that Mariana came to him flushed and expectant.

"Signor Morani sent for me," she explained. "I left Isolde with a daughter of the laundress and went. He has offered me an engagement in a comic opera."

Algarcife started and looked up.

"It seems that the manager heard me sing one day when I was at my lesson. He liked my dramatic power, Signor Morani says. At any rate, one of his troupe has given out, and he offers me the part."

"But, Mariana—"

Mariana did not look at him, but went rapidly on, as if waiving possible objections.

"We need the money. It might take Isolde away—and it is a chance. I am so young, you see—and—"

"Mariana!" cried Algarcife, sharply. There was a note in his voice which caused her to shrink away as if he had struck her. "Mariana," he put out his hand in protest, "you shall not do it. I will not let you. I could not bear it."

Mariana tapped her foot upon the floor impatiently. "I believe it is a child's part," she said.

"You shall not do it," he said, passionately.

Mariana turned her eyes upon him.

"But the money?"

"Oh, we will arrange it. I will leave The Gotham and take a room down-town, and you and Isolde shall go."

"Very well," said Mariana, sullenly, and left the room.

The next few days brought a wave of heat, and Algarcife made arrangements to send Mariana and the child away. He gave notice at The Gotham, and secured a room upon Fourth Street, and in spare moments assisted Mariana with the packing. Then there was some delay in the payment for the articles he had written, and Mariana's departure was postponed. "Get your things ready," said Algarcife, when the heat grew more intense and Isolde drooped. "The moment that the money arrives, you can start. It was due a week ago."

So Mariana continued her packing with nervous hands. She was divided between anxiety for Anthony and anxiety for the child, and she was profoundly depressed on her own account.

"If it wasn't for Isolde, I wouldn't go a step," she declared, standing before a trunk into which she was putting cans of baby's milk. "I feel as if I could weep gallons of tears—only I haven't time."

Miss Ramsey, who was rocking Isolde, smiled encouragingly. "The change will do you good," she responded, "and I am sure you need it. You are quite ghastly."

Mariana sighed and looked at herself in the glass. "I suppose so," she remarked, a little wistfully. "I might be thirty."

And she went on packing. "Of course we may not leave for weeks," she explained, "and yet I feel driven. The uncertainty is horrible."

But Algarcife, coming in at dusk, found her more cheerful. She kissed him with something of her old warmth, and talked almost animatedly while he ate his supper.

"I shall miss you so," she said, "and yet I do wish we could get off. Isolde has been very fretful all day, and is badly broken out with heat. She has just fallen asleep."

After supper Mariana went to bed, and Anthony returned to work. He had an article to do upon the moral effects of the bicycle, which was to be handed in

PHASES OF AN INFERIOR PLANET

in the morning, and this, with some additional work, would keep him writing far into the night. With a strong feeling of distaste he took up his pen, and his repugnance increased with every line. In a moment he rose, threw off his coat, and applied himself with dull determination. It was warm to oppression, and the noises of the city came distinctly through the open window. The elevated road grated upon him as if it were running along his nervous system, and he started at the shrill sounds which rose at intervals above the monotonous roar of the streets.

He had been writing some hours, and it was twelve o'clock when the door opened and Mariana came in. She was barefooted and in her night-gown. Her face shone gray in the lamplight, and there were heavy circles under her eyes. She spoke rapidly.

"The baby is ill," she said. "You must find a doctor. She can't breathe."

In an instant Algarcife had passed her and was bending over the crib. The child was lying upon its back, staring with a mute interrogation at vacancy. There was a purple tinge over its face, and its breath came shortly.

"In a moment," said Anthony, and, taking up his hat, went out.

Within half an hour he returned, followed by the doctor, a well-meaning young fellow, fresh from college and wholly in earnest.

He looked at the child, spoke soothingly to Mariana, wrote a prescription, which he himself had filled at the nearest druggist's, gave a multitude of directions, sat an hour, and departed with the assurance that he would return at daybreak.

"She looks easier now," said Anthony, with a nervous tremor in his voice. "It must have been the heat."

Mariana, with tragic eyes, was fanning the little,

flushed face, crooning a negro lullaby which she had treasured from her own childhood. The wavings of the palm-leaf fan cast a grotesque shadow that hovered like a gigantic hand above the baby's head, and, with the flitting of the shadow, the wistful little plantation melody went on. Ever since the birth of Isolde, Mariana had sung that song, and it fell upon Anthony's ears with an acute familiarity, like the breaking of happier associations against a consciousness of present pain.

> "Ba! ba! black sheep. Where yo' lef' yo' lamb?
> Way down yonder in de val-ley.
> De birds an' de butterflies a-peckin' out its eyes,
> An' de po' little thing cries: 'Mammy.'"

As Algarcife looked down upon the small and motionless body, he felt a sudden tightening of his heart. The infantile hands, with their waxen look of helplessness, caused him to draw his breath as he turned away, and to wonder how Mariana could sit there hour after hour, crooning the negro song and waving to and fro the palm-leaf fan.

And yet her figure in its pallid outline against the dim light was photographed upon his brain, and it was Mariana at that moment that he loved with the love more abundant, and that in the after-years he found it hardest to forget.

He saw her with the reddish glow from the night-lamp upon her profile, her drooping body in the shadow, the fixed look of pain upon her face softened by the look which fell upon the sick child. He saw the child lying mute and motionless, the wide eyes staring, the small hands folded, the soft rings of flaxen hair wet and dark with perspiration, and the moisture lying upon the fragile little chest which the gown left bare; and he saw it all shadowed and lightened by the wavings of Mariana's fan.

PHASES OF AN INFERIOR PLANET

Beyond this he saw the homely and disordered room, the articles dropped hastily as if in the start of sudden anxiety, the half-packed trunk with the piles of clothes upon the floor beside it, the tiny socks with the impress of the feet just learning to stand, the battered India-rubber doll with the crocheted frock of bright-hued worsteds, and at Mariana's hand the medicines which the doctor had left.

All these things were one with Mariana and himself. They were the heritage of their marriage, the memories which must always be inviolate—memories that could be shared by none other, could be undone by no stretch of time. In that atmosphere of common pain, which is more powerful both to sever and to unite than the less trenchant atmosphere of joy, he felt his heart leap into an invisible communion with the heart of Mariana. At that moment he was conscious of an additional sense-perception in the acuteness of his sympathy. He returned to his desk and took up his pen. The articles must be finished, and yet between himself and the unwritten page rose the vision of the still room, the pallid woman, and the sick child. The wavings of Mariana's fan seemed to obscure the light, and in his nervous tension he convinced himself that he heard the difficult breathing of a dying child—his child and Mariana's.

He swallowed an added dose of caffeine and looked at the page before him. The last written words stared him in the face and seemed so alien to his present train of thought as to have emanated from another person. He wondered what that other person's completion of the sentence would have been.

"Optimism is the first duty of the altruist." What in thunder had that to do with the effects of the bicycle? And what beastly rot it was. One might as well state that to be comfortable is the first duty of the damned.

"Optimism is the first duty of the altruist." He wrote on with the feeling that he was existing as an automaton, that while his hand was executing the result of some reflex action, his thinking entity was in the still room behind the closed door.

But with the absence of personality his senses were rendered doubly acute, and he seemed to see the rhythm of the atmospheric waves about him, while his ears were responsive to every sound in the night without—hearing them, not in a confused discord, but in distinct differentiation of note and key. Once his gaze encountered the grinning skull above the mantel, and, to his giddy senses, it seemed to wink with its hollow sockets. He found himself idly wondering if the skull had caught the trick of winking from its former accompaniment of flesh, and was forced to pull his thoughts together with a jerk. Then there came one of those sudden attacks of vertigo to which he had become subject, and he laid aside his pen and closed his eyes. "Too much caffeine," he muttered. But when it passed he went on again.

As the day broke he finished his articles, placed them in envelopes, stamped and addressed them, and rose to his feet. He blew out the lamp, and the faint odor of heated oil caused him a sensation of nausea. Crossing to the window, he raised the shade and stood inhaling the insipidity of atmosphere which is the city imitation of the freshness of a country morning. Without, a sombre, neutral-toned light flooded the almost deserted streets. In the highest heaven a star was still visible, and the vaguest herald of dawn flaunted itself beyond the chimney-pots.

As he lifted the shade he noticed that his hand trembled and that his head was unusually light. That massive sense of loneliness which the transition hour from darkness to day begets in the on-looker oppressed him with the force of an estrangement of hope. Such an

PHASES OF AN INFERIOR PLANET.

impression had been produced upon him a hundred times by the breaking of dawn after a sleepless night.

He turned away and opened the door softly.

The night-lamp was still burning, but the beginning of the morrow washed with a faint grayness the atmosphere. The objects he had dwelt upon the night before were magnified in size, and in an instant the unpacked trunks, the rubber doll, and the bottles of medicine obtruded themselves upon his vision.

Mariana was still sitting as he had left her, waving to and fro the palm-leaf fan. He wondered vaguely if she had sat thus since midnight. Then he laid his hand upon her shoulder.

" Mariana, you must lie down." And as he stooped nearer he saw that the child was dead.

CHAPTER XVIII

For the next six weeks Anthony was forced to listen to the distracted self-accusations of Mariana. When the little white coffin had been carried to Greenwood and laid in the over-grown plot beside the graves of Algarcife's parents, to be shadowed by the storied urns that redounded to the honor of a less impoverished generation, Mariana returned, and, throwing herself upon the floor, refused consolation.

"I want nothing," she said — "nothing, nothing. What could comfort me?"

At Anthony's protestations of love and grief she lifted dull and scornful eyes, wherein the triumph of motherhood showed supreme over all other emotions.

"How can you know?" she asked, between tearless sobs. "You did not nurse her, and hold her in your arms night and day; you did not bathe her while she laughed at the bubbles; you did not put on her little dresses and socks. Oh, my baby! my baby! I want my baby!"

Then she would rise and pace up and down in a sudden frenzy of despair, clinching her hands at her own impotence, tearing her wounds asunder with remorseless recollections. It was as if she found satisfaction in thus inflicting upon herself the added agony of recalling the minor details of her loss—in voicing the keenest passion of her grief.

Algarcife, writing in the adjoining room and wrung by a tortured brain, would listen to her unsteady tread as she walked ceaselessly back and forth, until the sound would madden him with its pauseless monotony —and then would come that half-choked cry for reckoning with fate, " Oh, my baby!"

To his more self-contained nature the violence of Mariana's grief was like the searing of the bleeding sores in his own heart. To avoid that cry of stricken motherhood he would have given the better portion of his life—to have been deaf to that impulsive expression of a pain he felt but could not utter he would have damned his soul.

And when, during the first few days, Mariana gathered together all the scattered little garments, and brooded over them with the passion of irremediableness, he would cry aloud out of his own bitterness,

"Put them away! If you love me, Mariana, hide them."

But Mariana, in the selfishness of loss, would glance at him with reproachful eyes, and turn to stroke the rubber doll in its bright-hued dress, and the half-worn socks with the impress of restless feet.

In the night she would start from a troubled sleep with corroding self-questionings. "Make a light," she would say, fretfully, sitting up and staring into the gloom. "Make a light. The darkness stifles me. I can't breathe."

Then, when the flame of the candle would flare up beside her, she would turn upon Anthony the blaze of her excited eyes, and play upon the sheet with feverish fingers. The loss of sleep which these spasms entailed upon Algarcife was an additional drain upon his wrecking system, and sometimes in sheer exhaustion he would plead for peace.

"Mariana, only sleep. Lie still, and I will fan you—or shall I give you bromide?"

But the hot questions would rush upon him and he would answer them as he had answered such questions for the past six weeks.

"Was it my fault? Could I have done anything? Was it taken away because I didn't want it to come?"

"Mariana!"

"Do you remember that I said I hoped it would die? You knew they were idle words, didn't you? You knew that I didn't mean it?"

"Of course, my dearest."

"But somebody told me once that for every idle word we would be held to account. Is this the account?"

"Hush."

For a moment she would lie silent, and then, rising again, the torrent would come.

"Perhaps if I had not left the window open that first warm day. And I did not send for the doctor at once. I thought it was only fretful. Perhaps—"

"You could have done nothing."

"I did not know. I was so ignorant. I should have studied. I should have asked questions."

Then she would turn towards him, laying her hot hand upon his arm.

"Tell me that it was not my fault. Tell me—tell me!"

"It was not. It was not."

"But I want her so. I want to feel her. I want to feel her soft and warm in my arms. Oh, my baby!"

And so the summer nights would wear away.

But as time went on a reactionary lethargy pervaded her. Her vitality being spent, she was left limp and devoid of energy. For hours she would lie motionless in the heated room, the afternoon sun, intensified by the reflected glare of pressed brick, streaming upon her, and she would appear to be indifferent to both heat and glare. From Algarcife she turned with an avoidance which was almost instinctive. When he touched her she shrank into silence, when he spoke she met his words with lethargic calm. It was as if the demands he made upon her emotional nature became irksome to her when that nature lay dormant.

"I suppose I love you," she said one day, in answer to his questions. "I think I do, but I don't feel it. I don't feel anything. I only want to forget."

"Not to forget me, Mariana?"

Mariana shook her head impatiently.

"Do you know," she continued, "that the thought of feeling makes me positively sick? I haven't any left, and I don't like it in other people. I am tired of it all."

"And of me?"

"I don't know. I think not, but I oughtn't to have married you."

"Mariana!"

"It would have been much better. You said so yourself once. But love is so strange. It makes people do such absurd things."

Algarcife did not reply. There was resentment in the look he bent upon her. He had not learned that even a woman in love is not a woman always in love —that love, in common with all other conditions, is subject to the forces which attract and repel, and that its equilibrium is maintained by a logical adjustment of opposites. To him Mariana's alienation betokened a fundamental failing in her nature, and with the thought he experienced a dull anger.

"I have felt so much in my life," continued Mariana, "that my capacity for sensations is lying fallow. The lack of ice in my tea and the heat in my room are of more importance than the excesses of affection. Were you ever that way?"

For a moment Algarcife did not reply; then he said, "You are very uncomfortable?"

"Yes."

"When we leave The Gotham it will be still worse. That room on Fourth Street is hellish."

"No doubt."

"How will you stand it?"

Mariana interlaced her fingers with impatient weariness and yawned.

"I don't know. As I stand it now, I suppose. We are poorer than ever, aren't we?"

"Poorer than ever."

She fingered her gown softly. "I suppose I shouldn't have bought this mourning," she said. "What a pity!"

When Anthony had gone she went out upon the fire-escape and looked down into the street below. The cry of a vender rolling his cart of over-ripe melons came up to her, and she followed his figure with curious intentness. From some indefinable cause, the vender suggested Signor Morani to her mind, and she recalled his warning, as she had recalled it in a different mood that rainy evening over a year ago. She realized now that Anthony's objection to her accepting Signor Morani's offer was still a canker within her heart. There remained, and there would always remain, the possibility that had she overruled his objection and entered into the engagement, Isolde might have been sent from the city, and might now be playing in some country meadow. The possibility, facing her as it did in all its ghastliness, produced a gnawing remorse, as invincible as a devil's thrust.

Upon this followed the conception that her marriage had doomed to failure not only her own life, but Anthony's; and there came a passionate regret for the part she had played in drawing him from his isolated abstraction into the turmoil of life and its passions. She blamed herself that she had gone to him that night, carrying the letter in her hand. She blamed herself that she had not resisted the appeal of her love, and, with a sudden pang, she realized all that the change had meant to him—the book that remained unwritten, the treadmill of uncongenial toil, the physical hardihood which was being slowly ground to dust. She realized this in its fulness, but with no determination of endeavor, no resolutions to battle more with fate. There was regret for the past, but there were no pledges for the future. The outcome was beyond her and beyond Anthony, this she knew. It was something to be left to the floodgates of hope that would be overborne by the press of time. In the lowered state of her vitality she felt almost indifferently her own inability to contest for larger measures of individual gain. She accepted destiny, and acquiesced, not in resignation, but in the apathy of one whom despair has drugged.

And above it all there rose the desire to escape, to be freed from it forever. "If he had never seen me!" she cried, passionately. "If he had never seen me!" Then colorless adumbrations of her own past blocked her horizon—and she confronted the ashes of her aspirations. She saw those illuminated dreams of her girlhood—the ideals which had crumbled at the corroding touch of care. She saw the demand for power which had been thwarted, the ambitions which had been undone, the cry for life more abundant which had been forced back upon her quivering lips. She saw herself walking day after day with empty arms along the way she had carried the child. She saw herself a drag upon her own existence and upon the existence of the man for whom she thought a love she had no power to feel. She saw the stretch of those monotonous and neutral-toned years, saw the sordid fight for bread, saw her sense of joy and beauty blunted, saw the masculine brain that was fitted to grasp universal laws decaying in the atmosphere of vulgar toil. And, woven and interwoven in her thoughts, was the knowledge that the affection to be invigorated by deprivations and to rise triumphant over poverty was not hers—that the love which in happier surroundings might have shown inviolable, which the great calamities of life might have left unassailed, had grown gray in the round of unsatisfied desires and victorious commonplaces. In the days to come, would not the jarring notes of their natures be exaggerated, the sympathetic ones suppressed? When old age came, as come it surely would, what would remain to them save a memory of discords and a present of unfulfilment? Was not death itself preferable to death in life?

Down on the sidewalk below a ragged urchin was turning somersaults in the shade. Suddenly, with a howl of delight, he pounced upon a half-rotten peach which a passer-by had thrown into the gutter. Mariana smiled faintly, left the fire-escape, and went indoors.

A week later they gave up The Gotham and moved into the room on Fourth Street. Algarcife made an attempt to sell the greater part of his library before moving, but the price offered was merely nominal, and at the last moment his heart misgave him. So he hired a dilapidated van, and the books were transported to the new lodgings and stacked along the south wall.

When the hour came for their departure, it was with a feeling of despair that he took Mariana's bag and descended for the last time the steps of The Gotham. A black finality seemed looming beyond their destination.

At the entrance, Mr. Nevins, with tears in his eyes, grasped Anthony's hand, and Miss Ramsey fell upon Mariana's neck.

Mariana laughed a little desperately.

"It reminds me of the time I saw a family move to the poor-house," she said; "only their friends weren't quite so affectionate."

"But you will come back," insisted Mr. Nevins. "Surely you will come back when things look a little brighter."

PHASES OF AN INFERIOR PLANET

"Which will be when the flames of spontaneous combustion illuminate this planet," remarked Ardly, cynically, but his eyes were sad as they rested upon Mariana.

"Or when a relation dies," said Mr. Nevins.

"How we shall miss you!" said Miss Ramsey.

Here Mr. Paul, who had sauntered up as if by chance, drew Algarcife aside.

"If you had only told me," he said, dryly. "I have a few thousands in bank, and I—"

Anthony caught his hand, but his voice was choked and he could only shake his head. Then Mariana said good-bye, and they left the house and ascended the steps to the platform of the elevated road.

As Mariana took her seat, she turned to the window and watched the little fire-escape upon the fourth story until The Gotham was lost to sight. Then she raised her veil and wiped a tear-drop from her eyelashes.

When the door was unlocked and she entered the new room, a fit of restlessness seized her. The barrenness of existence struck her with the force of a blow, and, with a swift return of impulse, she cried out in rebellion. The stale odor of cooking, which rose from the apartment below, the dustiness of the floor, the blackened ceiling, the hard and unyielding bed, gave her a convulsive shudder.

"I cannot bear it," she said. "I cannot bear it."

Algarcife left the window, where he had been standing, and came towards her. Between himself and Mariana a constraint had been growing, and he recalled suddenly the fact that their old warmth of intercourse had chilled into an indifferent reserve.

"It is bad," he said. "I am very sorry."

Mariana took off her hat and veil and laid them in one of the bureau drawers. The drawer creaked as she opened it, and the sound jarred upon Anthony's overwrought sensitiveness. He noticed suddenly that Mariana's expression had grown querulous, and that she had ceased to wear her hair becomingly.

"You can hardly think that I enjoy it," he added. "An existence composed of two-thirds nerves and one-third caffeine is hardly rose-color."

He looked gray and haggard, and the hand which he raised trembled slightly.

"Hardly," returned Mariana, shortly.

Both felt an instinctive desire to vent their wretchedness in words, and yet each felt an almost passionate pity for the other. The very pity emphasized the aggravation from which they suffered, and it was by a process of reflex action that, when goaded by thoughts of each other, they would strike out recklessly.

"No," repeated Mariana; "but it seems to be a case where two, instead of lessening the misery, increase the discomforts."

Immediately after supper she went to bed, tossing restlessly for hours because the mattress was uneven,. the sheets coarse, and the lamp, by which Anthony worked, shining in her face.

When she finally fell asleep, it was with a sob of revolt.

CHAPTER XIX

MARIANA's restlessness did not pass with the passing days. It developed until it gathered the force of a malady, and she lived in persistent movement, as if impelled by an invisible lash. As her aversion to their lodgings became more pronounced, her powers of endurance increased, and through the long, hot days she was rarely in-doors. Algarcife often wondered where she spent the morning and afternoon hours, but the constraint between them had strengthened, and he did not ask her. When breakfast was over, he would see her put on her hat, take her shabby black parasol, and go out into the street. At luncheon she would return, looking flushed and warm, as if from exercise in the summer sun; but when they had risen from the table she would move uneasily about, until, at last, she would turn in desperation and go out again. He seldom sought to detain her. Indeed, her absence was almost a relief, and he found it less difficult to work when the silence was unbroken by impetuous footsteps and the rustle of skirts.

Once he said: "It is too hot for you this afternoon."

And she answered: "No, I will go to a square."

He was silent, and she left in sudden haste.

That she walked miles in that fearful weather, driven on by sheer inability to rest, he realized pityingly. Occasionally he would go to the window as she descended the stairs, and the sight of the fragile, black-robed figure, making its rapid way through the fierce sunshine, would cause him a spasmodic contraction of pain. And yet the remembrance of her indifference would chill the words with which he greeted her return, and the knowledge that her heart had passed from him and was straining towards the outside world would veil his mental suffering in an assumption of pride. That Mariana's withered desires for the fulness of life had grown green again, he could but know. He had seen the agony inflicted upon her by every trivial detail of their lives—by the poorly cooked food, by the fly-specks upon the dishes, by the absence of a hundred superficial refinements. He had seen her flinch at the odors of stale vegetables, and set her teeth at the grating voices of the other lodgers. He had heard her moans in the night, rising from a wail for the small comforts of life to a wail for the child she had lost. He had marked every added line about her mouth, every bitter word that fell from her lips. And yet he had gone unswervingly on his way, and she had not known, but had thought him as pulseless to her presence as she to his.

"I am late," she said one day in September, coming in with more brightness than usual. "Have you had luncheon?"

"I waited for you," responded Anthony.

As she laid aside a roll of music she carried, he saw that it was the score of a light opera.

"You have been to Signor Morani's?" he asked.

"Yes, I have been taking lessons again."

Anthony glanced dubiously round.

"And you have no piano," he said. "You will miss it."

Mariana shook her head, and pushed away her tea with a gesture of disgust. "But I practise at Signor Morani's. He lets me use one of his rooms."

He noticed that she spoke cheerfully, and that a wave of her lost freshness had returned to her face. The instantaneous effect of her moods upon her appearance was an ever-recurring surprise to him. It was as if, by the play of her features, she unconsciously translated feeling into expression.

In a moment she spoke again.

"It is a part that I have been studying," she continued, "and I must commit the words to memory."

He picked it up. It was a serio-comic opera, entitled, "La Sorcière."

"Morani says that my voice has developed during the long rest. He was surprised when I sang."

"Was he?" asked Anthony, absently. He was wondering dully what would be the end of Mariana's ambitions—if there was any end for ambitions other than obliteration. Had fate anything to offer more durable than dust and ashes?

Mariana glanced about her and her face clouded. "It is that horrible cabbage again," she complained. "I believe those people down-stairs do nothing but fry cabbage. It makes me ill."

Anthony was recalled from his abstraction with a sense of annoyance.

"It seems to me," he retorted, sharply, "that, in our condition, to worry over a grievance of that order would be refreshing—when one's heels are hanging over the verge of starvation, it is a relief to be allowed to smell some one else's dinner."

"That depends upon what the dinner consists of," Mariana rejoined. "I may be reduced to living on dry bread, but I hope you will spare me the fried cabbage."

"You speak as if I had reduced you to this state for my own gratification." His temper was getting the better of him, and, with a snap, he set his teeth and was silent.

The mental distress, the stimulants he had used to spur a jaded brain into action, and his failing health had left him a prey to anger. An unexpected interruption, a jarring sound, a trivial mishap, were sufficient to cause him an outburst from which he often saved himself by flight.

Mariana replied tartly.

"I am sure I don't see how my objection to living upon fried cabbage could reflect upon you. I did not know you cared for it."

"You know I do not. But I don't see why you should make a fuss about a wholesome article of food."

"It is not wholesome. It is exceedingly indigestible."

"At any rate, it belongs to your neighbors. You aren't forced to eat it."

"No, but you implied that the time would come when I'd be glad to. I merely said it never would."

"Then let the cabbage be damned," said Algarcife.

"Gladly," responded Mariana, and they said no more.

Algarcife selected a manuscript from his desk and went out. He felt as if his nerves had quickened into ramifying wires through which a current of electricity was passing. He was not angry with Mariana. He was angry with no one, but he was racked by the agony of diseased sensibilities, and, though rationally he endeavored to be sympathetic in his bearing to his wife, his rational nature seemed ploughed by the press of his nerves, and for the first time in his life he found self-restraint beyond his grasp.

As he ascended the steps of the newspaper office where he was to leave the manuscript, he ran against a man whom he knew and who stared at him in astonishment.

"My God, Algarcife, you are a ghost! What have you been doing?"

"Wrestling with Providence," returned Algarcife, shortly. "Hardly a becoming job."

"Well, take my advice and leave off at the first round. If you don't mind the comparison, you bear

PHASES OF AN INFERIOR PLANET

a close resemblance to that Egyptian mummy in the museum."

"No doubt. But that Egyptian has a damned sight the best of it. He lived three thousand years ago."

And he passed on.

It was several nights after this that he started from a heavy sleep to find that Mariana had left his side. Rising upon his elbow, he glanced about the room, and saw her white-robed form revealed in nebulous indistinctness against the open window. Her head was resting upon her clasped hands and she was looking out into the night.

"Mariana," he said.

Her voice came with a muffled sound from the obscurity.

"Yes."

"What are you doing?"

The white figure stirred slightly.

"Thinking," she answered.

"Don't think. It is a confounded mistake. Go to sleep."

"I can't sleep. It is so hot."

"Lie down and I will fan you."

"No."

Algarcife turned over wearily, and for a time there was silence.

Suddenly Mariana spoke, her voice wavering a little.

"Anthony—are you asleep?"

"No."

Again she was silent, and again her voice wavered as it rose.

"I have been thinking about—about how poor we are. Will it ever be better?"

"I cannot say. Don't think of it?"

"But I must think of it. I am trying to find a way out of it. Is there any way?"

"None that I know of."

Mariana half rose and sat down again.

"There is one," she said, "and I—"

"What do you mean?" Algarcife demanded, starting up.

Her voice came slowly.

"I mean that I am—that it is better—that I am—going away."

For a moment the stillness seemed tangible in its oppressiveness. Mariana's head had fallen upon her hands, and as she stared at the electric light on the opposite corner she heard Anthony's heavy breathing. A moth circled about the ball of light, showing to her fixed gaze like some black spirit of evil hovering above a planet.

Algarcife's tones fell cold and constrained.

"To leave me, you mean?"

"It is the only way."

"Where will you go?"

Something that was not grief and yet akin to it choked Mariana as she answered.

"I have an offer. The one that—that I told you of. It is an excellent opening—so Morani says. The company goes abroad—next week. And I know the part."

"And you wish to go?" His voice hurt her with its absence of color.

She lifted her hands and let them fall in her lap. Her gaze left the electric light, where the moth was still revolving in its little orbit.

"It is not choice," she replied; "it is necessity. What else is there to do—except starve? Can we go on living like this day after day, you killing yourself with work, I a drag? It is better that I should go—better for us both."

He hesitated a moment as if in thought, and when he spoke it was with judicial calm.

PHASES OF AN INFERIOR PLANET

"And would you have gone—a year ago?"

She was silent so long that he would have repeated the question, but at his first word the answer came with a wave of self-abasement.

"I—I suppose not."

And that was all.

During the next few days the subject of Mariana's decision was not mentioned. Both felt a constraint in alluding to it, and yet both felt the inevitableness of the final hour. Anthony's pride had long since sealed his lips over the expressions of an unwished-for affection, and Mariana had grown chary of words.

But both went quietly along their daily lives, Anthony working at his desk while Mariana gathered together her shabby garments and made ready for the moment which by word and look they both ignored.

Then at last, when the night before her going came, Mariana spoke. They had just risen from the supper-table and the slipshod maid of work had carried off the unemptied tray. Mariana had eaten nothing. Her face was flushed, and she was moving excitedly about the room.

"I go to-morrow," she began, feverishly.

Algarcife looked up from a book through which he was searching for a date.

"So you have decided?" His lips twitched slightly and the veins upon his forehead contracted.

Mariana shook out a night-gown which she had taken from a drawer, folded it carefully, and laid it in the trunk.

"There is nothing else to do," she replied, mechanically, as if she were fencing with fate from a corner into which she had been driven.

Algarcife closed the book and rose to his feet. He pressed his hand upon his eyes to screen them from the glare of light. Then he moistened his lips before speaking.

"Do you realize what it means?" he asked.

Mariana lowered her head into the trunk and her voice sounded from among the clothes.

"There is nothing else to do," she repeated, as mechanically as before.

"I hope that it will be for your happiness," said Algarcife, and turned away. Then he went towards her in sudden determination.

"Is there anything that I can help you about?"

Mariana stood up and shook her head. "I think not," she answered. "Signor Moràni calls for me to-morrow at six."

Algarcife sat down, but the old sensation of dizziness came upon him and he closed his eyes.

"Have you a headache?" asked Mariana. "The tea was very bad. Shall I make you a cup?"

He shook his head and opened a book, but she crossed to his side and laid her hand upon his shoulder.

"It may not be for long," she said. "If I am successful—"

He flinched from her touch and shook her hand off almost fiercely. His eyes were bloodshot and his lips white.

"The room is so warm," he said, "it makes me dizzy. I'll go out."

And he went down-stairs.

Mariana stood where he had left her and looked down upon the pile of unpacked garments. A tear glistened upon her lashes, but it was a tear of impersonal sorrow and regret. For herself she was conscious only of a dulness of sensation, as if her usually vital emotions had been blunted and rendered ineffectual. In a mute way, as she stood there, she realized an almost tragic pity, but it was purely mental, and she recalled calmly the fact that a separation, which six months ago would have seared her soul with agony,

PHASES OF AN INFERIOR PLANET

she was now accepting with a feeling that was one of relief. The stress of accumulated griefs and anxieties had crushed her impressionable nature past all resemblance to its former responsiveness. Yet it is possible that even then, had Anthony returned to overpower her with his appeal, she would have wavered in her decision, but the wavering would have been the result of a fight between the instincts which were virile and the memory of the instincts which were buried with her buried passions, and it is doubtful where the victory would have rested. Her impulse for flight was as keen as the impulse which causes a bird to beat its breast against the bars that hold it. She wanted to flee from the sorrow she had known and all its associations; she wanted to flee from poverty and ugliness to beauty and bright colors. The artistic genius of her nature was calling, calling, and she thrilled into an answering echo.

But, for all that, a tear glistened upon her lashes as she looked down upon the unpacked clothes.

"O God! if you would only make a miracle!" she said—"if you only would!"

Her glance fell upon the desk where Anthony's work was lying. She saw the freshly written page upon which the ink was not dry. She lifted the pen in her fingers and felt the thick cork handle which was stained and indented by constant use. She sighed and turned slowly away.

The next afternoon, in hat and veil, with a small black satchel in her hand, she stood waiting for Signor Morani. Her trunk had already been carried down, and the carriage was turning the corner. She spoke lightly, dreading silence and dreading an accent of seriousness. "It is cooler," she said. "I hope a change is coming."

Then, as the carriage stopped beside the pavement below, she held out her hands. They shook slightly.

"Good-bye," she said.

"I hope you will be happy."

"And you. It will be easier for you."

"Good-bye."

She raised her veil, her eyes shining.

"Kiss me."

He kissed her, but his lips were cold, and there was no pressure upon hers.

She lowered her veil and went out. Algarcife stood at the window and heard her footsteps as she descended the stairs. He saw her leave the house, pause for an instant to greet Signor Morani, give the black bag into his hands, and enter the carriage. As she sat down, she leaned out for an instant and glanced up to where he stood. Then the carriage started, turned the corner, and was gone.

Still he did not leave the window. He stood motionless, his head bent, looking down into the heated streets, across which were stretching the slanting shadows from the west. A splash of scarlet, like the impress of a bloody hand, projected above the jagged line of tenement roofs, while a film of rising smoke obscured its lurid distinctness. He felt that complete sense of isolation, that loss of connection with the chain of humanity which follows a separation from one who has shared with us, night and day, the commonplaces of existence. The past and future seemed to have clashed together and shattered into the present.

In the street below men and women were going homeward from the day's work. He noticed that they wore, one and all, an aspect of despair, as if passing automatically along the endless round of a treadmill. He felt a vague wonder at the old, indomitable instinct of the preservation of self which seemed so alien to his mood. Situated as he was above it all, humanity assumed to his indifferent eyes a comic effect, and he found himself laughing cynically at the moving figures that blocked the sidewalk below. A physical disgust for the naked facts of life attacked him like nausea. The struggle for existence, the propagation of the species, the interminable circle of birth, marriage, and death, appeared to him in revolting bestiality. In his bodily and mental wreckage, all action became repellent and hideous, and the slanting sun-rays bespattering the human atoms in the street produced a giddiness in his brain. At that moment he was in the throes of a mental revolution, and his old philosophic sanity was ingulfed.

He remembered suddenly that he had eaten nothing all day, and, turning from the window, drank a cup of tea which had been left upon the table. The continual use of stimulants, in exciting his nervous system, had made sleep impossible, and he felt as if a furnace blazed behind his eyeballs. He sat down, staring blankly at the opposite wall. In the corner, upon a heap of books, the skull and cross-bones had been thrown, and they caught his glance and held it with a curious fascination. They seemed to typify his own life, those remnants of dry bones that had once supported flesh and blood. He regarded himself impersonally, as he might once have regarded a body for dissection. He saw that he had passed the zenith of his physical and mental power, and that from this day forth it would mean to him retrogression or stagnation. He saw that the press of untoward circumstances had forced his intellect from its natural orbit into a common rut from which there was no side-track of escape. He weighed his labors, his knowledge, his impassioned aims for truth, and, in the balance with a handful of dust, he found them wanting. He stirred the ashes heaped where once had been a vital passion, and he found a wasted skeleton and dry bones. He looked at his thin and pallid hand, and it seemed to him as incapable of work as the hand of one palsied.

PHASES OF AN INFERIOR PLANET

Before his tragic eyes, the years of his past stood marshalled, and, one and all, they bore the badge of failure.

As he rose from his chair in sudden desperation, the recurring faintness seized him and he steadied himself against the open drawer of the bureau. Looking into it as he turned away, he saw some loose articles which Mariana had forgotten—a bit of veiling, a single stocking, and a tiny, half-worn sock of pink worsted. He closed the drawer and turned hastily away.

Then he sat down beside his desk and bowed his head into his hands.

CHAPTER XX

FOR a week after Mariana's departure Algarcife worked on ploddingly. He closed his eyes to actualities and allowed his overwrought mind no cessation from labor. It was as if all molecular motion in his brain had been suspended save that relating to the subject in hand, and he wrote with mechanical readiness journalistic essays upon the "Advantages of a Vegetable Diet" and "The Muscular Development of the Body." Then, upon trying to rise one morning, he found that his shattered system was turning in revolt, and that no artificial spur could sting his exhausted brain into action.

Through the long, hot day he lay relaxed and nerveless, conscious of the glare of the sunshine, but dreading to draw the shades, conscious of the closeness of the atmosphere, and conscious of a beating, like the strokes of an anvil, in his temples. When his dinner was brought he drank a cup of tea and sat up. Then he reached for a phial of morphia pellets which he kept in his desk, and, dissolving one in water, swallowed it. For a moment the temptation to take the contents of the phial at a dose assailed him, but, more from inability to venture a decisive step than from any mental determination, he laid the bottle aside. Action of any kind appeared intolerably irksome, and he waived with disgust the solution of the simple problem of his life.

As he fell back upon the bed, his glance passed over the pillow beside him, and he pictured to himself the circle which Mariana's head had drawn upon the cotton. He remembered that she always slept lying upon her right side, her left knee bent, one hand under the pillow and one lying upon her breast, her profile shadowed by dreams. He remembered the nervous fear she felt of resting upon her heart, and that, having once turned upon her left side, she awoke with palpitating breaths and a smothered cry. He saw her calmer slumber, he felt her rhythmic breathing, and he recalled his sensation when one of her loosened braids had brushed his cheek. Again he saw her as she leaned over to soothe the child, and, raising it in her arms, hushed it upon her breast. He recalled it dully, as one recalls the incidents of long-past years over which the colorless mantle of time has been cast to deaden the flickering embers amid the ashes. In his mind there was no virility of passion nor intensity of bitterness—there was only an almighty melancholy. Life in its sufficiency of satisfied desires showed stale and unprofitable, and in its barrenness it was but a blank.

The sunshine, blazing through the open window, accelerated the throbbing in his temples. In the morbid acuteness of his senses, the cries of the vegetable venders in the street below harassed his ears. Along his whole body there ran a quivering flame of fever, and his thoughts spun like a revolving globe. The morphia had not stilled the beating in his head. It had produced a sensation of sickness, which seemed but the physical accompaniment of his mental syncope.

He surveyed the books stacked against the opposite wall and wondered vaguely at the energy with which he had attacked those volumes upon whose covers the dust was now lying like a veil. He tried to arouse a memory of the old intellectual exhilaration with which he had grappled with and vanquished an unexplored

PHASES OF AN INFERIOR PLANET

department of thought. He remembered that at such moments the printed lines before him had assumed an unusual degree of clearness, and that he had been reading *The Wealth of Nations* when a point in comparative morphology occurred to him. But the sensation itself he could not recover. The association of ideas was still unbroken, but the mental state was lost.

As he lay there, tossing restlessly upon the heated pillows, he reviewed unsympathetically his old pursuit of knowledge. What did it all mean? For what had he given his heritage of youth and manhood? For Truth. Granted, but what was Truth that he should follow it unswervingly until he passed from flesh and blood to a parcel of dry bones? How could he find it, and, finding, know it? That gray and ancient scepticism which had never appealed to him in health preyed now upon his wasting vitals. Since through the senses alone one could perceive, and the senses were but faulty instruments, what was perception worth? What were ideas but the figments produced by faculties which were at best deceptive? And in the infinite complexity of the self-sustaining reality, of what account were the abstractions of the finite intellect? In Truth itself, that all-pervading immateriality, were not the myriads of man's little truths ingulfed and lost? Were not true and false but symbols to express the differing relations of a great whole, as evolution and dissolution were symbols to express the recurring waves of a great force. As one man with his single hand barring the march of the seasons, was the man who by his single brain sought to hasten the advance of the Law which is Truth. And though he crumbled to dust, not one needful fact but would find its way into the moving world.

Stunned by despondency, he closed his eyes and groaned. In the absolute grasp of the futility of endeavor, he realized the lowest depths of human hopelessness. It was as if he had reached the ultimate nothing, the end to which his pathway led. Though he dashed his brains into the void, not one breath of the universal progress would swerve from its course.

And happiness? What was it but another symbol to signify the wistful yearning of the world? Where was it found? Not in love, which is the thirsting for a woman's spirit; not in passion, which is the burning for a woman's flesh. Did not bitterness follow upon the one, and upon the other satiety? His nature was deadened to the verge of obliviousness, and in his waning vitality the impulse of self-gratification had gone first. Physical desires shrank into decay, and mental ones passed with them. He wondered that he had ever sought in love other than calm reasonableness and a cooling presence. The emotion that sent scarlet thrills to his brain he analyzed with callousness. He remembered his mother as she lay upon the invalid's sofa, her Bible and a novel of Victor Hugo's upon the table beside her. He saw the placid beauty of her face, the slender, blue-veined hand which she laid upon his forehead when he went to her a wailing child; and it seemed to him that such a touch was the only touch of love with the power to console. Then he remembered Mariana's hand as she laid it upon her child and his, and he knew that the touch was the same. He thought of her as she sat beside the crib when the child lay dying. The passionate self-control about the mouth, the agony in her eyes, the tragic droop of her figure—these returned to soften him. He saw the black shadow of the palm-leaf fan, passing to and fro above the little bluish face, and he heard the labored breathing.

In sudden bitterness he opened his arms and cried aloud, "Mariana!"

Then the tears of weakness and despair stained the pillow where her head had lain.

PHASES OF AN INFERIOR PLANET

When the twilight fell he rose, dressed himself with an effort, and descended the stairs. His limbs trembled as he moved, and, upon reaching the open air, he staggered and leaned for support against the red brick wall. Then he straightened himself, and wandered aimlessly from street to street. As he passed among men and women he was aware of a strange aloofness, as if the links connecting him with his kind had snapped asunder; and he felt that he might have been the being of another planet to whom earthly passions and fulfilments bore no palpable relation, but were to be considered with cosmic composure. The thought jarred upon him insistently that these moving men and women, whom he brushed in passing, were each stirred by an entity akin to that which in himself lay drugged. He realized that the condition of a mind without the attraction of physical desires is as chaotic as the condition of a world suddenly freed from the attraction of gravitation.

He looked at his fellow human beings with forced intentness. It struck him with an almost hysterical shock that they were of ludicrous shapes, and he laughed. Then he glanced at a carriage rolling along the street, and it appeared absurd that one mortal should sit upon four wheels while a fellow-mortal of a nobler build should draw him. He laughed again. As he did so he had a quick perception that delirium was approaching, and he stopped to swallow another pellet. He reeled slightly, and a boot-black upon the corner surveyed him with interest.

"Air yer drunk, mister?"

He laughed aloud. "Damned drunk," he responded, and walked on. Some hours later he found himself in Whitehall Street, passing the lighted windows of the Eastern Hotel. Beneath the station of the elevated road he came upon a stand, with the words "Cider and Root-Beer" flaming in red letters on a white background, and for the first time he was conscious of a sensation of thirst. He stopped, felt in his pocket, and then, checking himself, passed onward to the Battery. A sharp wind struck him, blowing the damp hair from his forehead and chilling the drops of perspiration upon his face. With a feeling of relief he leaned against one of the stone pillars and bared his head to the incoming breeze. Far out the islands shone in iridescent lights, flashing through variations of green and amber, and over the water the ferryboats skimmed like gigantic insects studded with particolored eyes

Down below the water lay black and cold, the slow breakers flecked with light foam. He saw a glimmer as of phosphorescence rise suddenly upon the waves, and, looking deeper, he saw the eternal stillness. Between the throbs of fever the passion for death seized him in a paroxysm, and mentally he felt the quiet waters stir beneath him and the quietness close over him. His hand fastened upon the iron chain between the pillars; then he drew back.

He remembered the row of acids upon a shelf in his room, and his assurance returned. With a sensation of luxuriousness he recalled the labels with the large "Poison!" above, and the inscription "Hydrocyanic Acid" stared him in the eyes. When he had made that collection for experimental purposes how little had he foreseen the experiment in which it would play a part. He sat down upon a bench and stared idly at the stream of passers-by, some lovers who went arm-in-arm, some husbands and wives who walked apart, some fathers and mothers who carried sickly children —all bound and burdened with the flesh. The fretful wail of a baby came to him and mingled mechanically with his train of thought. It seemed the frail treble in the great symphony of human woe.

Beyond the men and women he saw the black water

PHASES OF AN INFERIOR PLANET

and the dancing lights, and, farther still, the misty islands.

Gradually the fever starts grew less, and calmness came back to him. With a wave of regret he looked back upon his lost serenity, and lamented that it had failed him. He knew that in his mental upheaval the opposing elements in his nature had waged a combat. The scientific tenor of his mind had for the past few weeks been crushed out by the virulence of his nerves. That physical force which he had so long held enthralled had at last asserted its supremacy, and for the time his mind was under the sway of bodily weakness.

This duality of being occurred to him in perplexing inconsistency. Had he been a pure mentality, his life would have been one steep and victorious ascent towards knowledge. Were he but a physical organism, carnality would have satisfied his cravings. Then the remembrance that stronger than will or flesh is necessity arose and smote him into silence.

Many of the people had gone, but he still sat plunged in thought. A hatless woman, fresh from a midnight carousal, with a bleeding cut upon her lip, took the seat beside him, and he found a forlorn comfort in the contact with alien wretchedness. When she laid her head upon the back of the bench and fell asleep, he listened to her drunken snores calmly and without aversion. He became aware that his old kinship to humanity was at the moment restored, that, losing it with the loss of desire, it was regained in despair. Suddenly the head of the woman beside him rolled forward and rested against his shoulder. She stirred slightly, heaved a sigh of satisfaction, and returned to her ribald dreams, while he, in numbness and pain, found consolation in this forced sacrifice of comfort.

He did not move, and through the long night the drunken woman slept with her head upon his shoulder.

For the next few days he dragged out a methodical

existence. In the mornings he would force himself to rise, swallow his food, and take his accustomed seat before his desk. With a failing hand he would take up his pen and endeavor to bend his fever-stricken brain to its task, but before a dozen lines were penned his strength would falter and the effort be abandoned. Then he would rise and finger the phials on the shelf, until, turning from them, he would say, "I will fight —fight until the last gasp—and then—"

At the beginning of the week, when his lodging bill was due, he carried by the armful a number of his books and pawned them for a nominal sum. Then he remembered his watch, and left that also. It was a heavy hunting-case of his father's, which he had always used from the nearness of the association, and as he laid it down something came into his throat. He opened the watch and took out the picture of his mother which was inside—a sketch in color, showing the lustrous Creole beauty in her first youth. Then he snapped the case and saw the initials "A. K. A." pass into the hands behind the counter.

Leaving the pawn-shop, he walked rapidly through the oppressive September sun until his limbs failed. Then turning with the throng of men that flowed into City Hall Square, he came to a sudden halt before the fountain. He was dazed and weakened, like a man who has recovered from a lapse into unconsciousness. The constant passing of the crowd bewildered him, and the sound of falling water in the fountain irritated him with the suggestion of thirst. He turned away and threw himself upon a bench beneath the shade of a tree. For an instant he closed his eyes, and when he opened them he found the scene before him to have intensified. The falling water sounded more distinctly, the sky was of a glaring blueness, and the dome of the *World* building glittered like a cloud of fire.

To his straining eyes the statue of Horace Greeley

seemed to grin at him from across the traffic in the street, and as he staggered to his feet he felt an impulse to shake his fist at it and say:

"Damn you! It is a chance that I want," but his muscles faltered, and he fell back.

Then his glance wandered to the man beside him, a filthy vagrant with the smell of grease about his clothes. Did not he want his chance as well? And a few feet away a boy with a scowl on his lips and a bruise above his eye—why not a chance for him? Then a gray haze obscured his vision and the noise of the street was dulled into a monotone.

The throbbing in his temples grew faster, and as he sat there he knew that he had fought to the final gasp and that the end had come. In his physical downfall there was room for neither alarm nor regret. He was lost to all vaguer impressions than the trembling of his frame, the icy starts through his limbs, the burning of his eyes, and the inevitable beating in his temples. Beyond these things he neither knew nor cared.

With the instinct for solitude, he started and rose to move onward, when he saw that the earth was undulating beneath his feet and that the atmosphere was filled with fog. The dome of the *World* building reeled suddenly and clashed into the flaming sky. He heard the sound of brazen-tongued bells ringing higher and higher above the falling of the water, above the tread of passing feet, and above the dull, insistent din of the traffic in the streets.

Then his name was called and he felt a hand upon his arm.

"Why, Anthony!"

He looked up bewildered, but straightened himself and stood erect, straining at the consciousness that was escaping him.

"How are you, Mr. Speares?" he asked. His voice was without inflection.

Father Speares spoke with impassioned pity. "What are you doing? You are ill—a ghost—"

Algarcife steadied himself against the bench and said nothing.

"What does it mean? Your wife—where is she?"

Anthony's voice came slowly and without emotion. "I am alone," he answered.

A quick moisture sprang to the older man's eyes. He held out his hand. "Come with me," he said, fervently. "I am alone also. Come to my house."

Algarcife left the bench and took a step from him.

"No," he replied. "I—I am all right."

Then he staggered and would have fallen but for the other's sustaining arm.

Phase Second

"And not even here do all agree—no, not any one with himself."
—MARCUS AURELIUS. (LONG.)

CHAPTER I

Two men passed the Church of the Immaculate Conception, wheeled suddenly round, and came back.

"By Jove, Driscoll, you have been outside of civilization!" said one, who was fair and florid, with a general suggestion of potential apoplexy polished by the oil of indulgence. "What! you haven't heard the Reverend Algarcife? Why, he rivals in popularity the Brockenhurst scandal, and his power is only equalled by that of—of Tammany."

John Driscoll laughed cynically.

"Let's have the scandal, by all means," he returned. "Spare me the puling priests."

"Bless my soul, man, don't tell me the Brockenhurst affair hasn't reached the Pacific slope! What a hell of a place! Well, Darbey was named corespondent, you know. You remember Darbey, the fellow who owned that dandy racer, La Bella, and lost her to Owens at cards? But the papers are full of it. Next thing you'll tell me you don't see the *Sun*."

"A fact. I don't read newspapers, I write them—or used to. But what about this priest? I knew an Algarcife in my green and ambitious youth, but he wasn't a priest; he was a pagan, and a deuced solemn one at that."

They stood upon the gray stone steps, and the belated worshippers trooped past them to vespers. A woman with a virginal calm face and a camellia in her hymnal brushed them lightly, leaving a trail of luxurious sweetness on the air; a portly vestryman, with inflated cheeks and short-sighted eyes, mounted the steps pantingly, his lean and flat-chested wife hanging upon his arm; a gray-browed gentlewoman, her eyes inscrutable with chastity unsurprised, held her black silk skirt primly as she ascended, carrying her prayer-book as if it were a bayonet.

In the street a carriage was standing, the driver yawning above his robes. From the quivering flanks of the horses a white steam rose like mist. Near the horses' hoofs a man born blind sat with a tray of matches upon his knee.

"Why, that's the jolliest part!" responded the first man, with a tolerant smile. "This one was an atheist once — or something of the sort, but the old man — Father Speares, I mean — got hold of him, and a conversion followed. And, by Jove, he has driven all the women into a religious mania! I believe he could found a new faith to-morrow if he'd be content with female apostles."

Driscoll shrugged his shoulders. "Religion might be called the feminine element of modern society," he observed. "It owes its persistence to the attraction of sex, and St. Paul was shrewd enough to foresee it. He knew when he forbade women to speak in public that he was insuring congregations of feminine posterity. Oh, it is sex — sex that moves the world!"

"And mars it."

"The same thing. Listen!"

As the heavy doors swung back, the voices of the choir swelled out into the faint sunshine, the notes of a high soprano skimming bird-like over the deeper voices of the males and the profundo of the organ.

When next Driscoll spoke it was with sudden interest. "I say, Ryder, if this is Algarcife, why on earth did he turn theologian? Any evidences of brain softening?"

"Hardly. It is a second Tractarian excitement,

with Algarcife for the leader. The High-Church party owes him canonization, as I said to the bishop yesterday. He is the best advertising medium of the century. After Father Speares died, he took things in hand, you know, and raised a thunder-cloud. The old man's mantle fell upon him, along with whatever worldly possessions he possessed. Then some physiologist named Clynn got him into a controversy, and it was like applying an electric-battery to the sluggish limbs of the Church."

Driscoll gave a low whistle.

"Well, as I'm alive!" he said. "What is it all for, anyway?"

"Let's go inside," said Ryder, drawing his collar about his throat. "Beastly chill for October. Wind's due east."

For an instant they paused in the vestibule; then Ryder laid his hand upon the door; it swung open, and they entered the church.

At first the change of light dazzled Driscoll, and he raised his hand to his eyes; then, lowering it, he leaned against a pillar and looked over the heads of the congregation. A mellow obscurity flooded the nave, lightening in opalescent values where the stained-glass windows cast faint glints of green and gold. The atmosphere was so highly charged with color that it seemed to possess the tangible qualities of fine gauze, drawn in transparent tissue from the vaulted ceiling to the gray dusk of the aisles. A single oblique ray of sunshine, filtering through a western pane, crept slowly along the walls to the first station of the cross, where it lay warm and still. Through the heavy luminousness the voices of the choir swelled in triumphant acclamation:

"And His mercy is on them that fear Him:
Throughout all generations.

PHASES OF AN INFERIOR PLANET

He hath showed strength with His arm:
He hath scattered the proud in the imagination of their hearts.
He hath put down the mighty from their seat."

Beyond the rood-screen in the chancel the candles on the altar flickered in yellow flames beneath a slight draught. Above them, from the window, a Christ in red and purple fainted beneath his crown of thorns. At the foot of the crucifix a heap of white chrysanthemums lay like snow.

Before the candles and the cross the priest stood in his heavy vestments, his face turned towards the altar, the sanctuary-lamp shining above his head. Around him incense rose in clouds of fragrant smoke, and through the vapor his dark head and white profile were drawn against the foot of the cross. The yellow candle-light, beside which the gas-light grew pallid, caught the embroideries on the hood of the cope, and they glistened like jewels.

He stood motionless when the censing was over, stray wreaths of mist encircling his head. Then, when the Magnificat was finished, he turned from the altar, the light rippling in the gold of his vestments. His glance fell for a moment upon his congregation, then upon the mute faces of his choristers seated and within the chancel.

Through the reading of the lesson he sat silently. There was no suggestion of emotion in his closed lips, and the composure in his eyes did not lessen when he rose and came forward, meeting the hush in the church. From the stillness of the altar his voice rose suddenly, sustaining the chant of the choir in a deep undertone of unwavering richness:

"I believe in God, the Father Almighty, Maker of heaven and earth. And in Jesus Christ, His only-begotten Son— ... I believe in the Holy Ghost, the Holy Catholic Church, the Communion of Saints—the forgiveness of sins, the Resurrection of the body—and the life everlasting—Amen."

PHASES OF AN INFERIOR PLANET

When the organ burst forth into the recessional hymn, Driscoll turned to his companion. "Come outside," he said. "I feel as if I had been drinking. And it was Algarcife—"

Half an hour later Father Algarcife left the church, and, crossing to Broadway, boarded a down-town car. At Twentieth Street he got out and turned eastward. He walked slowly, with long, almost mechanical strides. His head was bent and his shoulders stooped slightly, but there was a suggestion of latent vigor in his appearance, as if he carried a reserve fund of strength of which his brain had not yet taken account. Beneath the rich abundance of his hair his features struck one with peculiar force. They had the firm and compressed look which is the external mark of sterile emotions, and the traces of nervous wear on brow and lips showed like the scars of past experiences rather than the wounds of present ones. His complexion possessed that striking pallor resulting from long physical waste, a pallor warmed by tawny tones beneath the surface, deepening into bluish shadows about his closely shaven mouth and chin. In his long clerical coat he seemed to have gained in height, and the closest observer would perhaps have detected in his face only a physical illustration of the spiritual function he fulfilled. In another profession he would have suggested the possible priest — the priest unordained by circumstances. As it was, he presented the appearance of having been inserted in his ecclesiastical position from a mere æsthetic sense of fitness on the part of Destiny.

Although it was an afternoon in early October, the winds, blowing from the river along the cross-town blocks, had an edge of frost. Overhead the sky was paling into tones of dull lavender that shaded into purple where the west was warmed by stray vestiges of the afterglow. Through the dusk the street lights flickered here and there like swarming fire-flies. As he passed the Post-graduate Hospital at the corner of Second Avenue a man came down the steps and joined him.

"Good-afternoon, father," he said. "Your charge is coming on finely. Going in?"

His name was Salvers, and he was a rising young specialist in pulmonary troubles. He had met Father Algarcife in his work among the poor on the East Side.

"Not to-day," responded the other; "but I am glad to have good news of the little fellow."

He was known to have endowed one of the babies' cots and to feel great interest in its occupant.

Dr. Salvers returned his quiet gaze with one of sudden admiration. "What a wonder you are!" he said. "If there is a man in New York who does your amount of work, I don't know him. But take my advice and slacken speed. You will kill yourself."

Into Father Algarcife's eyes a gleam of humor shot. It went out as suddenly as it had come, and a tinge of sadness rose to the surface.

"Perhaps I am trying to," he answered, lightly.

"It looks like it. Here's Sunday, and you've come from a half-dozen services to run at the call of a beggar or so who might have had the politeness to wait till week-day. How is the Bowery Mission?"

"Very well," responded the other, showing an interest for the first time. "I have persuaded ten converts to take the pledge of a daily bath. It was tough work."

Salvers laughed. "I should say so. But, you know, that is what I like about your mission. It has the virtue of confusing cleanliness with godliness. Are you still delivering your sermons on hygiene?"

"Yes. You know we have been sending out nurses

to women in confinement in connection with those Sunday-night lectures on the care of children. The great question of the tenement-house is the one of the children it produces."

The light that fired his features had chased from them their habitual expression of lethargic calm.

"It is a great work," said the doctor, enthusiastically. "But, do you know, father, it seems to me odd that so intense a believer in the rules of the rubric should have been the first to put religion into practical use among the poor. It seems a direct contradiction to the assertion that the association of the love of beauty with the love of God destroys sympathy for poverty and disease."

A cloud passed over the other's face.

"My predecessor prepared the ground for me," he replied, constrainedly. "I hope to sow the seed for future usefulness."

"And capital seed it is. But, as I said, it saps the sower. You are running a race with Death. No man can work as you work and not pay the penalty. Get an extra assistant."

Father Algarcife shook his head.

"They cannot do my work," he answered. "That is for me. As for consequences—well, the race is worth them. If Death wins or I—who knows?"

His rich voice rang with an intonation that was almost reckless. Then his tone changed.

"I go a block or two farther," he said. "Good-day."

And he passed on, the old lethargy settling upon his face.

At some distance he stopped, and, entering a doorway, ascended the stairs to the second landing. A knock at the first door brought a blear-eyed child with straight wisps of hair and a chronic cold in the head. She looked at him with dull recognition.

"Is Mrs. Watson worse?" he asked, gently.

PHASES OF AN INFERIOR PLANET

A voice from the room beyond reached him in the shrill tones of one unreconciled to continual suffering.

"Is it the father?" it said. "Show him in. Ain't I been lying here and expecting him all day?" The voice was querulous and sharp. Father Algarcife entered the room and crossed to where the woman lay.

The bed was squalid, and the unclean odors of the disease consuming her flesh hung about the quilt and the furniture. The yellow and haggard face upon the pillow was half-obscured by a bandage across the left cheek.

As he looked down at her there was neither pity nor repulsion in his glance. It was merely negative in quality.

"Has the nurse been here to-day?" he asked, in the same gentle voice.

The woman nodded, rolling her bandaged head upon the pillow. "Ain't you going to sit down, now you've come?" she said.

He drew a chair to the bedside and sat down, laying his hand on the burning one that played nervously upon the quilt.

"Are you in pain?"

"Always—night and day."

He looked at her for a moment in silence; then he spoke soothingly. "You sent for me," he said. "I came as soon as the services were over."

She answered timidly, with a faint deprecation:

"I thought I was going. It came all faint-like, and then it went away."

A compassion more mental than emotional awoke in his glance.

"It was weakness," he answered. "You know this is the tenth time in the last fortnight that you have felt it. When it comes, do you take the medicine?"

She stirred pettishly.

PHASES OF AN INFERIOR PLANET

"I 'ain't no belief in drugs," she returned. "But I don't want to go alone, with nobody round but the child."

He held the withered hand in his as he rose. "Don't be afraid," he answered. "I will come if you want me. Has the milk been good? And do you remember to watch the unfolding of that bud on the geranium? It will soon blossom."

He descended the stairs and went out into the street. At Madison Avenue he took the car to Fortieth Street. Near the corner, on the west side, there was a large brown-stone house, with curtains showing like gossamer webs against the lighted interiors of the rooms. He mounted the steps, rang the bell, and entered through an archway of palms the carpeted hall.

"Say to Miss Vernish that it is Father Algarcife," he said, and passed into the drawing-room.

A woman, buried amid the pillows of a divan, rose as he entered and came towards him, her trailing skirts rustling over the velvet carpet. She was thin and gray-haired, with a faded beauty of face and a bitter mouth. She walked as if impatient of a slight lameness in her foot.

"So you got my message," she said. "I waited for you all day yesterday. I am ill—ill and chained to this couch. I have not been to church for eight weeks, and I have needed the confessional. See, my nerves are trying me. If you had only come sooner."

She threw herself upon the couch and he seated himself on a chair beside her. The heavily shaded lamplight fell over the richness of the room, over the Turkish rugs scattered upon the floor, over the hangings of old tapestries on the walls, and over the shining bric-à-brac reflected in long mirrors. As he leaned forward it fell upon his features and softened them to sudden beauty.

"I am sorry," he answered, "but I could not come

yesterday, and to-day a woman dying of cancer sent for me."

She crushed a pillow beneath her arm, smiling a little bitterly.

"Oh, it is your poor!" she said. "It is always your poor! We rich must learn to yield precedence—"

"It is not a question of wealth or of poverty," he returned. "It is one of suffering. Can I help you?"

The bitterness faded from her mouth. "You can let me believe in you," she said. "Don't you know that it is because you despise my money that I call for you? I might have sent for a hundred persons yesterday who would have outrun my messenger. But I could not bring you an instant sooner for all my wealth—no, not even for the sake of the church you love."

"How do you know?" he asked, gravely. "Call no man unpurchasable until he has been bargained for."

She looked at him passionately. "That is why I give to your church," she went on; "because to you my thousand counts no more than my laundress's dime."

"But it does," he corrected; "and the church is grateful."

"But you?"

"I am the instrument of the church."

"The pillar, you mean."

He shook his head. There was no feeling in voice or eyes—but there was no hardness.

"I love your church," she went on, more gently. "I love what you have made of it. I love religion because it produces men like you—

"Stop," he said, in a voice that flinched slightly.

She raised her head with a gesture that had a touch of defiance. "Why should I stop?" she asked. "Do you think God will mind if I give His servant his due? Yesterday religion was nothing to me; to-day it is everything, and it is you who have been its revelation. Why should I not tell you so?"

He was regarding her with intentness.

"And you are happier?" he asked.

"Happier! It is an odd word for a woman like me. I am fifty years old, I am alone, I am loveless. It has given me something to hope for, that is all."

"Yes?"

With a sudden yearning she stretched out her thin, white hands in appeal.

"Talk to me," she said. "Make me feel it. I am so alone."

When Father Algarcife descended the brown-stone steps an hour later, his face was drawn and his lips firmly closed. The electric light, shining upon his resolute features, gave them the look of marble.

He turned into Fifth Avenue and continued his way to Fifty-eighth Street. Before the door of the rectory, which was at the distance of a stone's-throw from the church, a carriage was drawn up to the sidewalk, and as he passed his name was called softly in a woman's voice:

"It is I—Mrs. Bruce Ryder. I have been waiting in the hope of seeing you."

He paused on the sidewalk and his hand closed over the one she gave him. She was a large, fair woman, with a superb head and shoulders, and slow, massive movements, such as the women of the old masters must have had.

"It is to force a promise that you will dine with me to-morrow," she said. "You have disappointed me so often—and I must talk with you." Her voice had a caressing inflection akin to the maternal.

He smiled into her expectant face.

"Yes," he said. "To-morrow—yes; I will do so. That is, if you won't wait for me if I am detained."

"That is kind," she responded. "I know you hate

PHASES OF AN INFERIOR PLANET

it. And I won't wait. I remember that you don't eat oysters."

The maternal suggestion in her manner had deepened. She laughed softly, pleased at the knowledge of his trivial tastes her words betrayed.

"But I won't keep you," she went on. "Thank you again—and good-bye."

The carriage rolled into the street, and he drew out a latch-key and let himself in at the rectory door, which opened on the sidewalk.

CHAPTER II

Mrs. Bruce Ryder unfolded her napkin and cast a swift glance over the heavy damask, sparkling with glass and silver.

"Yes; he is late," she said; "but he doesn't like to be waited for."

From the foot of the table Mr. Bruce Ryder smiled complacently, his eye upon his Blue Points.

"And his wish is law, even unto the third and fourth courses," he responded, pleasantly. "As far as Mrs. Ryder is concerned, the pulpit of the Church of the Immaculate Conception is a modern Mount Sinai."

"Bruce, how can you?" remonstrated his wife, upbraiding him across the pink shades of candles and a centre-piece of orchids. "And you are so ignorant. There is no pulpit in the church."

"The metaphor holds. Translate pulpit into altar-step—and you have the Mount Sinai."

"Minus Jehovah," commented Claude Nevins, who sat between a tall, slight girl, fresh from boarding-school, and a stout lady with an enormous necklace.

Ryder shook his head with easy pleasantry. He had been handsome once, and was still well groomed. His figure had thickened, but was not unshapely, and had not lost a certain athletic grace. His face was fair, with a complexion that showed a faint purplish flush beneath the skin, paling where his smooth flaxen hair was parted upon his forehead. On the crown of his head there was a round bald spot which had the effect of transparency. His deceptive frankness of manner was contradicted by an expression of secretiveness in his light-blue eyes.

He lifted the slice of lemon from his plate, squeezing it with his ruddy and well-formed fingers.

"Oh, but he's a divinity in his own right!" he retorted. "Apollo turned celibate, you know. He is the Lothario of religions—"

"Bruce!" said his wife again. A vexed light was shining in her eyes, giving a girlish look to her full and mature beauty. She wore a dress of black gauze, cut low from her splendid shoulders, above which her head, with its ash-blond hair, rose with a poise that was almost pagan in its perfection."

"For my part," said a little lady upon Mr. Ryder's right, "Mount Sinai or not, I quite feel that he speaks with God."

Her name was Dubley, and she was round and soft and white, suggesting the sugar-coated dinner-pills which rested as the pedestal of her social position, since her father, with a genius for turning opportunities to account, had coined into gold the indigestion of his fellows.

"Ah! You are a woman," returned Ryder, smilingly. "You might as well ask a needle to resist a magnet as a woman to resist a priest. I wonder what the attraction is?"

"Aberration of the religious instinct," volunteered Nevins, who had not lost his youthful look with his youthful ardor, and whom success had appeared to settle without surfeiting.

"On the contrary," interposed a short-sighted gentleman in eye-glasses, who regarded the oyster upon his fork as if he expected to recognize an old acquaintance, "the religious instinct is entirely apart from the vapid feminine sentimentalizing over men in long coats and white neckties. Indeed, I question if woman has developed the true religious instinct. I

PHASES OF AN INFERIOR PLANET

am collecting notes for a treatise upon the subject."

He stopped breathlessly, swallowed his oyster, and looked gloomily at the table-cloth. His name was Layton, and he was a club-man who had turned criminologist for a whim. Having convinced himself by generalizations from experience of the total depravity of the female sex, he had entered upon his researches in the hope of verifying his deductions.

The point he advanced being called in question by a vivacious and pretty woman who sat next him, there followed a short debate upon the subject. When it was ended, John Driscoll looked up languidly from Mrs. Ryder's left hand.

"My dear Layton," he advised, "return to the race-course if you value your sanity. The enigma of the Sphinx is merely the woman question in antiquity and stone." Then he turned to Mrs. Ryder. "How is the renowned father?" he inquired. "I was decoyed into buying a volume of his sermons this morning."

A smile shone upon him from her large, pale eyes. "Oh yes," she responded, her beauty quickening from its repose. "They are in answer to those articles in the *Scientific Weekly*. Are they not magnificent?"

Driscoll assented amiably.

"Yes," he admitted. "He has the happy faculty of convincing those who already agree with him."

She reproached him in impulsive championship, looking hurt and a little displeased. "Why, the bishop was saying to me yesterday that never before had the arguments against the vital truths of Christianity been so forcibly refuted."

"May I presume that the bishop already agreed with him?"

Mrs. Ryder's full red lips closed firmly. Then she appealed to a small, dark man who sat near her. "Mr.

Driscoll doesn't like Father Algarcife's sermons," she said. "I am disappointed."

"On the contrary," observed Driscoll, placidly, "I like them so well that I sent them to a missionary I am trying to convert—to atheism."

"But that is shocking," said Mrs. Dubley, in a low voice.

"Shocking," repeated Driscoll. "I should say so. Such an example of misdirected energy you never saw. Why, when I met that man in Japan he was actually hewing to pieces before the Lord one of the most adorable Kwannons I ever beheld. The treasures he had shattered in the name of religion were good ground for blasphemy. In the interest of art, I sought his conversion. At first I tried agnosticism, but that was not strong enough. He said that if he came to believe in an unknown god he should feel it his duty to smash all attempts to sculpture him. So I said: 'How about becoming an out-and-out infidel? Then you wouldn't care how many gods people made.' He admitted the possibility of such a state of mind, and I have been working on him ever since."

Mrs. Ryder looked slightly pained.

"If you only weren't so flippant," she said, gently. "I can't quite follow you."

Driscoll laughed softly.

"Flippant! My dear lady, thank your stars that I am. Flippant people don't go about knocking things to pieces for a principle. The religion of love is not nearly so much needed as the religion of letting alone."

"I am sure I shouldn't call Father Algarcife meddling," commented Mrs. Dubley, stiffly; "and I know that he opposes sending missionaries to Japan."

"As a priest he is perfection," broke in Mr. Layton, argumentatively.

"The chasuble does hang well on him," admitted Nevins in an aside.

PHASES OF AN INFERIOR PLANET

Mr. Layton ignored the interruption. "As a priest," he went on, "there is nothing left to be desired. But I consider science entirely outside his domain. Why, on those questions, the *Scientific Weekly* articles do not leave him a—a leg to stand on."

"The truth is that, mentally, he is quite inferior to the writer of those articles," remarked the short, dark gentleman in a brusque voice. "By the way, I have heard that they were said to be posthumous papers of Professor Huxley's. An error, of course."

At that moment the door was opened and Father Algarcife was announced. An instant later he came into the room. He entered slowly, and crossed to Mrs. Ryder's chair, where he made his excuses in a low voice. Then he greeted the rest of the table indifferently. He wore his clerical dress, and the hair upon his forehead was slightly ruffled from the removal of his hat. About the temples there were dashes of gray and a few white hairs showed in his heavy eyebrows, but eyes and mouth blended the firmness of maturity with an expression of boyish vigor. As he was about to seat himself at Mrs. Ryder's right, his eye fell upon Driscoll, and he paled and drew back. Then he spoke stiffly.

"So it is you, John?"

"I had quite lost sight of you," responded Driscoll.

There followed an awkward silence, which was abridged by Mrs. Ryder's pleasant voice.

"I like to watch the meeting of old friends," she said; "especially when I believed them strangers. Were you at college together?"

"Yes," answered Driscoll, his assurance returning. "At college—well, let me see—not far from twenty years ago. Bless me! I am a middle-aged man. What a discovery!"

"You were in the Senior class," observed Father

Algarcife, almost mechanically, and with little show of interest. "You were the pride of the faculty, I believe."

"I believe I was; and, like pride proverbial, I ended in a fall. Well, there have been many changes."

"A great many."

"And not the least surprising one is to find you in the fold. You were a lamb astray in my time. Indeed, I remember flattering myself in the fulness of my egoism that I had opened other channels for you. But a reaction came, I suppose."

"Yes," said Father Algarcife, slowly, "a reaction came."

"And my nourishing of the embryonic sceptic went for naught."

"Yes; it went for naught."

"Well, I am glad to see you, all the same."

"How serious you have become!" broke in Mrs. Ryder. "Don't let's call up old memories. I am sure Mr. Nevins will tell us that those college days weren't so solemn, after all."

Nevins, thus called upon, glanced up from his roast, with accustomed disregard of dangerous ground.

"I can't answer for Mr. Driscoll," he responded. "His fame preceded mine; but the first time I saw Father Algarcife he had just won a whiskey-punch at poker, and was celebrating."

Mrs. Ryder colored faintly in protest, and Driscoll cast an admonishing glance at Nevins, but Father Algarcife laughed good-naturedly, a humorous gleam in his eyes.

"So the sins of my youth are rising to confound me," he said. "Well, I make an honest confession. I was good at poker."

Nevins disregarded Driscoll's glance with unconcern.

"An honest confession may be good for the soul,"

he returned, "but it seldom redounds to the honor of the reputation."

"Happily, Father Algarcife is above suspicion," remarked Ryder, pleasantly. Then he changed the subject. "By the way, Mr. Nevins, I hear you have been displaying an unholy interest in the coming elections."

"Not a bit of it," protested Nevins, feelingly. "They might as well be electing the mayor of the moon for aught I care. But, you see, my friend Ardly has got himself on the Tammany ticket for alderman."

"What! You aren't working for Tammany?"

"Guess not. I am working for Ardly. The mayor is a mere incident."

"I wish he would remain one," announced the short, dark gentleman. "The Tammany tiger has gorged itself on the city government long enough."

"Oh, it has its uses," reasoned Driscoll. "Tammany Hall makes a first-rate incubator for prematurely developed politicians."

"And peoples the country with them," said Ryder. "I always look upon a politician as a decent citizen spoiled."

"And you really think they will elect Vaden?" asked the vivacious and pretty young woman at Layton's left. "It does seem a shame. Just after we have got clean streets and a respectable police force."

"But what does it matter?" argued Driscoll, reassuringly. "Turn about is fair play, and a party is merely a plaything for the people. In point of impartiality, I vote one ticket at one election and another at the next."

When Driscoll left, that evening, he joined Claude Nevins on the sidewalk, and they walked down the avenue together. For some blocks Nevins was silent, his face revealing rising perplexity. Then, as they paused to light cigars, he spoke:

"I believe Algarcife was a friend of yours at college?" he said.

Driscoll was holding his palm around the blue flame of the match. He drew in his breath slowly as he waited for a light.

"Yes," he responded, "for a time. But he has made his reputation since I knew him—and I have lost mine. By Jove, he is a power!"

"There is not a man of more influence in New York, and the odd part of it is that he does nothing to gain it—except work along his own way and not give a hang for opposition. I believe his indifference is a part of his attraction—for women especially."

"Ah, that reminds me," said Driscoll, holding his cigar between his fingers and slackening his pace. "I was under the impression that he married after leaving college."

Nevins's lips closed with sudden reserve. It was a moment before he replied.

"I believe I did hear something of the sort," he said.

When Mrs. Bruce Ryder turned back into the drawing-room, where Father Algarcife sat alone, the calm color faded from her face. "I am so glad," she said. "I have waited for this the whole evening."

She seated herself near him, resting one large, fair arm on the table beside her. With the closing of the door upon her guests she had thrown aside the social mask, and a passionate sadness had settled upon her face.

"I wanted to go to the sacristy on Friday," she went on, "but I could not. And I am so unhappy."

Brought face to face, as he often was, with the grinning skeleton that lies beneath the fleshly veil of many a woman's life, Father Algarcife had developed an almost intuitive conception of degrees in suffering. Above all, he had learned, as only a priest and a phy-

PHASES OF AN INFERIOR PLANET

sician can learn, the measures of sorrow that Fate may dole out to the victim who writhes behind a smile.

The sympathetic quality in his voice deepened.

"Have you gained no strength," he asked, "no indifference?"

"I cannot! I have tried, tried, tried so long, but just when I think I have steeled myself something touches the old spring, and it all comes back. On Thursday I saw a woman who was happy. It has tortured me ever since."

"Perhaps she thought you happy."

"No; she knew and she pitied me. We had been at school together. I was romantic then, and she laughed at me. The tears came into her eyes when she recalled it. She is not a wealthy woman. The man she married works very hard, but I envy her."

"Of what use?"

She leaned nearer, resting her chin upon her clasped hands. The diamonds on her fingers blazed in the lamplight. "You don't know what it means to me," she said. "I am not a clever woman. I was made to be a happy one. I believe myself a good one, and yet there are days when I feel myself to be no better than a lost woman—when I would do anything—for love."

"You fight such thoughts?"

"I try to, but they haunt me."

"And there is no happiness for you in your marriage? None that you can wring from disappointment?"

"It is too late. He loved me in the beginning, as he has loved a dozen women since—as he loves a woman of the town—for an hour."

A shiver of disgust crossed her face.

"I know." He was familiar with the story. He had heard it from her lips before. He had seen the whole tragic outcome of man's and woman's ignorance—the ignorance of passion and the ignorance of innocence. He had seen it pityingly, condemning neither the one

PHASES OF AN INFERIOR PLANET

nor the other, neither the man surfeited with lust nor the woman famished for love.

"I cannot help you," he said. "I can only say what I have said before, and said badly. There is no happiness in the things you cry for. So long as self is self, gratification will fail it. When it has waded through one mirage it looks for another. Take your life as you find it, face it like a woman, make the best of what remains of it. The world is full of opportunities for usefulness—and you have your faith and your child."

She started. "Yes," she said. "The child is everything." Then she rose. "I want to show him to you," she said, "while he sleeps."

Father Algarcife made a sudden negative gesture; then, as she left the room, he followed her.

As they passed the billiard-room on their way upstairs there was a sound of knocking balls, and Ryder's voice was heard in a laugh.

"This way," said Mrs. Ryder. They mounted the carpeted stairs and stopped before a door to the right. She turned the handle softly and entered. A night-lamp was burning in one corner, and on the hearth-rug a tub was prepared for the morning bath. On a chair, a little to one side, lay a pile of filmy, lace-trimmed linen.

In a small brass bedstead in the centre of the room a child of two or three years was sleeping, its soft hair falling upon the embroidered pillow. A warm, rosy flush was on its face, and the dimpled hands lay palms upward on the blanket.

Like a mounting flame the passion of motherhood illuminated the woman's face. She leaned over and kissed one of the pink hands.

"How quietly he sleeps!" she said.

The child stirred, opened its eyes, and smiled, stretching out its arms.

PHASES OF AN INFERIOR PLANET

The mother drew back softly. Then she knelt down, and, raising the child with one hand, smoothed the pillow under its head. As she rose she pressed the blanket carefully over the tiny arms lying outside the cover.

When she turned to Father Algarcife she saw that he had grown suddenly haggard.

CHAPTER III

FATHER ALGARCIFE withdrew the latch-key from the outer door and stopped in the hall to remove his hat and coat. He had just returned from a meeting of the wardens, called to discuss the finances of the church.

"Agnes!" he said.

A woman came from the dining-room at the end of the hall, and, taking his coat from his hands, hung it upon the rack. She was stout and middle-aged, with a face like a full-blown dahlia beneath her cap of frilled muslin. She had been house-keeper and upper servant to Father Speares, and had descended to his successor as a matter of course.

"Have there been any callers, Agnes?"

"Only two, sir. One of the sisters, who left word that she would return in the evening, and that same woman from Elizabeth Street, who wanted you to take charge of her husband who was drunk. I told her a policeman could manage him better, and she said she hadn't thought of that. She went to find one."

"Thank you, Agnes," replied Father Algarcife, with a laugh. "A policeman could manage him much better."

"So any fool might have known, sir; but those poor creatures seem kind of crazy. I believe they get you twisted with the Creator. They'll be asking you to bring back the dead next. Will you have dinner at eight?"

"Yes, at eight."

PHASES OF AN INFERIOR PLANET

He passed into his study, closing the door after him. A shaggy little cur, lying on the hearth-rug, jumped up at his entrance, and came towards him, his tail cutting semicircles in the air.

"How are you, Comrade?" said the man, cheerfully. He bent over, running his fingers along the rough, yellow body of the dog. It was a vagrant that he had rescued from beneath a cable-car and brought home in his arms. His care had met its reward in gratitude, and the bond between them was perhaps the single emotion remaining in either life.

The room was small, and furnished in a manner that suggested luxurious comfort. It had been left thus by Father Speares, and the younger man, moved by a sense of loyalty, had guarded it unchanged. Over the high mantel one of Father Speares's ancestors looked down from a massive frame, and upon the top of the book-shelves lining the four walls there was the marble bust of another. Heavy curtains of russet-brown fell from the windows, and a portière of the same material hung across the door. In the centre of the room, where the light fell full upon it while it was yet day, there was a quaint old desk of hand-carved mahogany. On the lid, covered by a white blotter, lay a number of unanswered letters, containing appeals for charities, the manuscript of an unfinished sermon, and the small black-velvet case in which the sermon would be placed upon its completion. In the open grate a fire burned brightly, and a table bearing an unlighted lamp was drawn into the glow.

The dog, trembling with welcome, curled upon the rug, and Father Algarcife, throwing himself into the easy-chair beside the table, stretched his hands towards the blaze. They were thin and virile hands, and the firelight, shining behind them, threw into relief the lines crossing and recrossing the palms, giving to them the look of hieroglyphics on old parch-

215

ment. His face, across which the flickering shadows chased, assumed the effect of a drawing in strong black and white.

Before the intense heat of the grate, a languor crept over him, a sensation of comfort inspired by the firelight, the warmth, and the welcome of the fellow-mortal at his feet. Half yawning, his head fell back against the cushion of the chair and his thoughts stirred drowsily.

He thought of the ruddy reflection dancing on the carving of the desk, of the text of the unfinished sermon, of a pamphlet on the table beside the unlighted lamp, and of a letter to his lawyer that remained unwritten. Then he thought of Mrs. Ryder in her full and unsatisfied beauty, and then of a woman in his congregation who had given a thurible of gold to the church, and then of one of the members of the sisterhood. He wondered if it were Sister Agatha who had called, and if she wished to consult him about the home of which she had charge. He feared that the accommodations were too crowded, and questioned if the state of the finances justified moving into larger quarters. In the same connection, he remembered that he had intended mentioning to the sacristan the insufficient heating of the church during services. From this he passed suddenly to the memory of the face of the woman who had died of cancer that morning. He recalled the dirt and poverty and the whimpering of the blear-eyed child with the chronic cold.

"What a life!" he said, and he glanced about the luxurious room calmly, half disdainfully. His eyes fell on the arm of the sofa which was slightly worn as if from friction, and he remembered that he never used it, and that it was the one on which Father Speares had been accustomed to take his daily nap. He shivered faintly, brushed by that near association with the dead which trivialities invoke.

PHASES OF AN INFERIOR PLANET

It seemed but yesterday, that morning eight years ago, when he had fainted in the crowded square. He could close his eyes now and review each detail with the dispassionateness of indifference. He could see the flaming blue of the sky, the statue of Horace Greeley across the way, and the confused blur of the bulletin-board before the *World* building. He could hear the incessant falling of the water in the fountain, and he could feel the old sensation of nausea that had blotted out the consciousness of place. He remembered the long convalescence from the fever that had followed—the trembling of his limbs when he moved and the weakness of his voice when he spoke—the utter vanquishment of his power of volition. He reviewed, almost methodically, that collapse into black despair and the mental and emotional stagnation that had covered all the crawling years. The fever, mounting to his brain, had left it seared of energy and had sapped the passion in his blood. It had consumed his old loves, with his old ambitions, and had left his emotions as sterile as his mind.

He remembered the struggle that had come, his resistance and his defeat, and he saw the joy in the older man's eyes when he had laid before him the remainder of his life — when he had said, "I no longer care. Make of me what you will."

The other had answered, "I will not take the sacrifice without sincerity or without the will of God."

"It is no sacrifice," he had replied. "It is a debt. If I can believe, I will."

And he had felt the words as a man half drugged by ether feels the first incision of the knife.

But he had not believed. Sitting now in his clerical dress, before the fire kindled by his ordination, he knew that it was his weakness, not his will, that had bent. Whether the motive was gratitude or despair he did not question. There had been a debt, and he had met it by the bond of flesh and blood. Yes, he had repaid it in full.

From the moment when he had been called into Father Speares's place he had striven untiringly to do honor to the dead. He had spared neither himself nor others. He had toiled night and day, as a man toils who loves a cause—or is mad. Though his heart was not in the work, his will was, and he was goaded to it by the knowledge that his intellect revolted. Because the life was loathsome to him he left not one detail unperformed. He had given a bond, and he fulfilled it, though his bond was a lie.

He lifted his head impatiently and looked before him. Then he smiled, half bitterly, in the flickering firelight. Across the drawn curtains at the window he could see the almost indistinguishable forms of people passing in the street. He felt suddenly that his whole existence was filled with such vague outlines, surrounded by gray dusk. The only thing that was real was the lie.

That was with him always, at every instant of the day. It lay in his coat, in his clothes, in his very necktie. It filled the book-shelves in the room and covered the closely written sheets upon his desk. It was in the cope and in the chasuble, in the paten and in the chalice, in the censer and in the Creed. Yes; he had sworn his faith to a myth, and had said "I believe—" to a fable.

The words of the Creed that he had chanted the day before rang suddenly in his ears:

"And in our Lord Jesus Christ, the only-begotten Son of God, begotten of His Father before all worlds, God of God, Light of Light, very God of very God—"

What if he had lived a lie decently, what if he had fought a good fight for a cause he opposed, what if he, in the name of that cause, had closed his eyes and his nostrils to the things that repel and had labored to cleanse the sewer at his door, was it any the less a lie?

"Father, dinner is served."

He raised himself and stood upon the hearth-rug. The dog awoke and circled about his feet. Then together they passed into the dining-room.

For a moment he stood before his chair, silently making the sign of the cross. Then he sat down and unfolded his napkin. It was a simple meal, and he ate it in silence. When the soup was finished and the meat brought on, he cut up a portion for the dog at his side, placing the plate upon the floor. Then he pushed his own plate away, and sat looking into his glass of claret as it sparkled in the light.

The bell rang, and the maid went to answer it. In a moment she came back.

"It is the sister," she said. "She is in your study."

"Very well," Father Algarcife responded.

He laid his napkin upon the table and passed out.

CHAPTER IV

JEROME ARDLY turned into one of the entrances leading to the Holbein studios, ascended the long flight of stairs, and paused before a door bearing a brass plate, on which was engraved

CLAUDE NEVINS

As the knocker fell beneath his touch the door swung open, revealing Nevins in a velvet smoking-jacket rather the worse for wear, his flaxen hair standing on end above his wrinkled brow.

"Hello!" was his greeting, taking the end of a camel's-hair brush from his mouth. "So you've turned up at last. I've been doing your dirty work all the morning."

Ardly entered with a swing, closing the door after him. He had grown handsomer in the last eight years, though the world had gone less well with him than with Nevins. His large brown eyes still held their old recklessness, and there had come into his voice a constant ring of bravado.

"Plenty for us both," he responded, blandly, throwing his hat on the divan and himself into a chair. "My hand hath found its share to do, and I have done it with all my might. I've been interviewing a lot of voters in the old Ninth Ward. If Tammany doesn't make a clean sweep of that district I'm a—a fool."

"I wish you were not. Then you wouldn't be polling round these confounded politicians. It seems to

PHASES OF AN INFERIOR PLANET

me your own district is more than you can manage, but somehow you seem to be attending to everybody else's. What under heaven does any self-respecting man want to be alderman for, anyway? I wouldn't look at it."

"My dear fellow, view it as a stepping-stone to greater glory."

"A deuced long step downward."

Ardly laughed, then, stretching himself, looked idly at the opening in the ceiling through which the daylight fell. It framed a square of blue sky across which a stray cloud drifted.

The room was large and oblong, and the atmosphere was heavy with the odors of oil and turpentine. The furniture consisted of a number of covered easels, several coarse hangings ornamented in bizarre designs, and a divan surmounted by an Oriental canopy. Over the door there was a row of death-masks in plaster, relieved against a strip of ebony, and from a pedestal in one corner a bust of Antinous smiled the world-worn smile of all the ages.

"Temper seems soured," remarked Ardly, raising himself and turning to survey Nevins. "What's up?"

Nevins smiled mysteriously, then waxed communicative.

"Saw Algarcife to-day," he said, carelessly.

"Oh! What did he say for himself?"

Nevins laughed.

"Does he ever say anything?" he demanded. "I asked him what he thought of the elections, and he replied that they did not come within the sphere of his profession."

Ardly grinned.

"Guess not," he ejaculated. "Was that all?"

"Oh, the rest was about as follows: I went to his house, you know, and told him I wanted his spiritual certificate as to your modesty and worth. I also observed that the newspapers had undertaken to throw moral search-lights indiscriminately around—"

"What did he say to that?" chuckled Ardly.

"He: 'Ardly can sustain them, I suppose.'

"I: 'Don't know, I'm sure. Would like to have your opinion.'

"He: 'It seems to me that you are in a better position to pass judgment on that point than I am.'

"I: 'But the standards are not the same, father.' (That 'father' ripped out as pat as possible.)

"He (rather bored): 'Oh, he is a fine fellow. I wish there were more like him.'"

"He is a fine fellow himself," retorted Ardly, loyally.

Nevins examined his brushes complacently. "If I were a Tammanyite," he said, "I'd post his certificate in the districts lying off the Bowery."

"It would be a shame," returned Ardly. Then he smiled. "By Jove! I believe if those districts knew Algarcife favored the little finger of a candidate, they would swallow the whole Tammany ticket."

"Queer influence, isn't it?"

"Well, I don't know. He works night and day over these people—and he knows how to deal with them. Leave it to the Bowery or to the ladies in his congregation, and he might turn this government into a despotism without a single dissenting vote."

"I believe you're right. By the way, you know he gave me that portrait of Father Speares to do for the church."

"Glad to hear it. But I never understood his conversion, somehow."

"Oh, I don't know. Men change like that every day."

"But not for logic. I say, it happened shortly after Mariana left, didn't it?"

"I think so."

"Heard anything of her?"

Nevins shook his head.

"Only what you know already," he answered.

"Deuced little, then."

"She came back, you know that, and went out West for a divorce. Then she married an ass of an Englishman, named the Honorable Cecil somebody."

"Good Lord! You've known that all these years?"

"Pretty nearly."

"Why in the devil didn't you tell me before?"

Nevins shrugged his shoulders. "My dear fellow, I don't feel the necessity to confide to you the secrets of my bosom."

"I call that a sneak."

"Why couldn't you find it out for yourself?"

"Because I don't go round diving into other people's affairs."

"Neither do I," responded Nevins, with dignity.

"How did you know, then?"

"It just came to me."

"Humph!" retorted Ardly, suspiciously.

Nevins squeezed a trifle of white-lead on his palette. Then he rose and drew the cord attached to the shade beneath the skylight. After which he stood to one side, studying the canvas with half-closed eyes, and shaking his dissatisfied head. As he returned to his seat he brushed the mouth of a tube of paint with his trousers, and swore softly. At last he spoke.

"I know something else," he volunteered, cautiously.

"About Mariana?"

"Yes."

"Let's have it, man."

Nevins laid his palette aside, and, seating himself astride the back of a chair, surveyed Ardly impressively.

"I can't see that there is any use," he remarked.

PHASES OF AN INFERIOR PLANET

Ardly threw the end of a cigar at him and squared up wrathfully. "Are you a damned fool or a utilitarian?" he demanded.

"She left the Honorable somebody," said Nevins, slowly.

"By Jove! what a woman!"

"She came to America."

"You don't say so!"

"She is in New York."

"What!"

Ardly left his chair and straightened himself against the mantel.

"How do you know?" he asked.

"I have seen her."

"Seen her!"

"Her photograph," concluded Nevins, suavely.

"Where?"

"In Ponsonby's show-case, on Fifth Avenue, near Thirtieth Street."

"How do you know it is she?"

"Well, I'll be damned! Don't I know Mariana?"

"Is it like her?"

"It is a gem; but you know she always photographed well. She knew how to pose."

"Has she changed?"

"Fatter, a trifle; fairer, a trifle; better groomed, a great deal—older and graver, I fancy."

"Well, I never!" said Ardly, and he whistled a street song between half-closed lips.

Nevins spoke again.

"She is a kind of rage with a lot of club-men," he said, "but the women haven't taken her up. I heard Mrs. Ryder call her an adventuress. But Layton told me Ryder was mad about her."

"Queer creatures, women," said Ardly. "They have a margin of morality, and a woman's virtue is determined by its difference in degree from the lowest stage

PHASES OF AN INFERIOR PLANET

worth cultivating. They imagine her not worth cultivating, I suppose."

"Oh, Mariana is all right," rejoined Nevins. Then he went on, reflectively: "Odd thing about it is her reputation for beauty. Judge her calmly, and she isn't even pretty."

"But who could judge her calmly?" responded Ardly. He picked up his hat and moved towards the door. "Well, I'll be off," he said.

"To the club?"

"No, just a little stroll down the avenue."

Nevins smiled broadly.

"Don't forget that Ponsonby's window-case is on the avenue," he remarked, placidly.

"Oh; so it is!"

Ardly went out into the crisp sunshine, a rising glow in his face. He walked briskly, with an almost impatient buoyancy. Near Thirtieth Street he stopped before the window-case and looked in.

From a square of gray card-board Mariana smiled at him, the aureole of her hair defined against a dark background. For a moment he stared blankly, and then an expression of hunger crept into his eyes—the hunger of one who has never been satisfied.

She was fairer, older, graver, as Nevins had said. There was a wistful droop in her pose, and in the splendor of her half-closed eyes there was something the old Mariana had never known—something left by the gathering of experience and the memory of tears.

He turned abruptly away, his face darkening and the buoyancy failing his step. He knew suddenly that the world was very stale and flat, and politics unprofitable. He crossed to Broadway and a few blocks farther down met Father Algarcife, who stopped him.

"Nevins was talking to me about you this morning," he said. "And so you are taking the matter seriously."

"As seriously as one takes—castor-oil."
The other smiled.
"Why, I thought you liked the chase."
"Like it! My dear sir, life is not exactly a question of one's likes or dislikes."
Father Algarcife looked at him with intentness.
"What! has not the world served you well?" he asked.
Ardly laughed.
"As well as a flute serves a man who doesn't know how to play it," he answered. "I am a master of discords."
"And so journalism didn't fit you?"
"Oh, journalism led to this. I did the chief a good turn or two, and he doesn't forget."
"I see," said Father Algarcife. Then he laughed. "And here is the other side," he added. Across the street before them hung a flaunting banner of white bunting, ornamented in red letters. Half mechanically his eyes followed the words:

SAMUEL J. SLOANE SAYS,
If I am elected Mayor, the government of New York will be conducted upon the highest plane of

EFFICIENCY! JUSTICE! AND RIGHT!

The wind caught the bunting and it swelled out as if inflated by the pledges it bore.
Ardly laughed cynically.
"I wish he'd drop a few hints to Providence," he remarked. "It is certainly a plane upon which the universe has never been conducted."
Father Algarcife walked on in silence, making his way along the crowded street with a slow yet determined step. The people who knew him turned to look after him, and those who did not stepped from before his way, moved by the virile dignity in his carriage,

which suggested a man possessed by an absorbing motive.

Ardly looked a little abashed, and laughed half apologetically.

"I have been in harness all my life," he said, "and now I'm doing a little kicking against the traces."

A boyish humor rushed to the other's lips.

"In that case, I can make but one recommendation," he replied: "if you kick against the traces—kick hard."

He drew out his watch and paused a moment as if in doubt.

"Yes, I'll go to the hospital," he said; "there is a half-hour before luncheon," and he turned into East Twentieth Street on his way to Second Avenue. When he reached the hospital, he entered the elevator upon the first floor and ascended to the babies' ward. As he stepped upon the landing, a calm-faced nurse in a fresh uniform passed him, holding a glass of milk in her white, capable hand.

His eyes brightened as he saw her, and under the serene system of the place he felt a sense of restfulness steal over him like warmth.

"How is my charge?" he asked.

A ripple of tenderness crossed the nurse's lips as she answered:

"He has been looking for you, and he is always better on the days that you come."

She passed along the hall and entered a large room into which the daylight fell like a bath of sunshine. In the centre of the room there was a tiny table around which a dozen children were sitting in small white chairs. Despite the bandaged heads and the weak limbs, there was no sign of suffering. It was all cheerfulness and sunshine, as if the transition from a tenement-house room to space and air had unfolded the shrunken little bodies into bloom.

In a cot near a window, where the sunlight flashed

across the cover, a boy of three or four years lay with a strap beneath his small pink wrapper, fastening him to a board of wood. At the head of the bed was printed the name, and below:

> "Pott's disease of the spine.
> Received, October, 1896; discharged..."

As he saw the priest he stretched out his pallid little hands with a gurgle of welcome, merriment overflowing his eyes.

Father Algarcife took the hands in his and sat down beside the cot. Since entering the room he seemed to have caught something of the infant stoicism surrounding him, for his face had lost its strained pallor and the lines about his mouth had softened.

"So it is a good day," he said. "The little man is better. He has been on the roof-garden."

The child laughed.

"It ith a good day," he made answer. "There ith the woof-garden and there ith ithe-cream."

"And which is the best?"

"Bofe," said the child.

"That's right, little soldier; and what did you do in the garden?"

The child clapped his hands.

"I played," he responded; "an' I'm goin' to play ball on my legs when I mend."

One of the nurses came and stood for a moment at the foot of the bed. "He has learned a hymn for you," she said. "He is teaching the other children to sing—aren't you, baby?"

"Yeth."

"And you'll sing for the father?"

The child's mouth quivered with pleasure and his eyes gleamed. Then his gay little voice rang out in a shrill treble:

PHASES OF AN INFERIOR PLANET

"Yeth, Jesuth lovths me,
Yeth, Jesuth lovths me,
Yeth, Jesuth lovths me,
The Bible tells me so."

He ended with a triumphant little gasp and lay smiling at the sunshine.

A quarter of an hour later Father Algarcife returned to the street. It was Friday, and at two o'clock he was to be in the sacristy, where it was his custom to receive the members of his parish. It was the most irksome of his duties, and he fulfilled it with a repugnance that had not lessened with time. Now it represented even a greater strain than usual. He had been soothed by his visit to the hospital, and he dreaded the friction of the next few hours—the useless advice delivered, the trivialities responded to, the endless details of fashionable foibles that would be heard. He wondered, resentfully, if there were not some means by which this office might be abolished or delivered into the hands of an assistant. Then his eyes shot humor as he imagined Miss Vernish, Mrs. Ryder, or a dozen others consenting to receive spiritual instruction from a lesser priest with a snub-nose.

As he passed a book-shop in Union Square, a man reading the posters upon the outside attracted his notice.

"Oh, I say, Mr. Algarcife!"

He stopped abruptly, recognized the speaker, and nodded.

The other went on with a heated rush of words.

"Those are fine things of yours, those sermons. I congratulate you."

"Thank you."

"Yes, they are fine. But, I say, you got the better of the *Scientific Weekly* writer. It was good."

"I don't know," responded Father Algarcife. "It is a good deal in the way you look at it, I suppose."

PHASES OF AN INFERIOR PLANET

"Not at all. I am not prejudiced—not in the least—never knew anybody less so. But he isn't your equal in controversy, by a long shot."

A sudden boyish laugh broke from Father Algarcife—a laugh wrung from him by the pressure of an overwhelming sense of humor. "I don't think it is a question of equality," he replied, "but of points of view."

CHAPTER V

The next afternoon Ardly burst into Nevins's studio without knocking, and paused in the centre of the floor to give dignity to his announcement.

"I have seen her," he said.

Nevins, who was stretched upon the divan, with his feet in the air and a cigarette in his mouth, rolled his eyes indolently in Ardly's direction.

"My dear fellow," he returned, "am I to presume that the pronoun 'her' refers to an individual or to a sex?"

"Don't be an ass," retorted Ardly. "I tell you I've seen Mariana."

Nevins turned upon his side and removed the cigarette from his lips.

"Where?" he responded, shortly.

"She was coming out of Thorley's. She wore an acre of violets. She has a footman in livery."

"How do you know it was she?"

"Well, I'll be damned! Don't I know Mariana?"

Nevins sat up and rested his head in his hands.

"How did she look?" he asked.

"Stunning. She has an air about her—"

"Always had."

"Oh, a new kind of air; the way a woman moves when she is all silk on the wrong side."

Nevins nodded.

"Speak to you?"

"I didn't give her a chance," returned Ardly, gloomily. "What's the use?"

The knocker rose and fell, and Mr. Paul entered, as unaltered as if he had stepped aside while the eight years slid by.

Nevins greeted him with a slight surprise, for they had drifted different ways.

"Glad to see you," he said, hospitably; "but this is an unusual honor."

"It is unusual," admitted Mr. Paul, seating himself stiffly on the edge of the divan.

"I am afraid to flatter myself with the hope that a whisper of my spreading fame has brought you," continued Nevins, nodding affably.

Mr. Paul looked up absently. "I have heard no such rumor," he replied, and regarded the floor as if impressed with facts of import.

"Perhaps it is your social charm," suggested Ardly; "or it may be that in passing along Fifty-fifth Street he felt my presence near."

Nevins frowned at him and lighted a fresh cigarette.

"I hope you are well, Mr. Paul," he remarked.

Mr. Paul looked up placidly.

"I may say," he returned, "that I am never well."

"Sorry to hear it."

There was a period of silence, which Mr. Paul broke at last in dry tones.

"I have occasion to know," he announced, "that the young woman whom we knew by the name of Mariana, to which I believe she had no legal title, has returned to the city."

Nevins jumped. "You don't say so!" he exclaimed.

"My information," returned Mr. Paul, "was obtained from the elevator boy who took her to the apartment of Miss Ramsey."

"Did she go to see Miss Ramsey?" demanded Nevins and Ardly in a breath.

Mr. Paul shook his head.

PHASES OF AN INFERIOR PLANET

"I do not know her motive," he said, "but she has taken Miss Ramsey away. For three days we have had no news of her."

The knocker fell with a decisive sound. Nevins rose, went to the door, and opened it. Then he started back before the apparition of Mariana.

She was standing near the threshold, her hand raised as when the knocker had fallen, her head bent slightly forward.

With an impulsive gesture she held out her gloved hands, her eyes shining.

"Oh, I am so glad!" she said.

Nevins took her hands in his and held them while he looked at her. She was older and graver and changed in some vital way, as if the years or sorrow had mellowed the temperament of her youth. There was a deeper thrill to her voice, a softer light in her eyes, and a gentler curve to her mouth, and over all, in voice and eyes and mouth, there was the shadow of discontent.

She wore a coat of green velvet, with ruffles of white showing at the loosened front, where a bunch of violets was knotted, and over the brim of her hat a plume fell against the aureole of her hair.

"I am so glad," she repeated. Then she turned to Ardly with the same fervent pressure of the hands.

"It is too good to be true," she went on. "It is like dropping back into girlhood. Why, there is dear Mr. Paul!"

Mr. Paul rose and accepted the proffered hands.

"You have fattened, madam," he remarked, with a vague idea that she had in some way connected herself with a title.

Mariana's old laugh pealed out.

"Why, he is just as he used to be," she said, glancing brightly from Ardly to Nevins in pursuit of sympathy. "He hasn't changed a bit."

PHASES OF AN INFERIOR PLANET

"The changes of eight years," returned Mr. Paul, "are not to be detected by a glance."

Mariana nodded smilingly and turned to Nevins.

"Now let me look at *you*," she said. "Come under the light. Ah! you haven't been dining at The Gotham."

"Took my last dinner there exactly six years ago next Thanksgiving Day," answered Nevins, cheerfully. "Turkey and pumpkin-pie."

She turned her eyes critically on Ardly.

"Well, he has survived his sentiment for me," she said.

Ardly protested.

"I don't keep that in the heart I wear on my sleeve," he returned. "You would need a plummet to sound the depths, I fancy."

Mariana blushed and laughed, the faint color warming the opaline pallor of her face. Then she glanced about the room.

"So this is the studio," she exclaimed, eagerly—"the studio we so often planned together—and there is the divan I begged for! Ah, and the dear adorable 'Antinous.' But what queer stuff for hangings!"

"If you had sent me word that you were coming," returned Nevins, apologetically, passing his hands over his hair in an endeavor to make it lie flat, "I'd have put the place to rights, and myself too."

"Oh, but I wanted to see you just as you are every day. It is so home-like—and what a delightful smell of paint! But do you always keep your boots above the canopy? They spoil the effect somehow."

"I tossed them up there to get rid of them," explained Nevins. "But tell me about yourself. You look as if you had just slid out of the lap of luxury."

"Without rumpling her gown," added Ardly.

"I was about to observe that she seemed in prosperous circumstances," remarked Mr. Paul.

PHASES OF AN INFERIOR PLANET

"Oh, I am," responded Mariana. "Stupidly prosperous. But let me look at the paintings first, then I'll talk of myself. What is on the big easel, Mr. Nevins?"

"That's a portrait," said Nevins, drawing the curtain aside and revealing a lady in black. "I am only a photographer in oils. I am painting everybody's portrait."

"That means success, doesn't it? And success means money, and money means so many things. Yes, that's good. I like it."

Nevins smiled, enraptured.

"You were the beginning," he said. "It was the painting of you and—and the blue wrapper that did it. It gave me such a push uphill that I haven't stood still since."

The wistfulness beneath the surface in Mariana's eyes deepened suddenly. Her manner grew nervous.

"Oh yes," she said, turning away. "I remember."

Mr. Paul, who had watched her gloomily, with traces of disapprobation in his gaze, took his leave with a stilted good-bye, and Mariana threw herself upon the divan, while Ardly and Nevins seated themselves on footstools at her feet and looked into her eyes.

"I want to hear all—all," she said. "Are you happy?"

"Are you?" asked Ardly.

She shook her head impatiently. "I? Oh yes," she answered. "I have clothes, and a carriage, and even a few jewels."

She slipped the long glove from her hand, which came soft and white from its imprisonment, with the indentation of the buttons on the supple wrist. She held up her fingers, where a blaze of diamonds ran. Then she smiled.

"But I never sang with Alvary," she added.

"Where is the voice?"

"It is dead," she replied; "but it was only a skeleton

when it lived. I learned that afterwards. I had the artistic temperament without the art."

Nevins and Ardly, watching the mobility of her face, saw the old half-disdainful weariness steal back.

"So you have learned that," said Nevins. "It is the greater wisdom—to learn what one has not."

"I don't idealize any longer," answered Mariana, playing with the glove in her lap. "I have lopped off an ideal every hour since I saw you."

"Sensible woman," returned Ardly. "We don't lop off our ideals—we distort them. Life is a continuous adjustment of the things that should be to the things that are."

"And middle-age shows the adjustment to be a misfit," added Nevins, his boyish face growing almost sad. "We grow tired of burnishing up the facts of life, and we leave the tarnish to mix with the triple-plate."

"Are you middle-aged?" asked Mariana.

"Not since you entered."

She smiled, pleased with the flattery. "So I am a restorer of youth. Do I look young?"

"There is a glass."

She turned towards it, catching the reflection of her face shadowed by the plume against her hair.

"Your eyes are older," said Nevins. "They look as if they had seen things, but your mouth is young. It could never hold an expression long enough for it to impress a line. Heavens! It is a mouth that would madden one to model, because of the impossibility! It is twenty mouths in one!"

"You never liked my nose," said Mariana, her eyes still on the glass. "Do you remember how you straightened it in the poster?"

"I have the poster still."

"And I have the nose."

Then she laughed. "It is so delightful to be here," she said.

PHASES OF AN INFERIOR PLANET

Ardly and Nevins talked rapidly, running over the years one by one, giving glimpses of the changes in their lives, meeting Mariana's gay reserve with fuller confidence. They had both grown boyish and more buoyant, and as they spoke they felt like an incoming tide the warmth of Mariana's manner. She seemed more lovable to them, more generous, more utterly to be desired. Her nature had ripened amid the luxury of her life, which, instead of rendering her self-centred, as poverty had done, had left her more responsive to the needs of others. She threw herself into the records of their lives with an impulsive fervor, stopping them at intervals to question as to details, and covering the past eight years with sympathetic searchlights.

And yet beneath the superficial animation in her voice there was a restless thrill, and the eagerness with which she turned to trivial interests was but the nervous veil that hid the weariness in her heart. It was as if she plunged into the thoughts of others that she might put away the memory of herself.

"So you have become a politician?" she said to Ardly. "I am so interested!"

"You wouldn't be if you knew as much of it as I do," remarked Nevins. "You'd be ashamed. It makes me blush every time I see his name on a ticket. I consider it an offence against the paths of our fathers."

"Why, Mr. Ryder told me you were working for him," Mariana returned; "but he did say that he couldn't reconcile it with your common-sense. He's for the other side, you know."

"So am I!" groaned Nevins; "but what has a man's convictions to do with his vote?"

"Or with his election?" laughed Ardly. "But Nevins is an unwilling accomplice of my aspirations."

"I wouldn't call them aspirations," remonstrated Nevins.

PHASES OF AN INFERIOR PLANET

Mariana buttoned her glove and rose. "I am going to work for you," she said, "and my influence is not to be scorned. I have not one vote, but dozens. I shall elect you."

"Don't," pleaded Nevins; "it will soil your hands!"

"Oh, I can wash them!" she laughed; "and it is worth a few smuts. I shall tell Mr. Ryder to canvass for you," she added.

Ardly shouted, "Good heavens! He is one of the best fighters the Republicans have!"

Mariana smiled inscrutably.

"But that was before I had a candidate," she answered.

They followed her to the sidewalk and tucked her carriage furs about her while the footman looked on.

"And you are coming to see me soon?" she insisted—"very soon?"

"We swear it!" they protested.

"And you will tell me all the news of the elections?"

"On our manly faith."

"That I will trust. Good-bye!"

"Good-bye!"

The carriage started, when suddenly she lowered the window and looked out, the plume in her hat waving black against the wind.

"I forgot to tell you," she said; "my name is Gore—Mrs. Cecil Gore."

With the light of audacity in his face, Nevins laid his hand upon the window.

"And where is the Honorable Cecil?" he asked.

A flash of irritation darkened Mariana's eyes. She laughed with a ring of recklessness.

"The Lord forbid that I should know!" she replied.

She motioned to the coachman, and the carriage rolled rapidly away. Nevins stood looking after it until it turned the corner. When the last wheel vanished, he spoke slowly:

PHASES OF AN INFERIOR PLANET

"Well, I'll be blessed!" he said.

Ardly stooped and picked up a violet that lay upon the curbing.

"And so will I," he responded.

"Have a whiskey?"

"All right."

They entered the building and mounted the stairs in silence.

CHAPTER VI

THE Reverend Anthony Algarcife had inspired his congregation with an almost romantic fervor.

When he had first appeared before them as assistant to Father Speares in his Bowery Mission, and a little later as server in the celebrations, they regarded him as a thoughtful-eyed young priest, whose appearance fitted into the general scheme of color in the chancel. When he read the lessons they noticed the richness of his voice, and when at last he came to the altar-step to deliver his first sermon they thrilled into the knowledge of his power.

But he turned from their adulations almost impatiently to throw himself into the mission in the slums. His eloquence had passed from the rich to the poor, and beyond an occasional sermon he became only a harmonious figure in the setting of the church. For the honors they meted out to him he had no glance, for their favors he had only indifference. He seemed as insensible to praise as to censure, and to the calls of ambition his ears were closed. He lived in the fevered haste of a man who has but one end remaining—to have life over.

But his indifference redounded to his honor. Because he shunned popularity, it fell upon him; because he put aside personal gains, he found them in the reverence of his people. His apathy was construed into humility, his compassion into loving-kindness, his endeavors to stifle memory into the fires of faith. At the end of six years his determination to remain a

PHASES OF AN INFERIOR PLANET

cipher in religion had made him the leader of his church, and the means which he had taken to annihilate self had drawn on him the wondering eyes of his world. Almost unconsciously he bowed his head to receive the yoke.

When, at the death of Father Speares, he was called to the charge, he accepted it without a struggle and without emotion. He saw in it but an opening to heavier labor and an opportunity to hasten the progress of his slow suicide.

So he took the work from the failing hands and devoted to it the fulness of his own frenzied vigor. The ritual which his predecessor loved became sacred to him, and the most trivial ceremonials grew mighty with memory of the dead. Each candle upon the altar, each silken thread in the embroidered vestments he wore, was a tribute to a sincerity which was not his.

He lent a sudden fervor to the decoration of the church and to the training of his choristers, passionately reviving lost and languishing rites of religion, and silencing the faint protests of his more conservative parishioners by an arrogant appeal to the "Ornaments Rubric" of the Prayer-book. In defiance of the possible opposition of the bishop, he transposed the "Gloria" to its old place in the Catholic Mass, hurling, like an avenging thunderbolt, at a priestly objector to the good old rule of St. Vincent, " Quod semper, quod ubique, quod ab omnibus."

"My dear father," his senior warden had once said to him, "I doubt if most priests put as much work into their whole lives as you do into one celebration."

"I know," replied Father Algarcife slowly. "If I have left anything undone it has been from oversight, not fear of labor."

The warden smiled.

"Your life is a proof of your industry as well as

your faith," he responded. "Only a man who loves his religion better than his life would risk himself daily. It is your great hold upon your people. They believe in you."

"Yes, yes," said the other.

"But I have wanted to warn you," continued the warden. "It cannot last. Give yourself rest."

Father Algarcife shook his head.

"I rest only when I am working," he answered, and he added, a little wistfully, "The parish bears witness that I have done my best by the charge."

The warden, touched by the wistfulness, lowered his eyes. "That you have done any man's best," he returned.

"Thank you," said Father Algarcife. Then he passed into the sacristy to listen to the confession of a parishioner.

It was a tedious complaint, and he followed it abstractedly — winding through the sick imaginings of a nervous woman and administering well-worn advice in his rich voice, which lent a charm to the truisms. When it was over, he advised physical exercise, and, closing the door, seated himself to await the next comer.

It was Miss Vernish, and as she entered, with her impatient limp, the bitterness of her mouth relaxed. She was supervising the embroidering of the vestments to be worn at Easter, and in a spirit of devotion she had sacrificed her diamonds to their ornamentation. Her eyes grew bright as she talked, and a religious warmth softened her manner.

"It has made me so happy," she said, "to feel that I can give something beautiful to the service. It is the sincerest pleasure I have known for years."

She left, and her place was taken by a young divinity student who had been drawn from law to theology by the eloquence of Father Algarcife. He had come to

PHASES OF AN INFERIOR PLANET

obtain the priest's advice upon a matter of principle, and departed with a quickening of his religious tendencies.

Then came several women, entering with a great deal of rustling and no evident object in view. Then a vestryman to talk over a point in business; then the wife of a well-known politician, to ask if she should consent to her husband's accepting a foreign appointment; then a man who wished to be confirmed in his church; and, after all, Mrs. Ryder, large and warm and white, to say that since the last communion she had felt herself stronger to contend with disappointment.

When it was over and he came out into the evening light, he drew himself together with a quick movement, as if he had knelt in a strained position for hours. Vaguely he wondered how his nerves had sustained it, and he smiled half bitterly as he admitted that eight years ago he would have succumbed.

"It is because my nerves are dead," he said; "as dead as my emotions."

He knew that since the pressure of feeling had been lifted the things which would have overwhelmed him in the past had lost the power to thrill his supine sensations, that from a mere jangled structure of nerve wires he had become a physical being—a creature who ate and drank and slept, but did not feel.

He went about his daily life as methodically as if it were mapped out for him by a larger hand. His very sermons came to him with no effort of will or of memory, but as thoughts long thought out and forgotten sometimes obtrude themselves upon the mind that has passed into other channels. They were but twisted and matured phrases germinating since his college days. The old fatal facility for words remained with him, though the words had ceased to be symbols of honest thought. He could still speak, it was only the ability to think that the fever had drained—it was only the power to plod with mental patience in the pursuit of a single fact. Otherwise he was unchanged. But as every sensation is succeeded by a partial incapacity, so the strain of years had been followed by years of stagnation.

He went home to dinner with a physical zest.

"I believe I have one sentiment remaining," he said, "the last a man loses—the sentiment for food."

The next evening, which chanced to be that of Election Day, Dr. Salvers came to dine with him, and when dinner was over they went out to ascertain the returns. Salvers had entered the fight with an enthusiastic support of what he called "good government," and the other watched it with the interest of a man who looks on.

"Shall we cross to Broadway?" he asked; "the people are more interesting, after all, than the politicians."

"The politicians," responded Salvers, "are only interesting viewed through the eyes of the people. No, let's keep to the avenue for a while. I prefer scenting the battle from afar."

The sounds grew louder as they walked on, becoming, as they neared Madison Square, a tumultuous medley issuing from tin horns and human throats. Over the ever-moving throngs in the square a shower of sky-rockets shot upward at the overhanging clouds and descended in a rain of orange sparks. The streets were filled with a stream of crushed humanity, which struggled and pushed and panted, presenting to a distant view the effect of a writhing mass of dark-bodied insects. From the tower of the Garden a slender searchlight pointed southward, a pale, still finger remaining motionless, while the crowd clamored below and the fireworks exploded in the blackness above.

Occasionally, as the white light fell on the moving throng, it exaggerated in distinctness a face here and

PHASES OF AN INFERIOR PLANET

there, which assumed the look of a grotesque mask, illuminated by an instantaneous flash and fading quickly into the half-light of surrounding shadows. Then another took its place, and the illumination played variations upon the changing features.

Suddenly a shrill cheer went up from the streets.

"That means Vaden," said Salvers. "Let's move on."

They left the square, making their way up Broadway. At the first corner a man offered them papier-maché tigers, at the second roosters, at the third chrysanthemums.

"Look at this," said Salvers, drawing aside. "Odd for women, isn't it? Half these girls don't know what they are shrieking about."

In the throng jostling past them there were a dozen school-girls, wearing yellow chrysanthemums in their button-holes and carrying small flags in their hands. The light from the windows fell upon their pretty faces, rosy from excitement. Behind them a gang of college students blew deafening blasts on tin trumpets, and on the other side a newsboy was yelling—

"*Eve-ning Wor-ld!* Vaden elected!—Va-den—!"

His voice was drowned in the rising cheers of men politically mad.

"I'll go to the club," said Salvers, presently; "this is too deuced democratic. Will you come?"

Father Algarcife shook his head.

"Not now," he replied. "I'll keep on to Herald Square, then I'll turn in. The fight is over."

And he passed on.

Upon a white sheet stretched along the side of the *Herald* building a stereopticon portrait of a candidate appeared, followed by a second, and then by the figures of the latest returns from the election boroughs. Here the crowd had stagnated, and he found difficulty in forcing his way. Then, as the mass swayed back, a woman fainted at his side and was carried into the nearest drug-store.

In the endeavor to reach Fifth Avenue he stepped into the centre of the street, where a cable car, a carriage, and a couple of hansom cabs were blocked. As he left the sidewalk the crowd divided, and the carriage started, while a horse attached to a cab shied suddenly. A woman stumbled beneath the carriage and he drew her away. As he did so the wheel of the cab struck him, stunning him for the moment.

"Look out, man!" called Nevins, who was seated beside the coachman upon the carriage-box; "that was an escape. Are you hurt? Here, hold on!"

At the same moment the door opened and a hand reached out.

"Come inside," said a woman's voice.

He shook his head, dizzy from the shock. Red lights flashed before his eyes, and he staggered.

Then the crowd pressed together, some one pushed him into the carriage, and the door closed.

"To Father Algarcife's house," said the voice. A moment more and the horses started. Consciousness escaped him, and he lay against the cushions with closed eyes. When he came to himself, it was to hear the breathing of the woman beside him — a faint insistence of sound that seemed a vital element in the surrounding atmosphere. For an instant it lulled him, and then, as reason returned, the sound brought in its train the pale survivals of old associations. Half stunned as he was, it was by feeling rather than conception that he became aware that the woman was Mariana. He was conscious of neither surprise nor emotion. There was merely a troublous sense of broken repose and a slight bitterness always connected with the thought of her—a bitterness that was but an after-taste of his portion of gall and wormwood.

He turned his head upon the cushions and looked at

her as she sat beside him. She had not spoken, and she sat quite motionless, her fitful breathing alone betraying the animation of flesh. Her head was in the shadow, but a single ray of light fell across her lap, showing her folded hands in their long gloves. He smelled the fragrance of the violets she wore, but the darkness hid them.

Surging beneath that rising bitterness, the depths of his memory stirred in its sleep. He remembered the day that he had stood at the window of that Fourth Street tenement, watching the black-robed figure enter the carriage below. He saw the door close, the wheels turn, and the last upward glance she gave. Then he saw the long street flecked with sunshine stretching onward into the aridity of endless tomorrows.

Strange that he remembered it after these eight years. The woman beside him stirred, and he recalled in that same slow bitterness the last kiss he had put upon her mouth. Bah! It meant nothing.

But his apathy was rended by a sudden fury—an instinct of hate—of cruelty insatiable. An impulse to turn and strike her through the darkness—to strike her until he had appeased his thirst for blood.

The impulse passed as quickly as it came, fleeing like a phantom of delirium, and in its place the old unutterable bitterness welled back. His apathy reclosed upon him.

The carriage turned a corner, and a blaze of light fell upon the shadow of the seat. It swept the white profile and dark figure of Mariana, and he saw the wistfulness in her eyes and the maddening tremor of her mouth. But it did not move him. He was done with such things forever.

All at once she turned towards him.

"You are not hurt?"

"It was nothing."

PHASES OF AN INFERIOR PLANET

She flinched at the sound of his voice, and the dusk of the cross-street shrouded them again. The hands in her lap fluttered nervously, running along the folds of her dress.

Suddenly the carriage stopped, and Nevins jumped down from the box and swung the door open.

"Are you all right?" he asked, and his voice was unsteady.

"All right," responded Father Algarcife, cheerfully. He stepped upon the sidewalk, staggered slightly, and caught Nevins's arm. Then he turned to the woman within the carriage. "I thank you," he said.

He entered the rectory, and Nevins came back and got inside the carriage.

"Will you go home?" he asked, with attempted lightness. "The returns from the Assembly districts won't be in till morning, but Ardly is sure."

Mariana smiled at him.

"Tell him to drive home," she answered. "I am very tired."

CHAPTER VII

THE morning papers reported that the Reverend Anthony Algarcife had been struck by a cab while crossing Broadway, and as he left the breakfast-table Mrs. Ryder's carriage appeared at his door, quickly followed by that of Miss Vernish.

By ten o'clock the rectory was besieged and bunches of flowers, with cards attached, were scattered about the hall. Dr. Salvers, coming in a little later, stumbled over a pile of roses, and recovered himself, laughing.

"Looks as if they mean to bury you," he remarked. "But how are you feeling? Of course, I knew it was nothing serious or I should have heard."

Father Algarcife rose impatiently from his chair.

"Of course," he returned. "But all this fuss is sufficient to drive a man mad. Yes, Agnes," to the maid who entered with a tray of carnations and a solicitous inquiry as to his health. "Say I am perfectly well—and please have all these flowers sent to the hospital at once. No, I don't care for any on my desk. I dislike the perfume." Then he turned to Salvers. "I am going out to escape it," he said. "Will you walk with me to the church?"

"With pleasure," responded the doctor, cheerfully; and he added: "You will find the church a poor protection, I fancy."

As they left the rectory they met Claude Nevins upon the sidewalk.

"I wanted to assure myself that it was not a serious accident," he said. "Glad to see you out."

Father Algarcife frowned.

"If I hear another word of this affair," he replied, irritably, "I shall feel tempted to regret that there is not some cause for the alarm."

"And you are quite well?"

"Perfectly."

"By the way, I didn't know that you felt enough interest in the elections to induce you to parade the streets on their account."

"Oh, it was the doctor's fault. He got me into the medley, and then deserted because he found it too democratic."

"It is democracy turned upsidedown that I object to," remarked Salvers. "There seems a lack of decency about it—as if we were to awake some morning to find the statue of Liberty on its head, with its legs in the air. I believe in the old conservative goddess of our fathers—Freedom shackled by the chains of respectability."

"So did Father Algarcife once," said Nevins. "He had an oration entitled 'The Jeffersonian Principles' which he used to deliver before the mirror when he thought I was asleep."

"I believe in it still," interrupted Father Algarcife, "but I no longer deliver orations. Greater wisdom has made me silent. Well, I suppose the result of last night was hardly a surprise."

"Hardly," responded Nevins. "What can one expect when everybody who knows the value of an office is running for it, and everybody who doesn't is blowing horns about the runners. But I won't keep you. Good-day."

"Good-day."

Nevins turned back.

"By the way," he said to Father Algarcife, "I wish you would drop in and look at that portrait the first chance you have. I am waiting for your criticism."

PHASES OF AN INFERIOR PLANET

"Very well. Congratulate Ardly for me."

And they separated, Salvers motioning to his coachman to follow him to the church.

Upon going inside, Father Algarcife found his principal assistant, a young fellow with a fair, fresh face, like a girl's, and a high forehead, surmounted by waves of flaxen hair. His name was Ellerslie, and his devotional sincerity was covered by a shy and nervous manner.

He greeted the elder priest with a furtive deprecation, the result of an innate humility of character.

"I went by the rectory as soon as I had seen the morning papers," he said. "Thank God you escaped unhurt!"

The irritation with which Father Algarcife had replied to Nevins's solicitude did not appear now.

"I hope you were not troubled by the report," he answered. "There was absolutely nothing in it except that I was struck by a vehicle and stunned slightly. But the exaggerated accounts have caused me a great deal of annoyance. By the way, John," and his face softened, "I have not told you how much I liked your last sermon."

The other flushed and shook his head. "They fall so far short," he returned, and his voice trembled. "I know now that I shall never be able to speak. When I face the people there is so much that I want to say that I grow dumb. My feeling is so strong that my words are weak."

"Time may change that."

"No," said Ellerslie; "but if I may listen to you I am content. I will serve God in humble ways. It is the service that I love, after all, and not the glory."

"Yes, yes," responded Father Algarcife, gently.

He went into the sacristy, where he sat for a few moments in reverie, his head resting upon his hand. Then he rose and shook himself free of the thought which haunted him.

PHASES OF AN INFERIOR PLANET

For several weeks after this he paid no calls except among his poor. The houses of his richer parishioners he appeared to shun, and his days were spent in active work in the mission districts. At all hours his calm black figure and virile face might be seen passing in and out of the grimy tenements or along the narrow streets. He had opened, in connection with his mission-house, a lodging for waifs, and it was his custom to spend several evenings of the week among its inmates. The house had been founded by funds which, until his call to the church, had been expended in Asiatic missions, but which, before his indomitable opposition, had been withdrawn. As the work went on it became of special interest to him, and a good half of his personal income went yearly to its support.

"It is not a charity," he had once said to Salvers. "I disapprove of such charities. It is merely a house where lodgings are let in as business-like a manner as they are around the corner, for five cents a spot; only our lodgings are better, and there is a bath thrown in."

"And a dinner as well," Salvers had answered, "to say nothing of breakfast and a bed to one's self. By the way, is your system of serving newsboys and boot-blacks on credit successful?"

Father Algarcife smiled.

"I have found it so," he replied; "but, you know, our terms are long, and we give good measure for the money."

It was in this work that he was absorbing himself, when, one day in early December, he received a note from Mrs. Ryder:

"I have secured a box at the opera for Thursday night" (she wrote), "that I might beg you to hear Madame Cambria, who sings Ortrude in 'Lohengrin.' Her contralto is superb, and I wish to engage her for our Christmas services, but I

PHASES OF AN INFERIOR PLANET

hesitate to do so until I have had your verdict upon her voice. This is a new charitable appeal, and one which I trust you will not refuse.

"Believe me to be,
"Always sincerely yours,
"FLORENCE VAN HORNE RYDER.

"The De Reszkes sing also."

He sent an acceptance, and the following day received an urgent request that he should dine quietly with Mr. Ryder and herself on Thursday evening. To this he consented, after some hesitation; and when the evening came he presented himself, to find Mrs. Ryder awaiting him with the pretty, vivacious young woman of the dinner-party, who was a guest in the house.

Mrs. Ryder crossed the room, with her large white hand outstretched, her satin gown rustling as she moved, and the lamplight shimmering over her massive shoulders in their setting of old lace. The vivacious young woman, whose name was Darcy, greeted him with a smile which seemed to blend in a flash of brightness her black eyes and white teeth.

"Mr. Ryder is a little late," his wife explained, "but he will not delay us long." And she passed to the subject of the Christmas services and the contralto she wished to secure.

While she was speaking, Ryder came in with his usual cordial pleasantries. He was looking fresh and a little flushed, as if he had just left a Turkish bath, and was dressed with an immaculateness of detail which carried a suggestion of careful polish. His sensitive skin, beneath which the purplish flush rose, was as fine as a child's, and his round, smooth hands had a suffusion of pink in the palms.

In a moment dinner was served, and they went into the dining-room. Ryder was easy and affable. He talked pleasantly about the events of the past few weeks, describing as if for the hundredth time the success of the Horse Show, and stating good-natured objections to the awards of the judges.

"It is a farce," he said—"a mere farce. They don't recognize the best horse-flesh when they see it." Then he smiled at his wife. "But who can blame them? It was really a puzzle to decide which were the most worth looking at, the horses or the women. It is hard to say where the blue ribbon belonged. Ah, father, you miss a great deal by being a saint."

Miss Darcy interrupted him with a pretty protest. "I am sure a saint may look at a horse," she said, "and a woman." And she added: "I have always forgotten to ask you who the lady in violet and silver-fox was who sat in Mr. Buisson's box? I did not recognize her."

Ryder's eyes narrowed slightly, but he answered easily, "Oh, that was Mrs. Gore, I believe."

Miss Darcy flashed a smile.

"The Englishwoman I have heard so much about? Why, I thought she was called a beauty!"

Ryder laughed.

"She is a beauty when you know her," he said, "or, rather, you get the idea that she is. But she isn't English, you know. She married an Englishman."

Then he changed the subject and drew Father Algarcife into a discussion of church decorations.

When dinner was over, Mrs. Ryder's maid appeared, bearing the opera-wraps, and the two women trailed down the steps and into the carriage. When Father Algarcife had stepped inside, Ryder closed the door and made his excuses.

"I'll look in a little later," he said; "but if Mr. Nevins finds you you won't need me, and a whole evening of it tires my nerves."

Then he lighted a cigar and strolled off leisurely, while the carriage started.

PHASES OF AN INFERIOR PLANET

When they entered the opera-house the curtain had risen, and the tenor was singing his farewell to the swan.

As Father Algarcife seated himself in the shadow of the box and looked over Mrs. Ryder's superb shoulders at the stage and the glittering foot-lights, he felt a quick impulse to rush away from it all. He hated the noise and the heat and the glare. The heavy atmosphere seemed oppressive and unnatural, and the women, sparkling brilliantly in the tiers of boxes, looked like beautiful exotics, fragrant with the perishable bloom of a hot-house. It was with a sensation of relief that he recalled the dull mission in the slums, where he had spent the morning.

On the stage, Elsa had cast herself into the arms of Lohengrin, and the voice of love dominant was translated into song. The music filled the house with a throbbing ecstasy—an ecstasy that had captured in its notes the joys of all the senses—the light to the eye of a spring morning, the perfume to the nostrils of fresh meadows, the warmth to the touch of falling sunshine. It was the voice of love ethereal—of love triumphant over flesh, of love holding to its breast the phantom of its dreams. It was the old, ever-young voice of the human heart panting for the possession of its vision—the vision realized in the land of legends.

The curtain was rung down, and in a moment Nevins came in and they fell to talking. They spoke of the tenor, of the fact that the prima donna's voice had strengthened, and of Madame Cambria, the contralto, who was a little hoarse. Then they spoke of the people in the boxes and of the absence of several whose names they mentioned.

Father Algarcife was silent, and he only aroused himself to attention when Miss Darcy, lowering her opera-glass, turned to Nevins inquiringly.

PHASES OF AN INFERIOR PLANET

"Do tell me if that is Mrs. Gore across from us—the one in green and violets?"

Nevins replied constrainedly. "Yes," he said; "I think so. The other is Miss Ramsey, I believe—a friend who lives with her."

Miss Darcy smiled.

"Why, I thought she lived alone," she returned; "but I have heard so many odd things about her that I may be mistaken in this one. She is evidently the kind of person that nobody possesses any positive information about."

"Perhaps it is as well," observed Mrs. Ryder, stiffly. "It is better to know too little on such subjects than too much."

Nevins was writhing in his chair, his mouth half open, when Father Algarcife spoke.

"In this case," he said, and his voice sounded cold and firm, "what is not known seems to be incorrectly surmised. I knew Mrs. Gore—before—before her marriage. She is a Southerner."

Mrs. Ryder looked up.

"Yes?" she interrogated, as he paused.

"And, although I cannot vouch for her discretion, I can for her innate purity of character."

Mrs. Ryder flushed, and spoke with a beautiful contrition in her eyes.

"I was wrong," she said, "to trust rumor. It makes me ashamed of myself—of my lack of generosity."

The curtain rose, and Father Algarcife turned to the stage. But he did not see it. The figures were blurred before his eyes and the glare tortured him. Across the circle of space he knew that Mariana was sitting, her head upraised, her cheek resting upon her hand, her face in the shadow. He could almost see her eyes growing rich and soft like green velvet.

Then, as the voice of the soprano rang out, he started

PHASES OF AN INFERIOR PLANET

slightly. Beneath the song of love he heard the cry of ambition—a cry that said:
"*I would give half my life for this—to sing with Alvary.*"

Whence the words came he did not know. He had no memory of them in time or place, but they struggled in the throat of the soprano and filled the air.

He turned and looked at her as she sat across from him, her cheek resting in her hand against a blaze of diamonds. She looked white, he thought, and wistful and unsatisfied. Then a fierce joy took possession of him—a joy akin to the gloating of a savage cruelty. She had failed. Yes, in spite of the brocade of her gown, in spite of the diamonds in her hair, in spite of the homage in the eyes of men that followed her—she had failed.

The blood rushed into his temples, and he felt it beating in his pulses. He was glad—glad that she was unsatisfied—glad of the struggle and of the failure—glad of the slow torture of famished aspirations.

And from the throat of the soprano the words rang heavy with throbs of unfulfilment:
"*I would give half my life for this— to sing with Alvary.*"

Then as he looked at her she stirred restlessly, and their eyes met. It was a blank look, such as two strangers might have interchanged, but suddenly he remembered the night they came together and sat in the fifth gallery. A dozen details of that evening flickered in his memory and reddened into life. He remembered the splendors of her eyes, the thrill in her voice, the nervous tremor of her hands. He remembered the violets in her bonnet, created from nothing after a chapter of Mill—and the worn gloves with the stains inside, which benzine had not taken away. He remembered her faintness when the opera was over, and the grocery-shop across from The Gotham, where they had bought ale and crackers. He saw her figure as she sat on the hearth-rug in her white gown, her hair hanging loose about her shoulders, her eyes drowsy with sleep. He saw her hands—bare then of jewels—as she unfastened the parcels, and heard her laugh as he drew the cork and the ale spilled upon the crackers. Good God! He had forgotten these things eight years ago.

Again he looked across at her and their eyes met. He turned to the stage and listened to the faltering of love as it struggled with doubt. The music had changed. It had deepened in color and a new note had throbbed into it—a note of flesh that weighed upon spirit—of disbelief that shadowed faith. The ideal was singing the old lesson of the real found wanting—of passion tarnished by the touch of clay. The ecstasy had fled. Love was not satisfied with itself. It craved knowledge, and the vision beautiful was fading before the eyes of earth. It was the song of the eternal vanquishment of love by distrust, of the eternal failure of faith.

When the curtain fell Ryder came into the box. He was looking depressed, and lines of irritation had gathered about his mouth. He pulled his fair mustache nervously. His wife rose and looked at him with a frank smile in her eyes.

"I have been watching Mrs. Gore," she said, "and she is very lovely. Will you take me to her box for a moment?"

Nevins looked up with quick gratitude, and Ryder grew radiant. He smiled on his wife in affectionate admiration.

"Of course I will," he answered, and as they left the box he added: "You are magnificent. There is not a woman in town with your neck and arms."

She smiled faintly, unmoved by his words. She had

learned long since that he still admired though he no longer desired her—and desire was the loadstar of his life.

Father Algarcife, looking at the box across from him, saw Mariana start suddenly and rise with an impulsive welcome as Mrs. Ryder entered. He could see the light on her face, and the frank pleasure of her greeting. Then, as the two women stood together, he saw Ryder glance from one to the other with his pleasant smile and turn to speak to Miss Ramsey. He heard Nevins breathing behind him, and he was conscious of a strange feeling of irritation against him. Why should he, who was at enmity with no man, cherish that curious dislike for one who was his friend?

"Mrs. Ryder is a creature to be adored," said Nevins to Miss Darcy. "She is Isis incarnate."

Miss Darcy responded with her flashing smile. "And Mrs. Gore's divinity?"

Nevins gave an embarrassed laugh.

"Oh, I am not sure that she is a goddess at all," he answered. "She is merely a woman."

CHAPTER VIII

As Mariana entered her house after the opera was over she unwound the lace scarf from her head, letting it trail like a silvery serpent on the floor behind her. Then she unfastened her long cloak, and threw it on a chair in the drawing-room.

"The fire is out," she said, looking at the ashes in the grate, "and I am cold—cold."

"Shall I start it?" asked Miss Ramsey, a little timidly, as she tugged awkwardly at her gloves, embarrassed by their length.

Mariana laughed absently.

"Start it? Why should you?" she questioned. "There are servants—or there ought to be—but no, I'll go up-stairs."

She went into the hall, and Miss Ramsey followed her. On the second landing they entered a large room, the floor of which was spread with white fur rugs, warmed by the reddish lights and shadows from an open fire.

Mariana crossed to the fire, and, drawing off her gloves, held her hands to the flames. There was a strained look in her eyes, as if she had not awaked to her surroundings.

Miss Ramsey raised the wick of the lamp, yawned behind her hand, and came to where Mariana was standing.

"Are you tired?" she asked. "The opera was very long."

Mariana started and looked at her.

PHASES OF AN INFERIOR PLANET

"You poor little thing," she said. "It half killed you. No, don't go. Sit down for a moment. I want to talk to you."

As she spoke she unfastened her gown, slipped it off, and threw it across a chair. Then she put on a wrapper of white flannel, and, seating herself on the rug before the fire, loosened her heavy hair.

"I want to talk," she repeated.

Miss Ramsey drew a chair beside her and sat down. She laid her hand on Mariana's hair.

"Shall I braid it?" she asked.

Mariana shook her head.

"I don't want you to wait on me," she replied, half pettishly. "Janet can do that. I want you to love me."

Miss Ramsey smiled.

"How shall I begin?" she inquired.

But Mariana was silent, staring moodily into the fire, where the ruddy coals assumed sharp and bizarre designs. As the light flickered over her face it brought out the changes in her eyes and the warmth of her mouth.

"Do you see that head in the fire?" she asked, suddenly. "It is the head of the Sphinx—and before it there is a burning desert—do you see?"

Then she laid her head in Miss Ramsey's lap, and her voice sounded faint and far off.

"I want to be told that I am good," she said; "that I have been good all my life—that I am a saint, like that splendid creature who came to speak to me tonight. Am I as good as she?"

"I do not know her," responded Miss Ramsey.

Mariana raised her eyes to her face.

"Am I like I used to be—at The Gotham?"

Miss Ramsey smiled.

"You are older."

"And wiser?"

PHASES OF AN INFERIOR PLANET

"I don't think you will ever be wise, my dear."

"I am afraid not," said Mariana. "I am wedded to folly." Then she sighed softly. "Am I better?" she asked.

"You are very good to me."

"Am I better—to look at?"

Miss Ramsey shook her head gently.

"Dress makes a good deal of difference," she returned, presently.

Mariana rose and kissed her good-night.

"Sleep well," she said. "And don't make your bed in the morning—please don't. Yes, I am very sleepy."

But when the door had closed after Miss Ramsey she sat looking into the grate until the crimson coals had waned to livid ashes. The room grew cold and the shadows deepened in the folds of the curtains at the windows, which were stirred by a faint draught. From the street below an occasional noise rose, vague, unseizable—the roll of a wagon or the tramp of a passer-by upon the sidewalk. In a distant room a clock struck twice, with a soft whirring sound. From her gown, thrown across the back of a chair, the bruised violets diffused a fading sweetness. The embers waned one by one, and the visions in the fire grew spectral, like living faces which the warm blood forsakes. As the last one died she rose and went to bed.

When she awoke in the morning it was to find Miss Ramsey standing beside her, holding her breakfast-tray.

"You were sleeping very soundly," she said. "Did you have a good night?"

"Oh yes," Mariana responded. She yawned and turned upon the pillows, stretching her arms above her head. The lace on her sleeves fell away from her bare elbows.

. "I slept very soundly, and I am sleepy still. The mere fact of getting up in the morning makes life a failure. Until I have had my bath I am always a pessimist."

She sat up drowsily, running her hands through her hair. Then she turned to her tea, which was placed on a table beside her.

"There are your violets also," remarked Miss Ramsey, pointing to a couple of florist's boxes; and, as an afterthought, she added: "Men are odd creatures."

Mariana laughed.

"Oh, they imagine that they are laying up treasures on earth," she answered, stirring her tea. "And they have overlooked the fact that moths corrupt. I shall advise them to transfer their attentions to Heaven. Who was it that called me 'unpropitious'?"

"I don't like it," said Miss Ramsey. "I may be old-fashioned, but I don't approve of married men living as if they had no responsibilities."

"Nor do I," agreed Mariana. "It bores one awfully."

"And it makes people say unkind things of you, my dear. It is so hard for them to draw the distinction between imprudence and infamy."

"Yes," admitted Mariana, pushing her cup aside. "I suppose it is—and I suppose I am imprudent."

"I wish you would try to be a little more careful."

Mariana caught her hand and pulled her down on the bed beside her.

"What a treasure you are!" she said. "Do you know you are the one woman I absolutely believe in? You might have made a fortune by reporting scandals about me, and you haven't done so."

The maid brought in several letters, and Mariana took them from her and broke the seals carelessly.

"Mr. Gore is coming forward again," she remarked, tossing an open sheet on the counterpane. "You knew he did not like that worshipful old uncle of his leaving me his property. He says it has made me too independent. Well, it has made me independent of him, for which Heaven be praised. When I heard of it I repeated the Thirty-nine Articles, fifty *Hail Mary's*, and as much of the Shorter Catechism as I could think of. I feel *so* thankful."

"I am sorry for that, Mariana."

"You wouldn't be if you knew him. You are too economical to squander emotions."

"But it does seem rather hard on him," said Miss Ramsey.

Mariana laughed.

"It would have been worse on me had I stayed with him," she responded. "And now, if Janet has my bath ready, I think I'll get up."

An hour later she came down-stairs in her hat and coat, and went for her morning walk in the park. When she returned she ordered the carriage, and went shopping, accompanied by Miss Ramsey.

"You are to have a heliotrope satin," Mariana declared, in a burst of generosity, "and I am to have one that is all amber and dull gold."

As she stood in the centre of the costumer's show-room, surveying the lustrous folds of heliotrope and amber, her eyes shone with pleasure. Miss Ramsey protested faintly.

"My dear Mariana, I beg of you," she said, "leave me the black silk. Colors confuse me."

But Mariana was obdurate.

"No," she replied, "I have selected it. We will go to the milliner's."

They drove to the milliner's, where they remained for a couple of hours — Mariana finding difficulty in deciding upon a bonnet. When the choice was made Miss Ramsey was threatened with hysteria, and they went home.

"I quite forgot," said Mariana, as they entered the house, a small brown-stone one on Fifty-seventh Street,

PHASES OF AN INFERIOR PLANET

which she had leased—"I quite forgot that I was to have sat for Mr. Nevins this morning. How provoking I am! But it is too late now, and, besides, I am looking a fright. My dear, good Miss Ramsey, I do wish you would express yourself more about the purchases I make."

"I did express myself," protested Miss Ramsey, looking jaded and harassed. "I expressed myself against that heliotrope satin, but it did no good."

"But that was absurd," responded Mariana. "I do hope luncheon is ready," and she went up-stairs to change her dress.

After luncheon Mrs. Ryder called, and Mariana went in to see her, a flush of pleasure suffusing her face.

"How very kind of you!" she said, taking the proffered hand, and there was a thrill of gratitude in her voice. They seated themselves near together and talked of mutual acquaintances, principally men, of the weather, and of the opera the evening before—all with the flippancy with which society veils the primordial network of veins coursing beneath its bloodless surface. Then, when Mrs. Ryder rose to go, she hesitated an instant, looking down at the smaller woman.

"I should like to be your friend," she said at last. "Will you let me?"

Mariana raised her eyes.

"I need them," she answered; and then she added, impulsively: "Do you know all that has been said of me—all?"

Mrs. Ryder drew herself up with a slow, gracious movement.

"But it is not true," she said.

"No, it is not true," repeated Mariana.

The other smiled and held out her hand.

"I want you to come to luncheon with me," she said. "I shall be alone to-morrow. Will you come?"

"Yes," Mariana responded, "to-morrow."

And after Mrs. Ryder had gone she sat down at her desk and wrote a note.

"You must not talk to me again as you did last evening," it said. "I have told you so before, but I may not have seemed in earnest. Now I am in earnest, and you must not—you shall not do it. I know it has been a great deal my fault, and I am sorry for it. Indeed, you must believe that I did not think of its coming to this."

Then she sealed it and gave it to the servant to mail, after which she went up-stairs and talked to Miss Ramsey until dinner.

The next day she went to Mrs. Ryder's, and they sat down to luncheon at a small round table and talked as women talk in whom feeling is predominant over thought, and to whom life represents a rhythmic series of emotions rather than waves of mental evolution.

They spoke in low, almost affectionate voices, conscious of one of those sudden outreaches of sympathy to which women are subject. When luncheon was over they went up to the nursery, and Mariana knelt upon the floor and romped with the child, who pulled her loosened hair, uttering shrill shrieks of delight. At last she rose hurriedly, and Mrs. Ryder saw that a tear trembled on her lashes.

The elder woman's heart expanded.

"You have had a child?" she asked, softly.

"Yes."

"And lost it?"

"Yes, I lost it."

Mrs. Ryder's eyes grew soft.

"I am so sorry for you," she said. The tear on Mariana's lashes fell upon her hand.

"It was eight years ago," she said. "That is a long time, but I suppose one never entirely forgets."

"No," answered the other, "one never forgets."

PHASES OF AN INFERIOR PLANET

She stooped suddenly, and, lifting her child, kissed it passionately.

Several mornings after this Mariana's carriage stopped before Nevins's studio, and Mariana got out and ascended the long flight of stairs. In response to the fall of the brass knocker, the door was opened and Nevins greeted her reproachfully. "Are you aware," he demanded, gravely, "that there has been sufficient time for the appearance of a wrinkle since your last sitting?"

"Portraits don't have wrinkles," returned Mariana, cheerfully, entering and unfastening her coat; "nor do I."

She removed her hat and gave an impatient little fluff to her hair.

"Do I look well?" she asked.

"Were you ever otherwise to me?" rejoined Nevins, in impassioned protest.

Mariana turned from him with a slight shrug of her shoulders.

"For the last week," she said, "I have had a horrible cold. It made my eyes red and my nose also. That is why I stayed away."

"And plunged me into a seven days' despair—for a cold."

"Oh, but such a cold!"

She seated herself on a low chair between two large curtained easels. Then she rose to examine the portrait.

"I suppose the touching-up makes a great deal of difference," she remarked.

"A great deal," assented Nevins; "but don't you like it?"

She hesitated, her head first on one side, then on the other.

"Oh yes," she said, "but I should like it to be ideal, you know."

PHASES OF AN INFERIOR PLANET

"Nonsense! You don't need to be idealized. To idealize means to wipe out character with turpentine and put in inanity with a paint-brush." Then he added: "Sit down just as you are, and turn your head towards the purple curtain on that easel. A little farther—there. I must have that expression."

He picked up his brush and worked steadily for twenty minutes. Then he frowned.

"You have suffered twelve changes of expression within the last sixty seconds," he said. "What are you thinking of?"

"Oh, lots of things."

"Keep to one, please."

She smiled.

"Which shall it be?"

His eyes lingered upon her in sudden brightness.

"Think of me," he responded.

"I do," returned Mariana, amiably; "but when I think of you I think of Mr. Ardly, and when I think of Mr. Ardly I think of The Gotham, and when I think of The Gotham I think of—Mr. Paul."

"Confound Mr. Paul!" retorted Nevins, crossly.

"Please don't," protested Mariana; and she added, "you know he disapproves of me very much."

"The scoundrel!"

"But a great many people do that."

"The scoundrels!"

"Oh no," said Mariana, plaintively; "it is only your kindness of heart that makes you say so."

He laid down his brush and looked at her.

"My God!—Mariana!" he exclaimed.

"Nevins," said a voice in the doorway.

He turned abruptly. Mariana, behind the curtained easel, paled suddenly.

"I knocked, my dear fellow," the voice went on, "and I thought you answered. So you *are* alone. I came to look at the portrait."

"I am not alone," returned Nevins, awkwardly; "but come in, a—a—Algarcife."

Mariana rose from behind the easel and came forward. Her face was white, but she was smiling.

"He is painting every one's portrait," she said, "and I am one of everybody." She held out her hand. He took it limply, and it fell from his grasp.

"I beg your pardon," he said; "I did not know."

"Oh, it doesn't matter," responded Mariana. "Please look at the portrait. I want to—to rest."

He turned from her coldly.

"Since Mrs. Gore is so kind," he said to Nevins, "I will look at it. It will only detain you a moment."

He crossed the room and drew aside the curtain from a large canvas, then he fell back from the light and examined it carefully for a few seconds, suggesting an alteration or two, and making a favorable comment.

Mariana followed him with her eyes, her hands clasped before her, her face pallid, and the red of her lips shining like a scarlet thread. "It—it is very like," she said, suddenly.

He bowed quietly, showing a slight surprise, as he might have done at the remark of a stranger. Then he turned to the door.

"I am sorry to have interrupted you," he said. "Good-morning."

When the door closed upon him Mariana stood for an instant with her head bent as if listening to his footsteps on the stairs. Then she turned to Nevins, a smile flashing across her face.

"We must go back to the portrait," she said. "It must be finished quickly—quickly. I am afraid of wrinkles."

CHAPTER IX

MARIANA was walking under the elms that skirt the park on Fifth Avenue. It was a mild December morning, and the sunshine fell in silvery waves through the bare branches of trees overhead and rippled lightly across the concrete sidewalk, while the slender shadows of the boughs assumed the effect of irregular lines drawn by crude fingers upon a slate. Far ahead, through the narrowing archway of naked elms, the perspective sloped in gradual incline, blending the changing shades of blue and gray into a vista of pale violet. On the low stone wall to her left the creepers showed occasional splashes of scarlet berries, glowing warm and vivid through the autumnal haze which tinted the atmosphere. December had reverted for a single day into the majesty of dead October.

Mariana walked slowly, the furs, which she found oppressive, open at the throat, and her muff hanging idly from her hand. There was a rapt expression upon her face, and her eyes were sombre. She had the strained and preoccupied air of one whose mind has winged back to long-past days, leaving the body adrift in its relation to present events. All at once a tiny child, rolling a toy along the sidewalk, stumbled and fell before her feet, uttering shrieks of dismay. The incident recalled her to herself, and, as she stooped to lift it, she smiled at the profuse apologies of the nurse. Then she glanced about her, as if uncertain of the number of blocks that she had walked.

Three aspens, standing together in the park, arrested her gaze, and she looked at them with momentary intentness. Their slender bodies shone like leprous fingers, pointing heavenward, and on the topmost point of one a broken spray of frosted leaves shivered whitely. They recalled to her with a shudder the little graveyard on the old plantation, where she had spent her earliest childhood, and she was seized with a spasm of memory. She saw the forgotten and deserted graves, with the rank periwinkle corroding the marble slabs, and she saw the little brown lizards that crept out to bask upon them in the summer sunshine. With the recollection, death appeared to her hideous and loathsome, and she walked on quickly, her eyes on the pavement. A group of street-cleaners were seated against the stone wall, eating their mid-day meal, and she looked at the hunks of bread and ham with a feeling of sympathy for the consumers. Then, as she passed, her thoughts swung to the owner of the house across the way whom she knew, and who was descending the front steps. At Sixty-seventh Street she turned into the park, her eyes drawn by the clump of pines darkly defined against the gray rock beyond. For the second time her errant thoughts went back to her childhood and to the great pine forest where the wind played lullabies through the white heat of August days. She felt a swift desire to throw herself beneath the little alien growth of pine, to lie on the soft grass, which was still like emerald deepened by bluish shadows, and to let the spicy needles fall upon her upturned face.

As she moved onward, a man crossing the park in a rapid walk approached her. It was Father Algarcife, and in a moment their glances met.

He raised his hat, and would have passed on, but she stopped him by a gesture.

"Won't you speak to me?" she asked, and her voice wavered like a harp over which the player has lost control.

As she looked at him she saw that he had grown thinner since she had last seen him, and that his eyes shone with an unnatural lustre.

"What is there for me to say?" he returned, arresting her wavering glance.

Her lips quivered.

"I may go away," she said, "and this is the last chance. There is something I must tell you. Will you turn and walk back with me?"

He shook his head.

"What is the use?" he asked, impatiently. "There is nothing to be said that cannot better be left—unsaid."

"No! No!" she said. "You must not think worse of me than—than I deserve."

He was smiling bitterly.

"What I think of you," he returned, "matters very little." Then the smile passed, and he looked at her gravely. "I have little time," he said. "My days are not my own." And he added, slowly: "If you wish it, I will walk back with you for a short distance."

"Thank you," she replied, and they passed the clump of pines on their way in the park.

For a time they were silent, he was looking ahead, and her eyes followed their shadows as they flitted before her on the ground. The two shadows drew nearer, almost melted into one, and fell away.

Suddenly he turned to her.

"There was something you wished to say?" he asked, as he had asked his parishioners a hundred times; then he added: "Even though it were better left unsaid?"

Her eyes left the shadows, and were raised to his face. She thought suddenly that there was a line of cruelty about his mouth, and shrank from him. Had she really seen that face illuminated by passion, or was memory a lie? She spoke rapidly, her words tripping upon one another.

PHASES OF AN INFERIOR PLANET

"I want you to know," she said, "how it happened—how I did it—how—"

He looked at her again, and the mocking smile flamed in his eyes.

"What does it matter how it happened," he questioned, "since it did happen? In these days we have become impressionists in all things—even in our experiences. Details are tiresome." Then, as she was silent, he went on. "And these things are done with. There is nothing between Mrs.—Gore and the Reverend Anthony Algarcife except a meeting in a studio and a morning walk in the park. The air is spring-like."

"Don't," she said, suddenly. "You are hard."

He laughed shortly.

"Hard things survive," he answered. "They aren't easy to smash."

She looked at the shadows and then into his face.

"Have you ever forgiven me?" she asked.

He did not answer.

"I should like to feel," she went on, "that you see it was not my fault—that I was not to blame—that you forgive me for what you suffered."

But he looked ahead into the blue-gray distance and was silent.

"Tell me that I was not to blame," she said, again.

He turned to her.

"It was as much your fault," he said, slowly, "as it is the fault of that feather that the wind is blowing it into the lake. What are you that you should conquer the wind?"

She smiled sadly.

"'And you have forgiven me?"

His eyes grew hard and his voice cut like steel.

"No."

"And yet you see that I was not to blame."

He smiled again.

s

"It is the difference," he answered, "between logic and life. What have they in common?"

She spoke almost passionately. "Do you think that I have not suffered?" she asked. "Do you think that you have had all—all the pain?"

He shook his head.

"I do not suffer," he replied. "My life is calm."

She paid no heed to him.

"I have been tortured," she went on; "tortured night and day with memory—and remorse."

His voice was cold, but a sudden anger blazed in his eyes.

"There are drugs for both," he said.

She shivered.

"I have tried to buy happiness as I bought diamonds," she continued. "I have gone from place to place in pursuit of it. I have cheated myself with the belief that I might find it. I did not know that the lack lay in myself—always in myself."

She was silent, and he softened suddenly. "And you have never found it?" he asked. "Of all the things that you craved in youth there is lacking to you now—only your ambition."

She raised her head.

"And love," she finished.

His voice grew hard again.

"We are speaking of realities," he returned, and added, bitterly: "Who should have had love—if not you?"

They had passed the lake, and were walking through the Ramble. The dead leaves rustled beneath their feet.

"It is not true," she said, passionately. "It is false."

"What is false?" he demanded, quietly. "That you have had opportunities for love?"

She did not reply. Her lips were trembling, and her hand played nervously with the ribbon on her muff.

PHASES OF AN INFERIOR PLANET

Suddenly she looked up.

"When I left you," she said, slowly, "I went with the opera troupe abroad. For several years I was very successful, and I believed it would end well. I was given a leading part. Then one winter, when we were in Paris, I was taken ill. It was pneumonia. I was very ill, and the pain was frightful. They thought it would go to my heart. But when I grew better the troupe went on. I was left at the hotel, ill and alone—except for one friend—an Englishman—"

He interrupted her harshly.

"You have made a mistake," he said, and his voice was dull and lifeless. "I have no right to know your story. You are not of my parish—nor am I your confessor."

She flinched, but went on steadily, though her tones drooped.

"He had followed me for a long time. He loved me—or thought he did. When I was deserted by the troupe he stayed with me. He paid my bills and brought me back to life. I grew strong again, but—my voice was gone."

She paused as if in pain.

"Sit down," he said.

And they sat down on a bench beneath the naked branches of an oak.

"I was penniless, alone, and very weak. He wanted me even then. At first he did not want to marry me, but when I would not yield, he begged me to come back with him and secure a divorce. I think he was mad with passion."

She hesitated and glanced at him, but he was looking away.

"At last the end came. There was nothing else to do—and I wrote to you."

He moistened his lips as if they were parched from fever.

"Did you get the letter?"

"Yes," he answered, "I got it."

"And you did not answer?"

"What was there for me to say? You were free." For an instant her eyes blazed.

"You never loved me," she said.

He smiled slightly.

"Do you think so?" he asked.

The anger died from her eyes and she spoke softly.

"I waited for the answer," she said; "waited months, and it did not come. Then I came back. We went out West. A divorce was very easy—and I married him. I owed him so much."

"Yes?"

"It was a mistake. I did not satisfy him. He thought me cold. We quarrelled, and he went to other women. He drank a great deal. I was much to blame, but I could not help it. I hated him. Then his uncle took my part and loved me—God bless him, he was a saint—and kind—oh, so kind. When he died he left me the money, and his nephew and I separated. I have not seen him since."

They were both silent. She could hear his heavy breathing, and her heart throbbed.

"It was all a mistake," she said. "My whole life has been a mistake. But there is no salvation for us who make mistakes."

His eyes grew dark as he looked at her.

"A mistake that one stands by may become the part of wisdom," he said. "Could you not go back to him and begin again?" His face had grown haggard.

Her wrath flamed out.

"If I begin again," she answered, "it must be from the beginning—to relive my whole life."

He looked at her restless hands.

"Then you must look to the future," he said, "since there is no present—and no past."

"There is a past," she returned, passionately.

He shook his head.

"A dead one."

Her mouth shone scarlet in the pallor of her face.

"And shall we forget our dead?" she asked.

His lips closed together with brutal force. His eyes were hot with self-control.

Then he stooped for her muff, which had rolled to the ground, brushing it lightly with his hand. As he gave it to her he rose to his feet.

"Shall we return?" he asked. "It has grown cloudy."

She rose also, but stood for an instant with her hand resting upon the back of the bench. Her lips opened, but closed again, and she turned and walked at his side in silence.

Suddenly he looked at her.

"It is late," he said, "as you doubtless know, and I have neglected a call. May I leave you to go on alone?" Then his voice softened. "Are you ill?" he asked—"or in pain?"

She laughed mirthlessly.

"You are too strong," she returned, "to stoop to irony."

"It was not irony," he answered, gently.

She smiled sadly, her eyes raised.

"Tell me that you will come to see me—once," she said.

He looked at her with sudden tenderness.

"Yes," he answered; "I will come. Good-bye!"

"Good-bye!"

And they went different ways.

CHAPTER X

Mariana went home with throbs of elation in her heart. She was thrilled with a strange, unreasoning joy—a sense of wonder and of mystery—that caused her pulses to quiver and her feet to hasten.

"I shall see him again," she thought—"I shall see him again."

She forgot the years of separation, her past indifference, the barriers between them. She forgot the coldness of his voice and his accusing glance. Her nature had leaped suddenly into fulness, and a storm of passion such as she had never known had seized her. The emotions of her girlhood seemed to her stale and bloodless beside the tempest which possessed her now. As she walked her lips trembled, and she thought, "I shall see him again."

At dinner Miss Ramsey noticed her flushed face, and, when they went into the drawing-room, took her hands. "You are feverish," she said, "and you ate nothing."

Mariana laughed excitedly.

"No," she answered, "I am well—very well."

They sat down together, and she looked at Miss Ramsey with quick tenderness.

"Am I good to you?" she asked. "Am I good to the servants?—to everybody?"

"What is it, dear?"

"Oh, I want to begin over again—all over again! It is but fair that one should have a second chance, is it not?"

PHASES OF AN INFERIOR PLANET

Miss Ramsey smiled.

"Some of us never have a first," she said; and Mariana took her in her arms and kissed her. "You shall have yours," she declared. "I will give it to you."

When she went up-stairs a little later she took down an old square desk from a shelf in the dressing-room and brought it to the rug before the fire. Kneeling beside it, she turned the key and raised the narrow lid of ink-stained mahogany. It was like unlocking the past years to sit surrounded by these memories in tangible forms, to smell the close, musty odor which clings about the relics of a life or a love that is dead.

She drew them out one by one and laid them on the hearth-rug—these faded things that seemed in some way to waft with the scent of decay unseizable associations of long-gone joy or sorrow. The dust lay thickly over them, as the dust of forgetfulness lay over the memories they invoked. There was a letter from her mother written to her in her babyhood, and the fine, faded handwriting recalled to her the drooping figure—a slight and passionate woman, broken by poverty and disappointments, with vivacious lips and eyes of honest Irish blue. There was a handful of mouldered acorns, gathered by childish fingers on the old plantation; there was the scarlet handkerchief her mammy had worn, and the dance-card of her first ball, with a colorless silk tassel hanging from one end. Then she pushed these things hastily aside and looked for others, as one looks beneath the sentiments for the passions of one's life. She found a photograph of Anthony, pasted on cheap card-board—a face young and intolerant, with the fires of ambition in the eyes and the lines of self-absorption about the mouth. Still looking at the boyish face, she remembered the man that she had seen that morning—the fires of ambition burned to ashes, the self-absorption melted into pain.

PHASES OF AN INFERIOR PLANET

With the photograph still in her hand, she turned back to the desk and took out a tiny cambric shirt with hemstitched edges, upon which the narrow lace was yellow and worn. As the little garment fell open in her lap she remembered the day she had worked the hemstitching—a hot August day before the child came, when she had lived like a prisoner in the close rooms, sewing for months upon the dainty slips, and dreaming in that subconscious existence in which women await the birth of a new life. She remembered the day of its coming, her agony, and the first cry of the child; then the weeks when she had lain watching the dressing and undressing of the soft, round body, and then the moist and feeble clutch upon her hand. She remembered the days when it did not leave her arms, the nights when she walked it to and fro, crooning the lullaby revived from her own infancy, and at last the hours when she sat in the half-darkness and watched the life flicker out from the little bluish face upon the pillow.

"Was that yesterday or eight years ago?"

Her tears fell fast upon the tiny shirt, and she folded it and laid it away with the photograph and the other relics—laid away side by side the relics and the recollections covered with dust.

She rose to her feet and carried the desk back to its place in the dressing-room. In a moment she returned and stood silently before the fire, her hand resting upon the mantel-piece, her head leaning upon her arm. She was thinking of the two things a woman never forgets—the voice of the man she has loved and the face of her dead child.

But when she went to bed an hour later there was a smile on her lips.

"I shall see him again," she said. "Perhaps to-morrow."

. The next day she went to Nevins's studio and sat

PHASES OF AN INFERIOR PLANET

for the portrait. Her face was aglow and she talked nervously. He noticed that she started at a noise on the stair, and that her attention wandered from his words. He made daring, if delicate, love to her, but she seemed oblivious of it, and, when she rose to go, remarked that he was depressed. In return, he observed that she was feverish, and advised consulting her physician. "Your eyes are too bright," he said. "What is it?"

"Your reflected brilliancy, perhaps."

"By no means. The lustre is too unnatural."

"Then it is sleeplessness. I lay awake last night."

"Anything the matter? Can I help you?"

She shook her head, smiling.

"I am adjusting a few difficulties," she answered; "chiefly matrimonial, but they belong to my cook."

He looked at her attentively.

"Don't worry," he said. "It is not becoming. The flush is all right, but in time it will give place to discontent. You will sow perplexities to reap—"

"Furrows," finished Mariana. Then she nodded gayly. "What a pessimist you are!" she said. "No, I am going to use the best cosmetic—happiness."

And she lifted her skirts and descended the stairs.

That afternoon she remained in-doors, wandering aimlessly from room to room, opening a book to turn a page or two and to throw it aside for another.

In the evening she went out to dinner, and Ryder, who was among the guests, remarked that he had never seen her in better form. "If there was such a thing as eternally effervescent champagne, I'd compare you to it," he said. "Are you never out of spirits?"

She looked at him with sparkling eyes. "Oh, sometimes," she responded; "but as soon as I discover it, I jump in again."

"And I must believe," he returned, his gaze warming, "that your element is one that cheers but not inebriates."

"You are very charitable. I wonder if all my friends are?"

He lowered his voice and looked into her eyes. "Say all your worshippers," he corrected, and she turned from him to her left-hand neighbor.

She laughed and jested as lightly as if her heart were a feather, and went home at last to weep upon her pillow.

For the next few days she lived like one animated by an unnatural stimulant. She talked and moved nervously, and her eyes shone with suppressed excitement, but she had never appeared more brilliant, and her manner was charged with an irresistible vivacity. To Miss Ramsey she was unusually gentle and generous.

Each morning, on rising, the thought fired her, "He may come to-day"; each night the change was rung to, "He may come to-morrow"; and she would toss feverishly until daybreak, to dress and meet her engagement, with a laugh upon her lips. To a stranger she would have seemed to face pain as she faced joy, with a dauntless insolence to fate. To a closer observer there would have appeared, with the sharper gnawing at her heart, the dash of a freer grace to her gestures, a richer light to her eyes. It was as if she proposed to conquer destiny by the exercise of personal charm.

At the end of the week she came down to luncheon one day with a softer warmth in her face. When the meal was over she went up to her room and called her maid. "I want the gray dress," she said; but when it was laid on the bed she tossed it aside. "It is too gloomy," she complained. "Bring me the red;" and from the red she turned to the green.

She dressed herself with passionate haste, arranging

and rearranging the coil of her hair, and altering with reckless fingers the lace at her throat. At last she drew back from the glass, throwing a dissatisfied glance at her reflection—at the green-clad figure and the small and brilliant face, surmounted by its coils of shining brown. Then she added a knot of violets to the old lace on her breast, and went down-stairs to walk the drawing-room floor. An instinctive belief in his coming possessed her. As she walked slowly up and down on the heavy carpet, the long mirrors suspended here and there threw back at her fugitive glimpses of her moving figure. In the dusk of the room beyond she saw herself irradiated by the glimmering firelight.

The hands of the clock upon the mantel travelled slowly round the lettered face. As she watched it she felt a sudden desire to shake them into swiftness. She touched the clock and drew back, laughing at her childishness. A carriage in the street caught her ears and she went to the window, glancing through the half-closed curtains. It passed by. Then a tall, black figure turning the corner arrested her gaze, and her heart leaped suddenly. The figure came on and she saw that it was an elderly clergyman with white hair and a benevolent face. She was seized with anger against him, and her impatience caused her to press her teeth into her trembling lip. In the street a light wind chased a cloud of dust along the sidewalk until it danced in little eddying waves into the gutter. An organ-grinder, passing below, looked up and lifted his hand. She took her purse from the drawer of the desk and threw him some change; but when the broken tune was ground out she shook her head and motioned him away. The sound grated upon her discordant nerves.

She left the window and crossed the room again. The hands of the clock had made a half-hour's progress in their tedious march.

PHASES OF AN INFERIOR PLANET

A book of poems lay on the table, and she opened it idly, her mental fever excited by the lighter words of one who had sounded the depths and sunk beneath.

"If Midge will pine and curse its hours away,
  Because Midge is not everything—for aye,
Poor Midge thus loses its one summer day,
  Loses its all—and winneth what, I pray?"

She threw the book aside and turned away—back to the window where there was dust and wind—back into the still room where the monotonous tick of the clock maddened her quivering mood. She walked to and fro in that silent waiting which is the part of women, and beside which the action of battle is to be faced with a song of thanksgiving.

The trembling of her limbs frightened her, and she flung herself upon a divan. The weakness passed, and she got up again. Another half-hour had gone.

All at once there was a ring at the bell. For an instant she felt her heart contract, and then a delirious dash of blood through her veins to her temples. Her pulses fluttered like imprisoned birds.

A footstep crossed the hall, and the door of the drawing-room opened.

"Mr. Ryder!"

She wavered for an instant and went forward to meet him with an hysterical laugh. Her eyes were like emeralds held before a blaze, and the intense, opaline pallor of her face was warm as if tinged by a flame.

He took her outstretched hand hungrily, his face flushing until the purplish tint rose to his smooth, white forehead.

"Were you expecting me?" he asked. "I would sell my soul to believe that you were—with that look in your eyes."

PHASES OF AN INFERIOR PLANET

She shook her head impatiently.

"I was not," she answered. "I was expecting no one. It is very warm in here—that is all."

He looked disappointed.

"Have you ever expected me?" he questioned, moodily—"or thought of me when I was not with you?"

She smiled. "Oh yes!" she returned, lightly. "When I had a note from you saying that you were coming."

He set his teeth.

"You are as cruel as a—a devil, or a woman," he said.

"What you call cruelty," she answered, gently, "is merely a weapon which we sometimes thrust too far. When you talk to me in this way, you force me to use it." And she added, flippantly, "Some day I may thrust it to your heart."

"I wish to God you would!"

But she laughed merrily and led him to impersonal topics, talking rapidly, with a constant play of her slim, white hands. She allowed him no time for protestations. It was all bright, frivolous gossip of the day, with no hint of seriousness. As she talked, there was no sign that her ears were straining for an expected sound, or her flesh quivering with impatience.

At last he rose to go.

"You are the only woman I know," he remarked, as he looked at her with his easy and familiar glance, "who is never dull. How do you manage it?"

"Oh, it is not difficult," she answered. "To laugh is much easier than to cry."

"And much more agreeable. I detest a woman who weeps."

Her brilliant laugh rang out.

"And so do I," she said.

When he had gone, and the house door had closed

after him, she crossed to the heavily hanging curtains, pushed them aside, and looked out.

Only dust and wind and gray streets and the sound of the footsteps of a passer-by. From out the blue mist a single light burst, then another and another. She held her head erect, a scornful smile curving her lips.

Again the bell rang, and again she quivered and started forward, listening to the steps that crossed the hall. The door opened.

" Mr. Buisson !"

She hesitated a moment, and then went forward with the same cordial gesture of her cold, white hand.

CHAPTER XI

FATHER ALGARCIFE was working like a man spurred by an invisible lash. At the breaking of the cold winter dawns he might be seen on his rounds in the mission districts, which began before the early Mass, to end long after dusk, when the calls of his richer parishioners had been treated and dismissed. During the morning celebrations one of the younger priests often noticed that he appeared faint from exhaustion, and attributed it to the strain of several hours' work without nourishment.

One morning, shortly after New Year, John Ellerslie joined him and went in with him to breakfast. It was then he noticed that Father Algarcife ate only cold bread with his coffee, while he apologized for the scantiness of the fare. "It is lack of appetite with me," he explained, "not injudicious fasting;" and he turned to the maid: "Agnes, will you see that Father Ellerslie has something more substantial?" But when cakes and eggs were brought, he pushed them aside, and crumbled, without eating, his stale roll.

The younger man remonstrated, his face flushing from embarrassment.

"I am concerned for your health," he said. "Will you let me speak to Dr. Salvers?"

Father Algarcife shook his head.

"It is nothing," he answered. "But I expect to see Dr. Salvers later in the day, and I'll mention it to him."

Later in the day he did see Salvers, and as they were parting he alluded to the subject of his health.

PHASES OF AN INFERIOR PLANET

"I am under a pledge to tell you," he said, lightly, "that I am suffering from loss of appetite and prolonged sleeplessness. I don't especially object to the absence of appetite, but there is something unpleasant about walking the floor all night. I don't want to become a chloral fiend. Can't you suggest a new opiate?"

"Rest," responded Salvers, shortly. "Take a holiday and cut for Florida."

"Impossible. Too much work on hand."

Salvers regarded him intently.

"The next thing, you'll take to bed," he said, irritably, "and I'll have all the ladies of your congregation besieging my office door." He added: "I am going to send you a prescription immediately."

"All right. Thanks. I stop at Brentano's."

He entered the book-shop, and came out in a few moments with a package under his arm. As he stepped to the sidewalk a lady in a rustling gown descended from her carriage and paused as she was passing him.

"I was just going in for a copy of your sermons," she said. "I am distributing quite a number. By the by, have you ever found out who the *Scientific Weekly* writer really is?"

He looked at her gravely.

"I have a suspicion," he answered, "but suspicions are unjustifiable things at best."

He walked home rapidly, unlatched his outer door, and entered his study. Going to his desk, he took a bunch of keys from his pocket, and, unlocking a drawer, drew out several manuscripts, which he glanced over with a half-humorous expression. One was the manuscript of the volume of addresses he had lately published, the other of the articles which had appeared in the pages of the *Scientific Weekly*. They were both in his handwriting, but one showed the impassioned strokes of a younger pen, and belonged to the time when he had written under the veil of anonymity, that it might not interfere with the plan of his great work. Now the great work lay at the bottom of the last drawer, with its half-finished sheets yellowed and sown with dust, while the lighter articles had risen after a silence of ten years to assault his unstable present with the convictions of his past.

He crossed to the fireplace and laid both manuscripts upon the coals. They caught, and the leaves curled upward like tongues of flame, illuminating the faded text with scrolls of fire. Then they smouldered to gray spectres and floated in slender spirals up the yawning chimney.

The next day a storm set in, and pearl-gray clouds swollen with snow drove from the northwest. The snow fell thickly through the day, as it had fallen through the night, blown before the wind in fluttering curtains of white, and coating the gray sidewalks, to drift in fleecy mounds into the gutters.

In the evening, when he came in to dinner, he received an urgent message from Mrs. Ryder, which had been sent in the morning and which he had missed by being absent from luncheon. Her child had died suddenly during the night from an attack of croup.

Without removing his coat, he turned and started to her at once, his heart torn by the thought of her suffering.

As he ascended the steps the door was opened by Ryder, who came out and grasped his hand, speaking hurriedly, with a slight huskiness in his voice.

"She has been expecting you," he said, leading him into the hall. "Come up to her immediately. I can do nothing with her. My God! I would have given my right hand to have spared her this." The sincerity in his voice rang true, and there were circles of red about his eyes.

They went up-stairs, and Ryder opened the door of

the nursery, and, motioning him inside, closed it softly after him. The room was faintly lighted, the chill curtain of falling snow veiling the windows. On the little bed, where he had seen it sleeping several months ago, the child was lying, its flaxen curls massed upon the embroidered pillow; but the flush of health on the little face had given place to a waxen pallor, and the tiny hands that had tossed restlessly in sleep were still beneath white rose-buds. A faint odor of medicine clung about the room, but the disorder of dying had been succeeded by the order of death.

Mrs. Ryder, sitting near the window, her profile dark against the storm, turned her heavy eyes upon him, and then, rising, came towards him. He caught her extended hands and held them firmly in his own. At that instant the past seemed predominant over the present—and the grief more his own than another's.

"You have come at last," she said. "Help me. You must help me. I cannot live unless you do. Give me some comfort—anything!"

His face was almost as haggard as her own.

"What would comfort you?" he asked.

She turned from him towards the little bed, and, falling on her knees beside it, burst into passionate weeping.

"It was all I had!" she cried. "All I had! O God! How cruel!"

He laid his hand upon her shoulder, not to stay her tears, but to suggest sympathy. Beyond her the sweet, grave face of the dead child lay wreathed in rose-buds.

At his touch she rose and faced him.

"Tell me that I shall see him again!" she cried. "Tell me that he is not dead—that he is somewhere— somewhere! Tell me that God is just!"

His lips were blue, and he put up his hand imploring mercy; then he opened his mouth to speak, but no sound came.

She clung to him, sobbing.

"Pray to God for me," she said.

He staggered for a moment beneath her touch. Then he knelt with her beside the little bed and prayed.

When he walked home through the storm an hour later he reeled like a drunken man, and, despite the cold, his flesh was on fire.

As he entered his door the wind drove a drift of snow into the hall, and the water dripping from his coat made shining pools on the carpet.

He went into his study and slammed the door behind him. The little dog sleeping on the rug came to welcome him, and he patted it mechanically with a nerveless hand. His face was strained and set, and his breath came pantingly. In a sudden revolution the passion which he believed buried forever had risen, reincarnated, to overwhelm him. He lived again, more vitally because of the dead years, the death of a child who was his and the grief of a woman who was his also. He, who had believed himself arbiter of his fate, had awakened to find himself the slave of passion—a passion mighty in its decay, but all victorious in its resurrection. He shivered and looked about him. The room, the fire, the atmosphere seemed thrilled with an emotional essence. He felt it in his blood, and it warmed the falling snow beyond the window. Before the consuming flame the apathy of years was lost in smoke. A memory floated before him. He was sitting again in that silent room, driving the heavy pen, listening to the breathing of his dying child, watching the still droop of Mariana's profile, framed by dusk. He felt her sobbing upon his breast, her hands clinging in pain when he lifted her from beside her dead—and his. He heard again her cry: "Tell me that I shall see her! Tell me that God is just!" The eternal cry of stricken motherhood.

Whatever the present or the future held, these things were locked within the past. He might live them over or live them down, but unlive them he could not. They had been and they would be forever.

The door opened and the servant came in.
"If you please, father, there is a lady to see you."
He looked up, startled.
"A lady? On such a night?"
"She came in a carriage, but she is very wet. Will you see her at once?"
"Yes, at once."
He turned to the door. It opened and closed, and Mariana came towards him.

She came like a ghost, pale and still as he had seen her in his memory, with a veil of snow clinging to her coat and to the feathers in her hat. Her eyes alone were aflame.

He drew back and looked at her.
"You?" he said.
She was silent, holding out her gloved hand with an impulsive gesture. He did not take it. He had made a sudden clutch at self-control, and he clung to it desperately.

"Can I do anything for you?" he asked, and his voice rang hollow and without inflection.

She still held out her hand. Flecks of snow lay on her loosened hair, and the snow was hardly whiter than her face.

"You must speak to me," she said. "You promised to come, and I waited—and waited."

"I was busy," he returned, in the same voice.

"We cannot be as strangers," she went on, passionately. "We must be friends. Can you or I undo the past? Can you or I undo our love—or our child?"

PHASES OF AN INFERIOR PLANET

"Hush!" he said, harshly.

"I came only to hear that you forgive me," she continued, a brave smile softening the intensity of her face. "Tell me that and I will go away."

He was silent for a moment; then he spoke.

"I forgive you."

She took a step towards the door and came back.

"And is that all?"

"That is all." Beneath the brutal pressure of his teeth a drop of blood rose to his lips. There was a wave of scarlet before his eyes, and he clinched his hands to keep them at his sides. A terrible force was drawing him to her, impelling him to fall upon her as she stood defenceless—to bear her away out of reach.

She looked at him, and a light flamed in her face.

"It is not all," she retorted, triumphantly. "You have not forgotten me."

He looked at her dully.

"I had—until to-night."

Tears rose to her eyes and fell upon her hands, while the snow on her hair melted and rained down until she seemed to weep from head to foot.

"I was never good enough," she said, brokenly. "I have always done wrong, even when I most wanted to be good." Then she raised her head proudly. "But I loved you," she added. "I never loved any one but you. Will you believe it?"

He shook his head, smiling bitterly. As he stood there in his priestly dress he looked like one in a mighty struggle between the calls of the flesh and of the spirit. The last wavering fires of anger flamed within him, and he took a step towards her.

"Do you think," he asked, slowly, forcing his words, "that I would have left you while there remained a crust to live on? Do you think that I would not have starved with you rather than have lived in luxury without you? Bah! It is all over!"

"I was too young," she answered — "too young. I did not know. I have learned since then."

His outburst had exhausted his bitterness, and a passionate tenderness was in his eyes.

"I would to God that you had been spared the knowledge," he said.

She shook her head.

"No," she responded. "Not that—not that."

She swayed, and he caught her in his arms. For an instant he held her—not in passion, but with a gentleness that was almost cold. Then he released her, and she moved away.

"Good-bye."

"Good-bye."

He followed her into the hall and opened the door. An icy draught blew past him.

"Wait a moment," he said. He took an umbrella from the rack, and, raising it, held it over her until she entered the carriage.

"I hope you will not take cold," he said, as he closed the door.

Then he went back into his study and walked the floor until dawn.

CHAPTER XII

ONE afternoon during the third week in January, Father Algarcife went to the studio of Claude Nevins, and found the artist smoking a moody pipe over a brandy-and-soda. His brush and palette lay upon the floor.

"How are you?" inquired Father Algarcife, with attempted lightness; "and what are you doing?"

Nevins looked up gloomily, blowing a wreath of gray smoke towards the skylight.

"Enjoying life," he responded.

The other laughed.

"It doesn't look exactly like enjoyment," he returned. "From a casual view, I should call it a condition of boredom."

He had aged ten years in the last fortnight, and his eyes had the shifting look of a man who flees an inward fear.

Nevins regarded him unsmilingly.

"Oh, I like it," he answered, lifting his glass. "Come and join me. I tell you I'd rather be drunk to-day than be President to-morrow."

"What's the matter?"

"Oh, nothing. I haven't done a damned stroke for a week; that's all. I am tired of painting people's portraits."

"Nonsense. Ten years ago you went on a spree because there were no portraits to paint."

"Yes," Nevins admitted, "history repeats itself—with variations. The truth is, Anthony, I can't work."

"Can't? Well, what are you going to do about it?"

"I am going to drink about it."

He drained his glass, laid his pipe aside, and rose, running his hand through his hair until it stood on end.

"Don't be an idiot. You gave all that up long ago."

Nevins filled his glass and looked up at the skylight.

>"'Indeed, indeed, repentance oft before
>I swore—but was I sober when I swore?'"

he retorted, with a laugh. Then he lowered his voice. "Between you and me," he said, "drinking is not what it is cracked up to be. To save my life, I can't detect a whiff of that old delicious savor of vice. I detect a twinge of gout instead. Coming conditions cast their claws before."

Father Algarcife glanced about the room impatiently.

"Come," he said, "I am hurried. Let's see the portrait."

Nevins tossed a silk scarf from a canvas in the corner, and the other regarded the work for a moment in silence.

"Yes, I like it," he said. "I like it very much indeed."

As he turned away, he stumbled against the easel containing the canvas on which Nevins had been working, and he started and drew back, his face paling. It was the portrait of Mariana, her profile drawn against the purple curtain.

Nevins, following him with his eyes, spoke suddenly.

"That also is good, is it not?" he asked.

Father Algarcife stared above the portrait to the row of death-masks on their ebony frame.

"Yes, that also is good," he repeated.

As he descended the stairs he met Ardly coming up, his eyes bright and his handsome face aglow.

PHASES OF AN INFERIOR PLANET

They stopped and shook hands.

"Politics agree with you, I see," said Father Algarcife. "I am glad of it."

Ardly nodded animatedly.

"Yes, yes," he returned, "there is nothing like it, and we are going to give you the best government the city has ever seen. There is no doubt of that."

"All right," and he passed on. When he reached the street he turned westward. It was the brilliant hour of a changeable afternoon, the sunshine slanting across the sidewalks in sharp lights and shadows, and the river wind entering the lungs like the incision of a blade. The people he met wore their collars close about their throats, their faces blue from the cold.

Then, even as he watched the crisp sunshine, a cloud crossed the sky, its shade descending like a gray blotter upon the shivering city.

At first he walked rapidly, but a sudden fatigue seized him, and his pace slackened. He remembered that he had not rested for six hours. In a moment he saw the cross on the steeple of his church emblazoned in fire upon the heavens where the sun had burst forth, and, crossing the street, he pushed the swinging doors and entered softly. It was deserted. With a sensation of relief he passed along the right side aisle, and seated himself within the shadow of the little chapel.

Atmospheric waves of green and gold sifted through the windows and suffused the chancel. Beyond the dusk of the nave he saw the gilded vessels upon the altar and the high crucifix above. A crimson flame was burning in the sanctuary lamp, a symbol of the presence of the sacrament reserved. Above the chancel the figure of the Christ in red and purple was illuminated by the light of the world without.

Suddenly the sound of the organ broke the stillness, and he remembered that it was the day of the choir practising. The disturbance irritated him. During all the years of his priesthood he had not lost his old aversion to music. Now he felt that he loathed it—as he loathed the lie that he was living.

He raised his eyes to the stained-glass window, where the Christ in his purple robes smiled a changeless smile. A swift desire stung him to see the insipid smile strengthen into a frown—to behold an overthrow of the strained monotony. Change for the sake of change were preferable. Only let the still red flame in the sanctuary-lamp send up one fitful blaze, one shadow darken the gilded serenity of the altar. Would it forever face him with that bland assumption of the permanence of creed—the damnation of doubt? Would time never tarnish the blinding brightness of the brazen cross? He shivered as if from cold.

Then the voices of the choir swelled out in a song of exhortation—the passionate and profound exhortation of the "Elijah." In an instant it filled the church, flooding nave and chancel with its anthem of adoration:

"Lift thine eyes. O, lift thine eyes unto the mountains whence cometh help. Thy help cometh from the Lord, the Maker of heaven and earth. He hath said thy foot shall not be moved. Thy Keeper will never slumber."

Over and over again rang the promise of the prophet:

"Thy Keeper will never slumber—thy Keeper will never slumber."

With the words in his ears he looked at the altar, the white altar-cloth, and the gilded vessels. He saw laid there as a sacrament the bonds of his service. He saw the obligations of a child to the one who had sheltered him, of a boy to the one who had shielded him, of a man to the one who had reached into the gutter and lifted him up. He saw the good he had done, the sick he had healed, the filthy he had made clean. He saw the love of his people—rich and poor—the faiths that would be shattered by the unsealing of his lips, the work of regeneration that would crumble to decay. Looking back, he saw the blessings he had left upon his pathway rotting to curses where they had fallen. Against all this he saw the lie.

"Thy Keeper will never slumber. He, watching over Israel, slumbers not, nor sleeps. He, watching over Israel, slumbers not, nor sleeps."

But was it really a lie? He did not believe? No, but he begrudged no man his belief. He had extinguished the last embers of intolerance in his heart. The good that he had done in the name of a religion had endeared that religion to the mind that rejected it.

He had taken its armor upon him, and he had borne it victoriously. He had worn unsullied the badge of a creed emblazoned upon his breast, not upon his heart. Was not this justification?

Then, with his eyes upon the altar and the crucifix, beneath the changeless smile of the Christ in purple robes, he knew that it was not. He knew that he had sinned the one sin unpardonable in his own eyes; that he had taken the one step from which for him there was no returning—that the sin was insincerity, and the step the one that hid the face of truth.

"He, watching over Israel, slumbers not, nor sleeps. Shouldst thou, walking in grief, languish, He will quicken thee—He will quicken thee."

He rose and left the church.

It was several days after this that, in unfolding the morning paper, his glance was arrested by the announcement, "The Honorable Mrs. Cecil Gore, who has been dangerously ill of pneumonia, is reported to be convalescent."

The paper shook in his hands, and he laid it hastily aside.

He went out and followed his customary duties, but the thought of Mariana's illness furrowed his mind with a slow fear. It seemed to him then that the mere fact of her existence was all he demanded from fate. Not to see her or to touch her, but to know that she filled a corner of space—that she had her part in the common daily life of the world.

It was Saturday, and the sermon for the next day lay upon his desk. He had written it carefully, with a certain interest in the fact that it would lend itself to oratorical effects—an art which still possessed a vague attraction for him. As he folded the manuscript and placed it in the small black case, the text caught his eye, and he repeated it with an enjoyment of the roll of the words. Then he rose and went out.

In the afternoon, as he was coming out of the church after an interview with the sacristan, he caught sight of Ryder's figure crossing towards him from the opposite corner. He had always entertained a distrust of the man, and yet the anxiety upon his ruddy and well-groomed countenance was so real that he felt an instantaneous throb of sympathy.

Ryder, seeing him, stopped and spoke. "We have been looking for you," he said, "but I suppose you are as much occupied as usual."

"Yes—how is Mrs. Ryder?"

"Better, I think—I hope so. She is going to Florida for February and March. Beastly weather, isn't it? Nevins got off a good thing the other day, by the by. Somebody asked him what he thought of the New York climate, and he replied that New York didn't have a climate—it had unassorted samples of weather."

PHASES OF AN INFERIOR PLANET

They walked on, talking composedly, with the same anxiety gnawing the hearts of both.

At the corner Ryder hailed the stage and got inside. "Come to see Mrs. Ryder," were his parting words. "She depends on you."

Father Algarcife kept on his way to Fifty-seventh Street, where he walked several doors west, and stopped before a house with a brown-stone front.

As he laid his hand on the bell he paled slightly, but when the door was opened he regained his composure.

"I wish to ask how Mrs. Gore is to-day?" he said to the maid, giving his card.

She motioned him into the drawing-room and went up-stairs. In a few minutes she returned to say that Mrs. Gore would receive him, if he would walk up.

On the first landing she opened the door of a tiny sitting-room, closing it when he had entered. He took a step forward and paused. Before the burning grate, on a rug of white fur, Mariana was standing, and through the slender figure, in its blue wrapper, he seemed to see the flames of the fire beyond. She had just risen from a couch to one side, and the pillows still showed the impress of her form. An Oriental blanket lay on the floor, where it had fallen when she started at his entrance.

For a moment neither of them spoke. At the sight of her standing there, her thin hands clasped before her, her beauty broken and dimmed, his passion was softened into pity. In her hollow eyes and haggard cheeks he saw the ravage of pain; in the lines upon brow and temples he read the records of years.

Then a sudden tremor shook him. As she rose before him, shorn of her beauty, her scintillant charm extinguished, her ascendency over him was complete. Now that the brilliancy of her flesh had waned, it seemed to him that he saw shining in her faded eyes the clearer light of her spirit. Where another man would have beheld only a broken and defaced wreckage, he saw the woman who had inspired him with that persistence of passion which feeds upon the shadows as upon the lights, upon the lack as upon the fulfilment.

Mariana came forward and held out her hand.
"It was very kind of you to come," she said.

The rings slipped loosely over her thin fingers. Her touch was very light. He looked at her so fixedly that a pale flush rose to her face.

"You are better?" he asked, constrainedly. "Stronger?"

"Oh yes; I have been out twice—no, three times—in the sunshine."

She seated herself on the couch and motioned him to a chair, but he shook his head and stood looking down at her.

"You must be careful," he said, in the same forced tone. "The weather is uncertain."

"Yes. Dr. Salvers is sending me South."

"And when do you go?"

She turned her eyes away.

"He wishes me to go at once," she said, "but I do not know."

She rose suddenly, her lip quivering.

He drew back and she leaned upon the mantel, looking into the low mirror, which reflected her haggard eyes between two gilded urns.

"I was very ill," she went on. "It has left me so weak, and I—I am looking so badly."

"Mariana!"

She turned towards him, her face white, the lace on her breast fluttering as if from a rising wind.

"Mariana!" he said, again.

He was gazing at her with burning eyes. His hands were clinched at his sides, and the veins on his temples swelled like blue cords.

Then his look met hers and held it, and the desire in their eyes leaped out and closed together, drawing them slowly to each other.

Still they were silent, he standing straight and white in the centre of the room, she shrinking back against the mantel.

Suddenly he reached out.

"Mariana!"

"Anthony!"

She was sobbing upon his breast, his arms about her, her face hidden. The heavy sobs shook her frame like the lashing of a storm, and she braced herself against him to withstand the terrible weeping.

Presently she grew quiet, and he released her. Her face was suffused with a joy that shone through her tears.

"You love me?" she asked.

"I love you."

She smiled.

"I will stay near you," she said. "I will not go South."

For a moment he was silent, and when he spoke his voice rang with determination.

"You will go South," he said, "and I will go with you."

Her eyes shone.

"South? And you with me?"

He smiled into her upturned face.

"Do you think it could be otherwise?" he asked. "Do you think we could be near—and not together?"

"I—I had not thought," she answered.

He held her hands, looking passionately at her fragile fingers.

"You are mine," he said—"mine as you have been no other man's. Nature has joined us together. Who can put us asunder?" Then he held her from him in sudden fear. "But—but can you face poverty again?" he asked.

"What will matter," she replied, "so long as we are together?"

"You will leave all this," he went on. "We will start afresh. We will have a farm in the South. It will be bare and comfortless."

She smiled.

"There will be peach-trees," she said, "all pink in the spring-time, and there will be the sound of cow-bells across green pastures."

"I will turn farmer," he added. "I will wring a living from the soil."

She lifted her glowing eyes.

"And we will begin over again," she said—"begin from the beginning. Oh, my love, kiss me!"

He stooped and kissed her.

CHAPTER XIII

WHEN Anthony descended Mariana's brown-stone steps the afterglow had faded from the west, and far down the street the electric lights shone coldly through frosted globes. He walked with a springing step, lifting his head as if impatient of restraint. His future was firm. There was no hesitancy, no possibility of retrenchment. In one breath he had pledged himself to break the bonds that held him, and this vow there was no undoing. He had sealed it with his passion for a woman. Already his mind was straining towards the freedom which he faced. The years of insincerity would fall away, and the lies which he had uttered would shrivel before one fearless blaze of truth. Fate had settled it. He was free, and deception was at an end. He was free!

In the effort to collect his thoughts before going to dinner he crossed to Broadway, walking several blocks amid the Saturday-evening crowd. He regarded the passing faces idly, as he had regarded them for twenty years. They were the same types, the invincible survivals from a wreck of individuals. He saw the dapper young fellow with the bloodless face, pale with the striving to ascend a rung in the social ladder; he saw the heavy features of the common laborer, the keen, quick glance of the mechanic, and the paint upon the haggard cheeks of the actress who was out of an engagement. They passed him rapidly, pallid, nervous, strung to the point of a breaking note, supine to placid pleasures, and alert to the eternal struggle of the race.

PHASES OF AN INFERIOR PLANET

When he had walked several blocks he turned and went back. The noise irritated him. He winced at the shrill voices and the insistent clanging of cable-car bells. He wanted to be alone—to think.

In the quiet of the side-street his thoughts assumed more definite shape. The mad thrill of impulse gave place to a rational joy. He possessed her, this was sufficient. She was his to be held forever, come what would. His in wealth and in poverty, in sickness and in health. His for better or for worse—eternally his.

He set his teeth sharply at the memory of her tear-wet face. He felt the trembling of her limbs, the burning pressure of her lips. Broken and worn and robbed of youth—was she not trebly to be desired? Was his the frail passion that exacts perfection? He had not loved beauty or youth; he had loved that impalpable something which resists all ravages of decay—which rises triumphant from death.

Yes, trebly to be desired! He remembered her as he had first seen her, lifting her head from her outstretched arms, her eyes scintillant with tears. He recalled the tremulous voice, the plaintive droop of the head. Then the night when he had held her in the shadow of the fire-escape, her loosened hair falling about him, her hands hot in his own. She had said: "I am yours—yours utterly," and the pledge had held. She was his, first and last. What if another man had embraced her body, from the beginning unto the end her heart was locked in his.

All the trivial details of their old life thronged back to him; struggle and poverty, birth and death, and the emptiness of the ensuing years yawned, chasm-like, before his feet. He was like a man suddenly recalled from the dead—a skeleton reclothed in flesh and reattuned to the changes of sensations. Yes, after eight years he was alive once more.

He entered the rectory, and in a few moments went

in to dinner. To his surprise he found that he was hungry, and ate heartily. All instincts, even that for food, had quickened with the rebirth of emotion.

He drank his claret slowly, seeing Mariana seated across from him, and the vision showed her pale and still, as she had come to him the night of the storm, the snow powdering her hair. Then he banished the memory and invoked her image as he had seen her in the afternoon, wan and hollow-eyed, but faintly coloring and tremulous with passion. She would sit opposite him again, but not here.

He had a farm in the South, a valueless piece of land left him by a relative of his mother. It was there that they would go to begin life anew and to mend the faith that had been broken. He would till the land and drive the plough and take up the common round of life again—a life free from action as from failure, into which no changes might ring despair.

He left the table and went into his study, seating himself before the fire. The little dog, with that subtle perception of mental states possessed by animals, pressed his cold nose into the palm of his master's hand, whimpering softly, a wistful look in his warm, brown eyes. Then he lay down, and, resting his head upon his paws, stared into the fire—seeing in the flames his silent visions.

Anthony leaned back upon the cushions, and the face of Mariana looked at him from the vacant chair on the hearth-rug. The reddish shadows from the fire flitted across her features and across the slim, white hand that was half outstretched. He saw the slippered feet upon the rug and a filmy garment in her lap, as the work had fallen from her idle hands.

The maid came in with his coffee and he lighted his pipe. In a moment the bell rang and Ellerslie entered, his face flushed, his hands hanging nervously before him. He sat down in the chair, still warm from the vision of Mariana, and Father Algarcife looked at him with a sudden contraction of remorse. For the first time he winced before the glance of another—of a girlish-looking boy with a tremulous voice and an honest heart. He was looking into the fire when Ellerslie spoke.

"I want you to meet my mother," he said. "You know she is coming to town next week. She is very anxious to know you; I have written so often about you."

The other looked up.

"Next week—ah, yes," he responded. He was thinking that by that time he would have passed beyond the praise or blame of Ellerslie and his mother—he would be with Mariana.

The younger man went on, still flushing.

"She often sends you messages which I don't deliver. She has never forgotten that illness you nursed me through five years ago."

Father Algarcife shook his head slightly, his eyes on the flames that played among the coals.

"She must not exaggerate that," he answered.

Ellerslie opened his mouth, but closed it without speaking. His shyness had overcome him.

For a time they were silent, and then Father Algarcife looked up.

"John," he said.

"Yes?"

"If—if things should ever occur to—to shake your faith in me, you will always remember that I tried to do my best by the parish—that I tried to serve it as faithfully as Father Speares would have done?"

Ellerslie started.

"Of course," he answered—"of course. But why do you say this? Could anything shake my faith in you? I would take your word against—against the bishop's."

Father Algarcife smiled.

"And against myself?" he asked, but added, "I am grateful, John."

When Ellerslie had gone, a man from the Bowery came in to recount a story of suffering. He had just served a year in jail, and did not want to go back. He preferred to live straight. But it took money to do that. His wife, who made shirts, and belonged to Father Algarcife's mission, had sent him to the priest. As he told his story he squirmed uneasily on the edge of Mariana's chair, twirling his shapeless hat in the hands hanging between his knees. The dog crouched against his master's feet, growling suspiciously.

Father Algarcife rested his head against the cushioned back, and regarded the man absently. He believed the man's tale, and he sympathized with his philosophy. It was preferable to live straight, but it took money to do so. Indeed, the wisest of preachers had once remarked that "money answereth all things." He wondered how nearly the preacher spoke the truth, and if he would have recognized a demonstration of his text in the man before him with the shapeless hat.

Then he asked his caller a few questions, promised to look into his case on Monday, and dismissed him.

Next came Sister Agatha, to bring to his notice the name of a child on East Twentieth Street, whom they wished to receive into the orphanage. He promised to consider this also, and she rose to go, her grave lashes falling reverently before his glance. After she had gone he pushed his chair impatiently aside and went to his desk.

On the lid lay the completed sermon, and he realized suddenly that it must be delivered to-morrow—that he must play his part for a while longer. At the same instant he determined that on Monday he would deed over his property to the church. He would face his future with clean hands. He would start again as penniless as when he received the vestments of religion.

PHASES OF AN INFERIOR PLANET

Save for the farm in the South and a small sum of rental, he would have nothing. He would be free!

There was no hesitancy, and yet, mixed with the elation, there was pain. Beyond Mariana's eyes, beyond the desire for honest speech, he saw the girlish face of young Ellerslie, and the grave, reverential droop of Sister Agatha's lashes. He saw, following him through all his after-years, the reproach of the people who had believed in him and been betrayed. He saw it, and he accepted it in silence.

Raising his head, he encountered the eyes of the ancestor of Father Speares. For an instant he shivered from a sudden chill, and then met them fearlessly.

CHAPTER XIV

THROUGH the long night Mariana lay with her hands clasped upon her breast and her eyes upon the ceiling. The electric light, sifting through the filmy curtains at the windows, cast spectral shadows over the pale-green surface. Sometimes the shadows, tracing the designs on the curtains, wreathed themselves into outlines of large poplar leaves and draped the chandeliers, and again they melted to indistinguishable dusk, leaving a vivid band of light around the cornice.

She did not stir, but she slept little.

In the morning, when Miss Ramsey came to her bedside, there was a flush in her face and she appeared stronger than she had done since her illness.

"Is it clear?" she asked, excitedly. "If it is clear, I must go out. I feel as if I were caged."

Miss Ramsey raised the shades, revealing the murky aspect of a variable day.

"It is not quite clear," she answered. "I don't think you had better venture out. There is a damp wind."

"Very well," responded Mariana. She rose and dressed herself hurriedly; then she sat down with Miss Ramsey to breakfast, but she had little appetite, and soon left the table, to wander about the house with a nervous step.

"I can't settle myself," she said, a little pettishly.

Going up-stairs to her room presently, she threw herself into a chair before the fire, and looked into the long mirror hanging on the opposite wall.

She was possessed with a pulsating memory of the evening before—of Anthony, and of the kiss he had left upon her lips. Then swift darts of fear shot through her that it might all be unreal—that, upon leaving her, he had yielded once more to the sway of his judgment. She did not want judgment, she wanted love.

As she looked at her image in the long mirror, meeting her haggard face and dilated eyes, she grew white with the foreboding of failure. What was there left in her that a man might love? What was she—the wreck of a woman's form—that she could immortalize a man's fugitive desire? Was it love, after all? Was it not pity, passing itself for passion? Her cheeks flamed and her pulses beat feverishly.

She turned from the glass and looked at her walking-gown lying upon the bed.

"I can't wait," she said, breathlessly. "I must see him. He must tell me with his own lips that it is true."

She dressed herself with quivering fingers, stumbling over the buttons of her coat. Then she put on her hat and tied a dark veil over her face.

As she came down-stairs she met Miss Ramsey in the hall.

"Mariana, you are not going out!" she exclaimed.

"Only a little way," said Mariana.

"But it has clouded. It may rain."

"Not before I return. Good-bye."

She opened the hall door. Pausing for an instant upon the threshold, a soft, damp air struck her, and overhead a ray of sunshine pierced the clouds.

She fastened the furs at her throat and descended to the street.

At first she had no definite end in view, but when she had walked a block the idea of seeing Anthony grew stronger, and she turned in the direction of his house. The contact of the moist air invigorated her,

PHASES OF AN INFERIOR PLANET

and she felt less weak than she had believed herself to be. When she reached the rectory she hesitated a moment with her hand upon the bell, trembling before the thought of seeing him—of hearing him speak. She rang, and the door was opened.

"Can I see Father Algarcife?" she asked.

Agnes eyed her curiously.

"Why, he's at church!" she responded. "He's been gone about a half-hour or so. Is it important?"

"No, no," answered Mariana, her voice recovering. "Don't say I called, please. I'll come again."

"Perhaps you'll step in and rest a bit. You look tired. You can sit in the study if you like."

"Oh no, I will go on. I will go to the church." She started, and then turned back. "I believe I will come in for a few minutes," she said.

She entered the house and passed through the open door into the study. A bright fire was burning, and the dog was lying before it. She seated herself in the easy-chair, resting her head against the cushions. Agnes stood on the rug and looked at her.

"You are the lady that came once in that terrible storm," she said.

"Yes, I am the one."

"Would you like a glass of water—or wine?"

Mariana looked up, in the hope of dismissing her.

"I should like some water, please," she said, and as Agnes went into the dining-room she looked about the luxurious study with passionate eyes.

It was so different from the one at The Gotham, that comfortless square of uncarpeted floor, with the pine book-shelves and the skull and cross-bones above the mantel.

The desk, with its hand-carving of old mahogany, recalled to her the one that he had used when she had first known him, with its green baize cover splotched with ink. The swing of the rich curtains, the warmth of the

PHASES OF AN INFERIOR PLANET

Turkish rugs, the portraits in their massive frames, jarred her vibrant emotions. How could he pass from this to the farm in the South—to the old, old fight with poverty and the drama of self-denial? Would she not fail him again, as she had failed him once before? Would she not shatter his happiness in a second chance, as she had shattered it in the first?

The tears sprang to her eyes and scorched her lids. She rose hastily from her chair.

When the servant returned with the glass of water she drank a few swallows. "Thank you," she said, gently. "I will go now. Perhaps I will come again to-morrow."

She passed to the sidewalk and turned in the direction of the church, walking rapidly. She had not thought of his being at church. Indeed, until entering his study she had forgotten the office he held. She had remembered only that he loved her.

As she neared the building an impulse seized her to turn and go back—to wait for him at the rectory. The sound of the intoning of the gospel came to her like a lament. She felt suddenly afraid.

Then several persons brushed her in passing, and she entered the heavy doors, which closed behind her with a dull thud.

After the grayness of the day without, the warmth and color of the interior were as vivid as a revelation. They enveloped her like the perfumed air of a hot-house, heavy with the breath of rare exotics—exotics that had flowered amid the ardent glooms of mediævalism and the colorific visions of cloistered emotions. Entering a pew in the side-aisle, she leaned her head against a stone pillar and closed her eyes in sudden restfulness. That emotional, religious instinct which had always been a part of her artistic temperament was quickened in intensity. She felt a desire to worship —something—anything.

PHASES OF AN INFERIOR PLANET

When she raised her lids the colors seemed to have settled into harmonious half-tones. The altar, which had at first showed blurred before her eyes, dawned through the rising clouds of incense. She saw the white of the altar-cloth, and the flaming candles, shivering from a slight draught, and above the crucifix the Christ in his purple robes, smiling his changeless smile.

Within the chancel, through the carving of the rood-screen, she saw the flutter of the white gowns of the choristers, and here and there the fair locks of a child.

Then the priest came to the middle of the altar, his figure softened by circles of incense, the sanctuary lamp burning above his head.

He sang the opening phrase of the Creed, and the choir joined in with a full, reverberating roll of male voices, while the heads of the people bowed.

Mariana did not leave her seat, but sat motionless, leaning against the pillar of stone.

From the first moment that she had seen him, wearing the honors of the creed he served, her heart had contracted with a throb of pain. This was his life, and what was hers? What had she that could recompense him for the sacrifice of the Eucharistic robes and the pride of the Cross?

He came slowly forward to the altar steps, his vestments defined against the carving of the screen, his face white beneath the darkness of his hair.

When the notices of the festivals and fasts were over, he lifted his head almost impatiently as he pronounced the text, his rich voice rolling sonorously through the church:

"For who knoweth what is good for man in this life, all the days of his vain life which he spendeth as a shadow? For who can tell a man what shall be after him under the sun?"

And he spoke slowly, telling the people before him

PHASES OF AN INFERIOR PLANET

in new phrases the eternal truth—that it is good for a man to do right, and to leave happiness to take care of itself—the one great creed to which all religions and all nations have bowed. He spoke the rich phrases in his full, beautiful voice—spoke as he had spoken a hundred times to these same people—to all, save one.

She stirred slightly. It seemed to her that a wind blew from the altar where the candles fluttered, chilling her flesh. She shivered beneath the still smile of the painted Christ.

The stone pillar pressed into her temple, and she closed her eyes. Her head ached in dull, startled throbs.

As she listened, she knew that the final blow had fallen—that it is not given one to begin over again for a single day; that of all things under the sun, the past is the one thing irremediable.

The sermon was soon over. He returned to the altar, and the offertory anthem filled the church. Pressed against the pillar, she raised her hand to her ear, but the repetition was driven in dull strokes to her brain:

"Thy Keeper will never slumber. He, watching over Israel, slumbers not, nor sleeps."

CHAPTER XV

SEVERAL hours later Mariana was wandering along a cross-street near Ninth Avenue. Rain was falling, descending in level sheets from the gray sky to the stone pavement, where it lay in still pools. A fog had rolled up over the city. She had walked unthinkingly, spurred at first by the impulse to collect her thoughts and later by the thoughts themselves. It was all over; this was what she saw clearly—the finality of all things. What was she that she should think herself strong enough to contend with a man's creed?—faith?—God? She might arouse his passion and fire his blood, but when the passion and the fire burned out, what remained? In the eight years since she had left him a new growth had sprung up in his heart—a growth stronger than the growth of love.

The memory of him defined against the carving of the screen, the altar shining beyond, his vestments gilded by the light, his white face lifted to the cross, arose from the ground at her feet and confronted her through the falling rain. Yes, he had gone back to his God. And it seemed to her that she saw the same smile upon his face that she had seen upon the face of the painted Christ, whose purple robes tinted the daylight as it fell upon the chancel.

As she reached Ninth Avenue, an elevated train passed with its reverberating rumble, and the reflection of its lights ran in a lurid flame along the wet sidewalk. Clouds of smoke from the engine were blown westward, scudding like a flock of startled

PHASES OF AN INFERIOR PLANET

swans into the river. Straight ahead the street was lost in grayness and the lamps came slowly out of the fog. A wagon-load of calves was driven past her on the way to slaughter, and the piteous bleating was borne backward on the wind. Suddenly her knees trembled, and she leaned against a railing.

A man passed and spoke to her, and she turned to retrace her steps. From the wet sidewalk the standing water oozed up through her thin soles and soaked her feet. A pain struck her in the side—sharp and cold, like the blow of a knife. In sudden terror she started and looked about her.

A cab was passing; she hailed it, but it was engaged, and drove on.

She leaned against the railing of a house, and, looking up, saw the cheerful lights in the windows. The idea of warmth invigorated her, and she moved on to the next, then to the next. At each step her knees trembled and she hesitated, fearing to fall and lie dead upon the cold sidewalk. The horror of death gave her strength. Beyond the desires of warmth and light and rest, she was unconscious of all sensation.

Then the pain in her side seized her again, and the shrinking of her limbs caused her to pause for a longer space. The monotonous cross-town blocks sloped upward in a black incline before her, seeming to rise perpendicularly from before her feet to a height in the foggy perspective. She clung to the railing and moaned softly. A woman, passing with a bundle on her arm, stared at her, hesitated an instant, and went on.

At Broadway the lights of the moving cars interchanged like the colors of a kaleidoscope, swimming amid the falling rain before her eyes.

At Sixth Avenue she steadied herself with sudden resolve, beginning that last long block with a kind of delirious joy. To stimulate her faltering feet she

PHASES OF AN INFERIOR PLANET

glanced back over the terrible distance that she had come, and she found that the black incline of blocks now sloped in the opposite direction. She seemed to have descended a hillside of slate. Good God! How had she lived? Her own door came at last, and she crawled up the slippery steps, steadying herself against the stone balustrade. The door was unlatched. She opened it and went inside. At the first suffusion of warmth and rest her waning thoughts flickered into life.

Then she raised her eyes and uttered a shriek of joy. "Anthony!"

He was standing on the threshold of the drawing-room, and, as she cried out, he caught her in his arms.

"My beloved, what is it? What does it mean?"

But as he held her he felt the wet of her clothing, and he lifted her and carried her to the fire.

"Mariana, what does it mean?"

He was kneeling beside her, unfastening her shoes with nervous fingers. She opened her eyes and looked at him.

"I went out in the rain," she said. "I don't know why; I have forgotten. I believe I thought it was all a mistake. The blocks were very long." Then she clung to him, sobbing.

"Don't let me die!" she cried—"don't let me die!"

He raised her in his arms, and, crossing to the bell, rang it hastily. Then he went into the hall and upstairs. On the landing he met the maid.

"Where is Mrs. Gore's room?" he asked, and, entering, laid her upon the hearth-rug. "She is ill," he went on. "She must be got to bed and warmed. Put mustard-plasters to her chest and rub her feet. I will get the doctor."

He left the room, and Miss Ramsey came in, her eyes red and her small hands trembling.

They took off her wet things, while she lay faint and

PHASES OF AN INFERIOR PLANET

still, a tinge of blueness rising to her face and to her fallen eyelids.

Suddenly she spoke.

"Give me the medicine on the mantel," she said—"quick!"

It was tincture of digitalis. Miss Ramsey measured out the drops and gave them to her. After she had swallowed them the color in her face became more natural and her breathing less labored. Miss Ramsey was applying a mustard-plaster to her chest, while the maid rubbed her cold, white feet, which lay like plaster casts in the large, red hands.

Mariana looked at them wistfully. "I have done foolish things all my life," she said, "and this is the most foolish of all."

"What, dear?" asked Miss Ramsey, but she did not answer.

When Anthony came in, followed by the doctor, she was lying propped up among the pillows, with soft white blankets heaped over her. Her eyes were closed and she was breathing quietly.

Salvers took her hand and bent his ear to her chest.

"She must be stimulated," he said. "You say she has already taken digitalis—yes?"

He took Miss Ramsey's seat, still holding Mariana's hand, and turning now and then to give directions in his smooth, well-modulated voice. Anthony was standing at the foot of the bed, his eyes upon the blankets.

A light fall of rain beat rhythmically against the window-panes. The fire crackled in the grate and sent up a sudden, luminous flame, transfiguring the furniture in the room and the faces gathered in the shadow about the bed. Mariana stirred slightly. Presently Salvers rose and drew Miss Ramsey aside.

"It is very serious," he said. "The danger is heart failure. In another case I should say that it was hopeless—but her constitution is wonderful. She may pull

PHASES OF AN INFERIOR PLANET

through." Then he asked a few questions concerning the cause of the relapse, and turned to go. "Keep her stimulated, as I have said," he continued; "that is all that can be done. I would stay until morning, but several of my patients are at critical points. As soon as I have seen them I will come back." He started, paused to repeat several directions, and left the room softly, the sound of his footsteps lost in the heavy carpets.

Anthony took the chair beside the bed and laid his hand on the coverlet. He thought Mariana asleep. She was lying motionless, her heavy hair tangled in the lace on the pillow, her lashes resting like a black shadow upon her cheeks, her lips half parted.

He remembered that she had looked like this after the birth of Isolde, when he sat beside the bed and the child lay within the crook of her arm.

A groan rose to his lips, but he choked it back. The hand upon the coverlet was clinched, and the nails, pressed into the livid palm, had become purple. Still he sat motionless, his head bent, his muscles quivering like those of one palsied.

The flame of the fire shot up again, illuminating Mariana's face, and then died slowly down. The rain beat softly against the window.

Miss Ramsey went noiselessly into an adjoining room and came back, a glass in her hand. From across the hall a clock struck.

Suddenly Mariana opened her eyes, moaning in short sobs. A blue wave was rising over her face, deepening into tones of violet beneath the shadows of her eyes. They measured the medicine and gave it to her and she lay quiet again. He put his arm across her.

"Anthony!" she said.

He bent his ear.

"My beloved?"

"Hold me, the bed is going down. My head is so low."

He caught her passionately, his kisses falling distractedly upon her eyes, her lips, the lace upon her breast, and her cold hands.

"And you do love me?"

"Love you?" he answered, fiercely. "Have I ever loved anything else? O my love! My love!"

His tears stung her face like fire.

"Don't," she said, gently; and then, "It would have been very nice, the little farm in the South, and the peaches, and the cows in the pastures, but," she smiled, "I am not very thrifty—the peaches would have rotted where they fell, and the cows would never have been milked."

"Mariana!"

She lay in his arms, and they were both silent.

The clock struck again. In the street a passer-by was whistling "Oh, Nellie's blue eyes."

She spoke drowsily: "Speak softly. You will wake the baby."

In the glimmer of dawn Salvers entered. A sombre mist penetrated the curtains at the windows, and in the grate a heap of embers reddened and waned and reddened and waned again. A light dust had settled over the room, over the mantel, the furniture, and the blankets on the bed—a fine gray powder, pale like the ashes of yesterday's flame.

He crossed to the bed and took Mariana from Anthony's arms. Her head fell back and the violet shadows in her face had frozen into marble. She was smiling faintly.

"My God!" said Salvers, in a whisper. "She has been dead—for hours."

He laid her down and turned to the man beside him, looking at him for a moment without speaking. Then he laid his hand upon his arm and spoke to him as if to a child. "You must go home," he said, emphasizing the syllables. "It is over. You can do no good. You must go home."

The other shook his head. His eyes were blank, like those of a man in whom the springs of thought have been suddenly paralyzed.

"You must go home," repeated Salvers, his hand still upon his arm. "I will be with you in an hour. You must go."

Beneath his touch Anthony moved slowly into the hall, descending the stairs mechanically. Salvers gave him his hat and opened the outer door. Going to the sidewalk, he motioned to his coachman.

"Take Father Algarcife home," he said.

He slammed the door and looked after the carriage as it rolled down the block and rounded the corner. Then he turned and re-entered the house.

When Father Algarcife reached the rectory, he went into his study, locking the door after him. Then he seated himself at his desk and rested his head in his hands. His mind had cleared from the fog, but he did not think. He remained staring blankly before him.

The room was cold and damp, the fire had not been kindled, and the burned-out coals lay livid upon the hearth. The easy-chair was drawn before the fender where he had sat yesterday, and the lamp which he had not lighted the evening before stood on the little marble-top table. An open book, his pipe, and an untasted cup of coffee were beside it.

On the desk his yesterday's sermon lay unrolled, the text facing him in bold black and white:

"For who can tell a man what shall be after him under the sun?"

The dull, neutral tones of advancing dawn flooded the room. There was a suggestion of expectancy about it, as of a world uncreate, waiting for light and birth.

PHASES OF AN INFERIOR PLANET

He raised his eyes, not his head, and stared over the desk at the wall beyond. From above the mantel the portrait of Father Speares's ancestor glared at him from its massive frame, wearing the fierce and faded aspect of a past century. Near the window stood the sofa, with the worn spot on the leather arm where the head of the dead man had rested. It was all chill and leaden and devoid of color.

Presently he moved, and, opening a drawer of the desk, drew out a small dark phial and placed it upon the unfolded leaves of the sermon. Through the blue glass the transparent liquid gleamed like silver. His movements were automatic. There was no haste, no precipitation, no hint of indecision. He looked at the clock upon the mantel, watching the gradual passage of the hands. When the minute-hand reached the hour he would have done with it all—with all things forever.

The colorless liquid in the small blue phial lay within reach of his grasp. It seemed to him that he saw already a man lying on that leathern sofa—saw the protruding eyes, the relaxed limbs, the clammy sweat, and saw nothing more that would be after him under the sun. The hands of the clock moved on. A finger of sunlight pierced the curtains and pointed to the ashes in the grate. Outside the noise of a crowded city went on tumultuously. He removed the cork of the bottle, inhaling a pungent and pervasive odor of bitter almonds.

At the same instant a voice called him, and there was a knock at his door.

"Father!"

He replaced the stopper, still holding the phial in his hand. For a moment the heavy silence hung oppressively, and then he answered: "What is it?" His voice sounded lifeless, like that of one awakening from heavy sleep or a trance.

PHASES OF AN INFERIOR PLANET

"You are there? Come quickly. Your men at the Beasley Rolling Mills have gone on a strike. A policeman was shot and several of the strikers wounded. You are wanted to speak to them."

"To speak to them?"

"I have a cab. You may prevent bloodshed. Come."

Father Algarcife returned the phial to its drawer, withdrew the key from the locker, and rose. He opened the door and faced the messenger. His words came thickly.

"There is no time to lose," he said. "I am ready."

He seized his hat, descended the steps, and rushed into the street.

THE END

By MARY E. WILKINS

JEROME, A POOR MAN. A Novel. 16mo, Cloth, Ornamental, $1 50.
MADELON. A Novel. 16mo, Cloth, Ornamental, $1 25.
PEMBROKE. A Novel. Illustrated. 16mo, Cloth, Ornamental, $1 50.
JANE FIELD. A Novel. Illustrated. 16mo, Cloth, Ornamental, $1 25.
A NEW ENGLAND NUN, and Other Stories. 16mo, Cloth, Ornamental, $1 25.
A HUMBLE ROMANCE, and Other Stories. 16mo, Cloth, Ornamental, $1 25.
YOUNG LUCRETIA, and Other Stories. Illustrated. Post 8vo, Cloth, Ornamental, $1 25.
GILES COREY, YEOMAN. A Play. Illustrated. 32mo, Cloth, Ornamental, 50 cents.

Mary E. Wilkins writes of New England country life, analyzes New England country character, with the skill and deftness of one who knows it through and through, and yet never forgets that, while realistic, she is first and last an artist.—*Boston Advertiser.*

Miss Wilkins has attained an eminent position among her literary contemporaries as one of the most careful, natural, and effective writers of brief dramatic incident. Few surpass her in expressing the homely pathos of the poor and ignorant, while the humor of her stories is quiet, pervasive, and suggestive.—*Philadelphia Press.*

It takes just such distinguished literary art as Mary E. Wilkins possesses to give an episode of New England its soul, pathos, and poetry.—*N. Y. Times.*

The pathos of New England life, its intensities of repressed feeling, its homely tragedies, and its tender humor, have never been better told than by Mary E. Wilkins.—*Boston Courier.*

The simplicity, purity, and quaintness of these stories set them apart in a niche of distinction where they have no rivals.—*Literary World*, Boston.

The charm of Miss Wilkins's stories is in her intimate acquaintance and comprehension of humble life, and the sweet human interest she feels and makes her readers partake of, in the simple, common, homely people she draws.—*Springfield Republican.*

Studies from real life which must be the result of a lifetime of patient, sympathetic observation. . . . No one has done the same kind of work so lovingly and so well.—*Christian Register*, Boston.

NEW YORK AND LONDON:
HARPER & BROTHERS, PUBLISHERS

☞ *The above works are for sale by all booksellers, or will be sent by the publishers, postage prepaid, on receipt of the price.*

By LILIAN BELL

FROM A GIRL'S POINT OF VIEW. 16mo, Cloth, Ornamental, Uncut Edges and Gilt Top, $1 25.

Miss Bell's former books have proved conclusively that she is a shrewd observer, and in the series of character studies which she has brought together under the title "From a Girl's Point of View" she is at her best. The book is an intimate analysis of the manner of the modern man, as seen with the eyes of the modern woman; and it is of interest not only to those from whose stand-point it is written, but to those at whom its good-humored shafts are directed. The best of it is that Miss Bell, while she may be severe, is never unjust, and her observations are so apt that the masculine reader cannot but laugh, even while he realizes that she is dealing with one of his own shortcomings.

THE UNDER SIDE OF THINGS. A Novel. With a Portrait of the Author. 16mo, Cloth, Ornamental, Uncut Edges and Gilt Top, $1 25.

Miss Bell's little story is very charming. . . . Miss Bell has plenty to say, and says it, for the most part, in a fashion engaging and simple, with touches of eloquence and passages of real strength. She has gifts of a sort far from common, and an admirable spirit. Her observation of life is keen, shrewd, and clear; it is also sympathetic. She has a strong and easy hold on the best realities.—*N. Y. Times.*

This is a tenderly beautiful story. . . . This book is Miss Bell's best effort, and most in the line of what we hope to see her proceed in, dainty and keen and bright, and always full of the fine warmth and tenderness of splendid womanhood.—*Interior*, Chicago.

THE LOVE AFFAIRS OF AN OLD MAID. 16mo, Cloth, Ornamental, Uncut Edges and Gilt Top, $1 25.

So much sense, sentiment, and humor are not often united in a single volume.—*Observer*, N. Y.

One of the most charming books of its kind that has recently come under our notice. From its bright "Dedication" to its sweet and gracious close, its spirit is wholesome, full of happy light, and one lingers over its pages.—*Independent*, N. Y.

NEW YORK AND LONDON:
HARPER & BROTHERS, PUBLISHERS

☞ *The above works are for sale by all booksellers, or will be sent by mail by the publishers, postage prepaid, on receipt of the price.*

www.ingramcontent.com/pod-product-compliance
Lightning Source LLC
Chambersburg PA
CBHW030737230426
43667CB00007B/744